TOWARD A NEW
WORLD ORDER

THE COUNTDOWN TO ARMAGEDDON

UPDATED EDITION

TOWARD A NEW WORLD ORDER

THE COUNTDOWN TO ARMAGEDDON

UPDATED EDITION

Don McAlvany

*Western Pacific
Publishing Co.*

P.O. Box 84900, Phoenix, AZ 85071

All scripture references are from the King James Version unless otherwise stated.

Toward a New World Order:
The Countdown To Armageddon
Second Edition, 1992
Copyright © by **Donald S. McAlvany**

Printed in the United States of America

Published by:
Western Pacific
Publishing Co.
P.O.Box 84900, Phoenix, AZ 85071

ISBN 1-879366-26-6

Contents

Foreword
Dr. Tim LaHaye

It is scary to hear the president of the United States, the president-dictator of Russia, and the head of the Eastern Establishment, who has for years controlled the Council on Foreign Relations and founded its stepchild, the Trilateral Commission, all promoting the same thing—the New World Order!

How can a committed communist, an arch capitalist, and the head of the freest and richest nation on earth have the same vision for our world? The communist is an atheist; consequently, he doesn't believe in God. The capitalist worships money and power, and the president of the United States claims he is a Christian.

Either these three men do not mean the same thing by the New World Order, or there is a conspiracy to lead the people of this world into a one-world government that needs to be exposed! If that is true, Don McAlvany is the ideal man to do it. He has a thorough knowledge of both geopolitics and the world of finance and is a committed Christian who knows what the prophets have said about the one-world government of the Antichrist who will one day rule the world.

I have been an avid reader of Don's *McAlvany Intelligence Report* for years. I find things in it that are not found in many other such reports, even my own. He has an incredible memory for detail and an interesting writing style. You will discover that for yourself in this book. But what you will also notice is that he documents everything he says . . . he has to—some of it is so shocking you wouldn't believe it otherwise.

From all indications, this world is rapidly moving to the very times our Lord and His disciples predicted would exist at the end of this age. Whether the New World Order is the means of bringing the world toward the one-world government of the last days is for you to judge. Reading this book will help you decide, for you will find information here you have never read before. In fact, you can hardly understand the real meaning of the New World Order until you have read this book. Don is one of the most widely read men of our times. Since he remembers so well what he has read, your reading of this book will equip you to understand what on earth is really happening.

Introduction

"For my part, whatever anguish of spirit it may cost, I am willing to know the whole truth, to know the worst, and to prepare for it."
—Patrick Henry, 1776

Planet earth seems to be spinning faster and faster with each week and month that passes as political, economic, and monetary turmoil not only increases, but the *rate of change accelerates*. It is not only the events which are taking place which are significant, but also the tremendous speeding up or acceleration of these events which needs to be considered. It is said that man has amassed more knowledge in the past 35 years than throughout all prior history. One large super computer can store quantities of information equivalent to thousands of years of prior knowledge and research, and process more data than all former computers combined. Instantaneous global communication today connects all points of the globe via satellite and other high technology, so that all events everywhere can be instantly known and viewed by everyone. A globe that once took months to circle can now be traversed in hours and every square inch of the planet can now be reached by destructive nuclear weapons within fifteen minutes, each with more explosive power than the world has seen in toto prior to 1945.

The acceleration or snowball factor can be seen in the deteriorating world debt pyramid where personal and business bankruptcies, S&L and bank failures, and Third

3

World defaults are accelerating at a breakneck pace. It can be seen in the incredible upheaval and change in the Soviet Empire and in the accelerating communist revolutions in Central and Latin America, South Africa, the Philippines, and the Middle East. It can be seen in the stampede toward political, economic, and monetary union in Western Europe; and in the plunge toward a New World Order and "the merger of the common interests of the U.S. and U.S.S.R." (targeted for the mid-1990s by the liberal Eastern Establishment).

The acceleration factor can be seen in the rapid spread of the New Age movement which promises to usher in a global government by the year 2000 and in the explosion of the occult, satanism, and New Age philosophy. In short, the world is careening toward incredible change, convulsions, and chaos in the 1990s. While peace, prosperity, brotherhood, and world government are being promised and sold to the masses by American, Western, and Soviet leaders, this writer believes that something quite different is approaching like a freight train out of control. The 1990s will be the most chaotic and convulsive decade in modern, or perhaps all of history. The title of a recent book captures this period well, *Peace, Prosperity, and the Coming Holocaust*. Remember to watch not just *what* is happening, but the *rate* at which those events are happening. It's called the *acceleration factor*.

For those who strive to be obedient to the commands of the Lord, Jesus said in Matthew 24 to "watch" the signs of the times. It is very difficult today to keep up with all of these accelerating developments. Unfortunately for the Christian, things must appear to get darker before the glorious light and Blessed Hope, the return of the Lord Jesus is observed. This book will, at first blush, perhaps seem overwhelmingly negative but the believer can be optimistic in looking up, for his redemption could very well be drawing nigh.

Jesus also instructed us in Matthew 24:44 to "be ready." We must be, as Issachar of old (1 Chron. 12:32) who understood the times to ". . . *know what Israel ought to do.* . . ."This book will hopefully provide a keen insight for Christians into our time and, as Francis Schaeffer said, "how then shall we live" in the 1990s—the decade of destiny.

Chapter One

The Decline of America

Remember Back When:

Teenagers answered "Yes, Sir," and "No, Sir" to their elders?

When helping the enemy was treason and punishable by death?

When a farmer could plant what he wanted to?

When you left the front door unlocked?

When the New York Times *was pro-American?*

When our government was the servant of the people, instead of the master?

When a handshake was as good as a written contract?

When the poor were too proud to take charity?

When what you made was yours?

When, before the "new math," two plus two was indubitably four, and not "probably" four?

When the doctor's first question was, "Where does it hurt?" instead of, "Do you have insurance?"

When it was preposterous to believe that America could lose a war?

When you went to church and heard a preacher who believed in the divinity of Christ and preached from the Bible?

When you could go abroad with the assurance that your government would stand up for you?

When a white wedding gown meant something?

*When the courts protected society, rather than the
    criminal?*
When there was such a thing as treason?
*When charity was a virtue, instead of a $30 billion
    business?*
When people used the phrase "sound as a dollar"?
*When pornography in the schoolroom was illegal, but
    prayers were not?*
When you could depend on what you read in the papers?
*When only cowards and traitors traded with, visited, and
    appeased the enemy?*

The rise and fall of civilizations can be described in
the following cycle: "From bondage comes spiritual faith,
and from spiritual faith comes courage. From courage
comes liberty, and from liberty comes abundance. From
abundance comes complacency, and from complacency
comes apathy. From apathy comes dependency, and from
dependency comes bondage."

The United States essentially falls very late in this
cycle, somewhere in the apathy/dependency stage, and is
rapidly descending down a secular humanistic, socialistic
path. As more government controls are invading all
aspects of our lives, and as America is declining in many
different areas, we could lose most, if not all, of our
freedoms before the decade of the 1990s is over.

The Perspective Triangle

While the civilization cycle described above covers a
period of about 200 years, America is in real decline in
almost every area in which a country can be in decline:
politically, financially, socially, morally, and spiritually.
A useful illustration is the "perspective triangle." The left

side of the triangle is the monetary/economic decline of the Western world. This decline is based on the false premise that we can create wealth out of thin air. For the past 20 years, our government has continually printed paper money and created a great deal of inflation. Other governments in the West have done this as well. There has also been the greatest debt binge in world history, with America's debt pyramid more than quadrupling from $3 trillion in 1980 to $14.2 trillion in 1990. This debt pyramid is beginning to unravel and will likely take the country into either major recession or depression. We are in the early stages of economic decline at the present time. This will be covered in great depth in later chapters.

TRIANGLE ILLUSTRATION

The right side of the triangle represents the social/political decline, which is based on the false premise that all men are created equal. This was the great lie of the French revolution: "liberty, equality, fraternity." All men are not created equal. God made each of us very different and very individual. But the socialists say that each person should be equal, even if they have to take from one person and give to another. They want to redistribute the wealth and control the "greedy businessmen" who obviously cannot be trusted. Rapidly accelerating socialism has been seen in the last 20 to 30 years in the United States. Communism has seized over 35 percent of the world's land mass and population and killed over 130 million people. There is a very powerful movement in the world toward a world, or global, government. Certain leaders are encouraging a New World Order, and New Agers believe a global government will emerge by A.D. 2000. The Russians are also continuing their quest for global domination of the world by communism. This side of the perspective triangle will also be covered thoroughly in Chapter Two.

The base of the triangle, the problem which has created all the other problems, represents the spiritual/ moral decline. The United States has moved away from its biblical, Christ-centered foundation. This country's beginnings were based on the principles of the Scriptures and the Lord Jesus Christ, and as a country we've moved away from that. The United States is still a religious country, but does not have the spiritual foundation and depth that we had 100 to 200 years ago.

Alexander Solzhenitsyn was asked on BBC radio a few years ago, "Why did the Russian people lose their freedom?" He replied, "Because we forgot God." This has happened to a certain extent in the United States, because of the vast prosperity this country has experienced over the past 40 years. God has blessed this country incredibly. The uninterrupted prosperity the United States has had since the end of World War II has caused Americans— Christians included—to become fat, dumb, and lazy. We wouldn't know what to do in tough times. If the television set goes out and we miss the finals in the basketball game or the Sunday afternoon football game, that's a major crisis for us. Americans have become very soft, and as we have, we've moved away from the basics. There are always consequences to our actions, and the result has been an overall moral decline in this country. The United States is the world leader in homosexuality, pornography, promiscuity, drug use, alcoholism, and violent crime. The moral decline is a result of the spiritual decline, and the spiritual decline in turn has contributed to the social/ political and monetary/economic decline.

People have short memories. Going back 40 to 50 years in this country, most Americans believed everything just stated. But today, Americans have forgotten the fundamentals—the basic political and biblical principles which made us a great nation. Santayana once said that "we learn from history, or we learn nothing from history." What is happening in the United States today is very similar to what happened in the Roman Empire when it was in decline. It had been the greatest empire in the world, but moral decay set in, and it began to rot from within. Characteristic of a country in decline is that most people cannot see or discern the decline. The handful of people that can see it and who try to warn others are ridiculed as gloom-and-doomers, reactionaries, or right-wing fearmakers.

The Moral Decline of America

The moral decline is tied together with the spiritual decline which is the basis for all the other areas of decline in our country. We've forgotten our spiritual foundations and where we came from. The moral decline in this country is amazing. The United States is the per capita leader in the Western world for drug usage. We have only 5 percent of the world's population and 55 percent of the world's drug usage. That's incredible! Of the marijuana consumed in the United States, 80 percent is also grown in the United States. This is one of our larger cash crops.

The United States is also the per capita leader in the Western world in teenage pregnancies, teenage suicide, and divorce. Our divorce rate is 25 times higher than Japan's. America publishes more pornography than any other country in the world. In the past, pornography was shipped into the United States from Scandinavia. Now in places as remote as Australia, New Zealand, and South Africa, pornographic movies and literature published in the United States are widespread.

In the last few decades, we have seen the break-up of the family and increasing problems for teenagers. In schools 35 years ago, the problems were chewing gum in class and being sent to the principal's office for scuffling. Today, the problems range from teenagers killing teachers in school to drug usage. Sex education is taught in schools; teenagers are taught how to have safe sex so they won't contract AIDS. Movies and television programs are saturated with sex and anti-family, anti-traditional values. The amount of violence and sex in television is increasing. Much of the rock music promotes rebellion, depression, suicide, sex, and drugs.

Our culture is in decline. Anyone over 40 years old can look back to their childhood and remember what it was like growing up in the 1940s and '50s, and then look at the sharply contrasting society which teenagers are growing up in today. In Denver, Colorado for example, over 25 percent of teenagers in high schools are said by officials to be involved in satanism.

The manifestations of America's decline and plunge toward slavery continue to proliferate. A Gallup poll recently conducted a survey of 539 students from 100 schools across America and the following results illustrate our moral dilemma: 69 percent said that premarital sex is *not* wrong, and 56 percent said they approve of living together in "trial marriages"; 9 percent of the women admitted to having had one or more abortions; and 15 percent of the men knew that at least one of their sexual partners had had an abortion; 51 percent said they approved of abortion (while 37 percent opposed it); half of the students reported having had more than one sex partner, and 24 percent had had five or more; half said they have sex occasionally, and 26 percent participate regularly.

A recent study by the University of Wisconsin shows that among 13,000 people who had "trial marriages" (it used to be called "shacking up") before marriage, 38 percent were divorced within 10 years. Only 27 percent of those who were married before living together were divorced.

When Lenin came to power in Russia, one of the first things he (and later, Stalin) determined to do was to destroy and restructure the family. Easy (no-fault type) divorce was instituted, and sexual immorality and abortion were encouraged. The family broke down and so did the entire Russian society.

It's not just students or the younger generation who are involved. In Washington, the illicit heterosexual escapades of John, Bobby, and Ted Kennedy, Wilbur Mills, John Tower, and Gary Hart have been followed by more recent scandals involving a Republican representative from Ohio who was recently convicted of having sex with a child; and Democratic representatives from Illinois and California who were sexually involved with women employees and a Peace Corps worker.

The Homosexual Revolution

A homosexual revolution is now emerging in Washington and across America. In recent years three prominent homosexual Washingtonians have contracted and died of AIDS: Terry Dolan, head of the National Conservative Political Action Committee; Dan J. Bradley, head of the leftist Legal Services Corp.; and Rep. Stuart McKinney (R-CT). McKinney had two gay lovers who died of AIDS and lived with a third for five years on Capitol Hill. A former congressman from Maryland, a gay who was forced from office in the early 1980s when caught cruising for teenage boys, says that at that time there were at least a dozen closet gays in the Congress. Since then, a congressman was ruined by a gay scandal involving murder; another was caught having sex with a 16-year-old male page; another was caught having sex in a Capitol Hill men's room; and another has been caught with his male lover running a call boy/girl ring from his apartment.

It seems that this last representative, Rep. Barney Frank (D-MA), a long-time homosexual, answered an ad in Washington's *Gay Blade* newspaper in 1985. The male prostitute who placed the ad, and who was convicted in 1975 of cocaine distribution, and in 1982 on four counts of production of obscene items involving a juvenile, possession of obscene materials, oral sodomy, and possession of cocaine, moved in with Congressman Frank. For two years, Rep. Frank had him on his payroll at $20,000 per year, while the prostitute used the representative's apartment as a homosexual/heterosexual sex-for-hire whorehouse.

Since this bizarre story has become public, liberal politicians have come to Frank's defense, calling him "one of America's top congressmen," "a great American leader," etc. The Congressional Ethics Committee gave him a minor slap on the wrist for his behavior, and he has continued as a powerful liberal leader in Congress.

Meanwhile, his homosexual call boy lover is beginning to talk about other congressmen and senators who have been his customers for either male or female prostitutes at his Capitol Hill bordello. Gay activist leaders in Washington estimate that there are *at least 30 homosexual congressmen on Capitol Hill.* It seems that homosexual activity is rampant in Washington. A Washington gay lobbyist even brought male prostitutes into the White House on four occasions for midnight tours. On July 11, 1990, the U.S. Senate voted to force restaurant owners to hire AIDS infected homosexuals as food handlers. Jesse Helms led the losing effort (the vote was 61 to 39). The bill was heavily lobbied by the militant homosexual lobby.

The liberal acceptance of homosexuality in Washington has translated into hundreds of millions of dollars in taxpayer funding for gay activist organizations in recent years. The federal government is now calling on churches to "adjust their teaching on homosexuality." A recent report from the Department of Health and Human Services states:

> *"Religion presents another risk factor. . . . Many traditional fundamentalist faiths still portray homosexuality as morally wrong. . . . Religion needs to re-assess homosexuality in a positive context within their belief systems."*

Indeed, government and private legal action is now being taken against churches and businesses for "alleged" discrimination against homosexuals. In New York, former Mayor Ed Koch issued an executive order granting "bereavement leave rights" to homosexuals whose "domestic partners" die. As local, state, and federal governments have come to accept and protect the homosexual/sodomite movement, public sentiment has also become more sympathetic.

A recent *Newsweek* poll asked the question, "Should being a homosexual keep someone from holding the following positions?" The percent saying *it should not* was: president—50 percent; member of the clergy—48 percent; teacher—50 percent; cabinet member—57 percent; judge—59 percent; member of Congress—60 percent; city government official—60 percent; policeman—61 percent. *So, between 48 and 61 percent (over half of Americans on average) believe that being a homosexual shouldn't keep you from holding high public office.* This is called the "new morality."

The moral decline and homosexual revolution is also evident in the arts. The U.S. taxpayer-funded National Endowment for the Arts reflects the moral plunge in Washington and the influence of homosexuality and other liberal moral standards. Only Sen. Jesse Helms (R-NC) had the courage to stand up (alone, among 100 senators and 435 representatives) and say: "Enough is enough!"

Helms' anger was aroused (according to the *Washington Times*) by two exhibitions by the National Endowment for the Arts:

1. The late photographer Robert Mapplethorpe's celebration of homosexuality, an exhibition which portrayed such poignant sights as a man urinating into another's mouth and the artist posing with the long end of a bullwhip dangling from a well-known body cavity.
2. Andre Serrano's work entitled "Piss Christ," a large photograph of a crucifix immersed in the artist's most recent medium, his own urine.

When asked by the press, since he worked with urine, what his next medium would be, Serrano replied: "Semen." The Mapplethorpe and Serrano works both got money from the taxpayer-funded National Endowment for the Arts, and Sen. Jesse Helms wants to see that it doesn't happen again. But he stands alone in the liberal *avant garde*, degenerate, immoral atmosphere in Washington, where he is laughed at, called a religious bigot, and accused of "violating our First Amendment right of free expression." Even President Bush has refused to condemn the federally-funded "progressive art" and has called for more taxpayer funding—which will continue.

Seattle First National Bank, whose parent bank is Bank of America, has agreed to offer a gay affinity MasterCard for homosexuals throughout Washington, Oregon, Idaho, Montana, and Alaska. The card is designed to help raise funds for gay and lesbian groups throughout the Pacific Northwest. Congressman William Dannemeyer (R-CA) says in his book, *Shadow In the Land*:

> *"Homosexuals are now insisting that young people be taught how to perform homosexual acts as well as heterosexual acts. They demand that such instruction be mandatory in our public schools and that the courses also teach that homosexuality is a normal and desirable appetite. Many schools have instituted such sex education."*

The communists recognize that a country in moral decline is an easy target. In 1960, they told their cadres in America:

> *"Eliminate all laws governing obscenity by calling them 'censorship' and violation of 'free speech' and 'free press.' Break down cultural standards of morality by promoting pornography and obscenity in books, magazines, motion pictures, radio, and TV. Present homosexuality, degeneracy, and promiscuity as 'nor-*

mal, natural, healthy' " (see *The Naked Communist* by W. Cleon Skousen, p. 260).

Of all human behavior besides murder, the Bible condemns homosexuality the most severely, and states that no society can survive the widespread practice *and acceptance* of homosexuality. It is very specific about the judgment which will fall upon a nation or people which so indulges. Could the present AIDS plague (spread primarily by homosexual lifestyles) be the beginning of that judgment?

The Legal Decline of America

Yet another area deserving special attention as indicative of society's decline is the legal system. This is critical, as well, since Christians are imperiled by the direction and influence of this degeneration. America's legal system has turned into a nightmare—a monster which is sapping the strength of our country and people. With *90 percent of the world's lawyers, more court litigation than the rest of the world put together,* and the free world's largest prison population, there would seem to be truth in the old saying, "the worse the society, the more the law." As America has plunged into moral decline, it has become common to see the legal system used for legal plunder, whereby millions of Americans sue millions of other Americans over some small legal technicality or imagined offense, in order to plunder the target of the lawsuit's financial wealth.

Literally tens of thousands of laws on the books and a myriad of legal interpretations have made this legal plunder by greedy individuals and lawyers one of America's top economic realities today. Virtually all economic, social, and human endeavors in America today are predicated on "what is the potential for a lawsuit." Every doctor, accountant, businessman, and person of any financial means must live with the constant fear of a lawsuit that will decimate his finances. It is part of our socialist, something-for-nothing mentality in America today that someone (e.g., the government, the legal system) must protect us from all physical and financial harm. So, suing people has become America's top growth industry today, and hundreds of thousands of lawyers exist primarily to encourage, exacerbate, and facilitate this process. Today, America graduates 100 times more lawyers than Japan, and Japan graduates 100 times more engineers than America. Which country is in economic decline and which is in economic ascent? Our lawsuit-saturated legal system is one of the chief causes of America's current economic decline.

Over 30 years ago, liberals, secular humanists, and communists began to move into our nation's law schools (much as they did into our journalism schools) in order to socialize and move the country to the political left. Today, most law school graduates are liberal, and it is almost impossible to find a conservative law school, lawyer, or judge in America. *Out of this liberal/left legal educational system for over three decades have come all of our judges and the vast majority of our politicians, whose primary goal is to pass more laws and change the face and character of America.*

The result of this liberalization of our legal system has been a criminal justice system which has completely broken down—one which encourages crime by lenient penalties against the criminal and harasses businessmen, conservatives, Christians, and the producers of our country. It has resulted in tens of thousands of laws being placed on the books which harass and restrict the average American, curtail his freedoms on an accelerating basis, and have become the foundation of a government bureaucracy which wants to control and dictate every aspect of our lives.

Three classic illustrations of leftist legal groups which have emerged to change the face of America are:

1. *The National Lawyers Guild*—widely believed to be a communist legal front and for decades a defender of communist causes in America;
2. *The Legal Services Corp*—a government/taxpayer-funded legal organization used by the political left to push leftist social causes in America; and
3. *The American Civil Liberties Union (ACLU)*—the number one *legal* purveyor and defender of leftist causes in America.

Recently, the Indiana *Evansville Courier* carried an excellent article by attorney Jack Schroeder on what the ACLU stands for, and indeed has pushed for 30 years in our legal system:

1. Legalization of drugs;
2. Abolition of the death penalty;
3. Fines as a preferred form of criminal penalty;
4. Abolition of tax benefits for churches and other religious groups;
5. Abolition of all laws restraining obscenity, indecency, and pornography (including child pornography);
6. Abolition of all restraints and discrimination against homosexuals; and, legalization of gay marriages, all the rights and benefits of heterosexual couples—including child custody and adoption rights;

7. Legalization of prostitution and elimination of all legal restraints on homosexual activities—e.g., abolition of all state sodomy laws;
8. Elimination of "under God" from the Pledge of Allegiance;
9. Removal of "in God we trust" from U.S. coinage; and
10. Registration and confiscation of all guns by abolition of American gun ownership.

Current targets of America's legal/political left include businesses, and conservative and Christian individuals, leaders, and groups. Examples of such leftist legal attacks are legion. For example, in early October 1989, a Georgia judge sentenced anti-abortion activist and Operation Rescue leader Randall Terry to two years in jail for criminal trespassing and unlawful assembly related to a sit-in in front of an abortion clinic. The same week in Atlanta, a drug dealer convicted of killing another drug dealer (he shot him 58 times) received a one-year jail sentence.

This is incredible! The American legal system has facilitated the murder of 25 million babies, and Christian/conservative protestors against this carnage can now be jailed and fined more severely than drug dealers, murderers, rapists, extortionists, and burglars (who often receive much lighter sentences). That is our American liberal/left legal system in action. Thousands of other anti-abortion protestors are being jailed and heavily fined by liberal judges across America. Many are receiving very rough and abusive treatment by local law enforcement officials as well.

On October 10, 1989, the U.S. Supreme Court ruled that a federal anti-racketeering law (RICO—the Racketeering Influenced and Corrupt Organizations Act), originally passed to help the government fight organized crime, can now be used against anti-abortion protestors. In Philadelphia, 26 anti-abortion protestors were convicted under the RICO racketeering law and fined $108,000. A RICO conviction allows triple damages to the plaintiff if they can prove "a pattern of illegal activities."

So now an unholy alliance of abortion clinics and liberal judges have combined to label anti-abortion demonstrators as criminal racketeers. Similar RICO lawsuits have been filed against pro-life activists by abortionists in Pittsburgh, Chicago, and Brookline, Massachusetts. Molly Yard of the National Organization for Women (NOW) responding to the RICO ruling said:

> *"Militant anti-abortion protestors are in the same league with gangsters and racketeers, so 'we' shall treat them that way."*

Such rulings, of course, violate conservative/ Christian Americans' First Amendment rights of free speech. They would never be applied against leftist anti-apartheid, anti-nuke/pro-disarmament demonstrators. Under these rulings, Martin Luther King would have been a racketeer when he trespassed on private property and conspired with others to bring about civil rights changes through mass demonstrations. Don't the civil rights of 25 million unborn babies carry any legal or moral rights in liberal America today? Obviously not!

How do these rulings differ from similar rulings against democracy demonstrators in Russia? In the U.S.S.R. there is a catch-all law against "hooliganism," which justifies the Soviet authorities arresting, convicting, and jailing Soviet citizens for virtually anything. The

RICO statutes are being used in the same way more and more in the U.S. to curtail the "undesirable" activities of Christians, conservatives, and businessmen who cannot be convicted on any other existing statutes.

In another related legal ruling, on October 5, 1989, the Florida Supreme Court struck down a Florida law requiring pregnant girls to get parental consent before having an abortion. Saying that a 15-year-old girl had the right to privacy, the liberal judges ruled that her parents had no right to know about the abortion in advance. What does that ruling do to our traditional concepts of parental authority, the family, etc.? Remember what Lenin said: "Destroy the family, and the society will collapse."

The legal left is also targeting religious holidays such as Christmas. The next major issue to be targeted by the political left through the courts is (believe it or not) religious holidays such as Christmas. A coalition of 16 leftist religious and educational groups, including the National Education Association, the National Council of Churches, etc., is targeting the holiday and other Christmas activities (e.g., trees, pageants, creches, songs, decorations, etc.) in schools, the work place, government facilities, etc. Lawsuits will follow!

The Legal Attack Against Christianity

The American Bar Association has declared war on Christianity. On May 4-5, 1989, the ABA hosted a seminar in San Francisco on how the legal profession can effectively sue Christians and Christian organizations (using tort law), because of religious fraud and *the detrimental impact (emotional, financial, and civil rights-wise) of religion and religious beliefs on American society*. This is incredible—this is the ABA, not the ACLU!

Topics and specific lectures of the seminar included: "Expanding Use of Tort Law Against Religions"; "Tort Law As an Ideological Weapon"; "Tort Law As Essential Restraint on Religious Abuses"; "Liability of Clergy and Spiritual Counselors"; "Tort Liability for Fraud, Emotional Distress, and Harm to Reputation Arising from Religiously Motivated Conduct"; "Tort Liability for Brainwashing"; "Liability for Sexual Conduct of the Clergy"; "Liability Arising Out of the Employment Relationship"; "Institutional Liability for Negligent Hiring/Retention"; "Piercing the Corporate Veil—Liabilities of Religious Bodies and Affiliated Organizations"; etc.

What is a tort? A tort is a private or civil wrong or injury, independent of contract. Suits involving personal injuries, wrongful death, or defamation are tort suits. A tort claim usually has three elements:

1. A legal duty to others;
2. A breach of that duty; and
3. Damages as a result of that breach of duty.

Liberal judges in recent decades have been creating new duties based on what they perceive to be societal norms. Thus, as society becomes more antagonistic toward Christianity (e.g., as in the wake of the Bakker/ Swaggart scandals), the courts will create new duties and become more receptive to litigation against Christians and Christian organizations.

The ABA seminar (and another held on the same topic in 1990) holds dire implications for American Christians. For example, there may be tort liability for brainwashing, coercive persuasion, or mind control. The Supreme Court of California has already ruled that there is a compelling state interest in preventing its citizens from unknowingly being subjected by religious organizations to coercive persuasion, brainwashing, or mind control. The court wrote that "where a person is subjected to coercive persuasion without his knowledge or consent," the state has a duty to intervene and entertain corrective litigation.

Psychiatrists now describe coercive persuasion as involving guilt manipulation, indoctrination, fear inducement, and peer pressure. *Voluntary* exposure to the persuasion by the listener/victim in no way alleviates the guilt of the perpetrator. By this definition, Billy Graham and every other evangelistic crusader in America, and a large portion of the teachings of American fundamental/ evangelical religious denominations and churches, can be construed to be in violation of tort law. Psychiatric testimony, according to attorney Barry Fisher in his presentation, "Tort Law As an Ideological Weapon," is now the most powerful and persuasive force in the courtroom on the issues of acceptable behavior. *Thus, a genuine Christian conversion/salvation experience is now being redefined by America's legal left as the result of guilt manipulation, indoctrination, fear inducement, and peer pressure.* The evangelist, pastor, para-church organizations (e.g., Campus Crusade for Christ, Billy Graham Evangelistic Association, etc.) responsible for such brainwashing or manipulation will be construed to be guilty of committing a tort.

A second implication is that the making of "allegedly" false statements is considered fraud. "Unprovable" religious doctrines such as eternal security and concepts of Heaven and Hell can be considered to be fraud. Stanley Leak, a personal injury lawyer, maintained in his lecture that when a religious organization fails to disclose accurately its identity and *what it teaches "before" a person attends any of its functions*, fraud has occurred.

Under this concept, liability is predicated on *what is "not" said,* as opposed to making false statements. Before you say that this would never stand up in court, the ruling should be noted regarding a Maryland real estate promoter who simply omitted Blacks from his advertisement and was *found guilty of discrimination based on what he "didn't" say.*

A third implication is that intentional infliction of emotional stress, as per a ruling by the California Supreme Court, is legally construed to be a tort. The elements of this emotional distress are: outrageous conduct or *intention* to cause emotional distress or suffering. An anti-Christian legal system will surely find a Sunday school teacher giving a lesson to young children on Jesus' teachings on Hell and eternal separation to be guilty of causing emotional distress. People who hear the preaching of the gospel of Jesus Christ often do come under emotional distress. Therefore, this concept, like brainwashing, coercive persuasion, mind control, and fraud, can be used to strike at the core of orthodox Christianity.

There is also a serious concern about the liability of clergy as spiritual counselors. The California Supreme Court ruled against John MacArthur's Grace Community Church, which gave spiritual counseling to a man who later committed suicide. The spiritual counseling was deemed to be the cause of the suicide and held to be inferior to secular counseling. The Supreme Court held that by counseling the man on the biblical doctrine of eternal security, that the church contributed to his suicide "by committing outrageous conduct," which led to a tort. The ruling was later reversed by a higher court, but it shows the direction the U.S. legal system is moving.

This concept will lead to the courts controlling the spiritual/biblical content of counseling, just as other

*concepts advocated by the ABA will control the content
of what pastors and evangelists can say from their
platforms or pulpits.*

Note: Red China claims to have religious freedom,
but it is illegal to mention the biblical doctrines of sin or
the second advent in religious services. How does this
newest U.S. legal attack against Christianity differ from
similar religious censorship in communist countries?

Additionally, the ABA seminars argue that when
there is sexual misconduct by a member of the clergy, *the
entire church organization, or denomination, is guilty of a
tort.* Courts are now beginning to rule this way, with
gigantic potential financial liabilities for church/para-
church organizations. Throughout the seminars, speakers
kept referring to going for the "deep pockets" in litigation
involving religious organizations (e.g., after the parent
organization or denomination with larger financial assets
than the individual accused).

Trial lawyers are urged to examine the assets of the
individual who has committed the wrong conduct, then
look at the assets of the organization, and finally, look at
the assets of individuals who are responsible for the organization (e.g., directors, elders, deacons, officers, etc.) in
order to obtain the largest possible monetary settlements.
Another wrinkle advocated by the ABA seminars is the
extension of liability beyond an individual to a group that is
associated with the group to which the individual belongs.
California courts have already ruled that major denominations (i.e., the United Methodist Church) are legally liable
for the actions of a pastor or employee way down the line in
a local church. In one case this was ruled due to the firing of
a homosexual employee in a local church.

In summary, there is an accelerating attack (i.e., war
has been declared) by the liberal left dominated legal

system in America on conservative and Christian individuals and organizations. Like the pro-abortion, disarmament, nuclear freeze, anti-apartheid movements, this onslaught is not spontaneous. It is well-orchestrated and organized by the political left. The legal system in America, with its leftist law schools, hundreds of thousands of parasitic lawyers, thousands of liberal lenient judges, a panoply of people-controlling laws, rules, and regulations, and millions of lawsuits is like a cancer eating away at America's financial/religious freedoms.

In many ways, America is taking a giant step toward a Soviet-type legal system, which is designed to stifle political and religious dissent. Patriotic Americans and complacent, apathetic Christians need to wake up and realize that the noose is rapidly tightening. We are like the frog that is being slowly boiled, but today the heat is being rapidly turned up.

The present thrust of the legal left in America to attack and neutralize the Christian church is the most dangerous attack on Christianity in U.S. history. Today tort law is civil. But there is a trend in the U.S. legal system to criminalize civil violations. So, before the decade of the 1990s is over, many religious freedoms and activities which we take for granted here in America could become illegal and subject to severe civil or criminal penalties. Could this be the beginning of Christian persecution and of driving the true Christian church in America underground by the mid- to late-1990s—as it is in the Soviet Union and Red China today?

It should also be noted that no new laws need to be passed to implement this ABA/legal left broadside against Christianity in America. There is an army of liberal left lawyers and judges just waiting to go on the attack against Christians and Christian organizations via *litigation,* liberal interpretation of, and rulings on existing laws. In other words, the attack is not in the nebulous future—*it has already begun.*

The moral decline in America can also be observed in the patriotic decline. For example, in June of 1990, the Supreme Court ruled that it is permissible to burn the American flag, our symbol of freedom and sovereignty, in public. They ruled that the freedom to burn the flag was part of our "free speech" guarantees under the First Amendment to the Constitution. Civil rights groups have cheered the decision. Incredibly, the liberal logic says we should have the freedom of speech to burn the U.S. flag, but not the freedom of speech to pray in school.

In July 1989, the Supreme Court (in an ACLU suit) severely limited Christmas nativity scenes and other religious displays on government property. Justice Henry Blackman, writing for the majority, said:

> *"The placement of the creche violates the Constitution because nothing in the context of the display detracts from the creche's religious message. The city's [i.e., Pittsburgh's] overall display must be understood as conveying the city's secular recognition of different traditions for celebrating the winter holiday season."*

Justice Arthur Kennedy said in a minority dissenting opinion that by blocking the nativity scenes the Supreme Court showed "an unjustifiable hostility toward religion, a hostility inconsistent with our history and precedents."

We are also witnessing an educational decline. The American education system and television are today producing functional illiterates. Only 7 percent of American 17-year-olds are ready for college math; 21

percent of adult Americans believe the sun goes around the earth; 17 percent think the earth orbits around the sun in one day; 78 percent cannot name a single member of Bush's Cabinet; only 10 percent of Americans know that the U.S. secretary of state is James Baker; 40 percent of U.S. college students cannot locate Japan on a map; only 1,300 out of 70,000 U.S. high schools have a global education component in their curriculum, etc.

Additionally, the U.S. Supreme Court has ruled, and our government and people have acquiesced, that 25 million babies (1.5 million per year) could be murdered in their mother's wombs, that prayer in school is illegal, but that pornography in school or on television is legal and part of our free speech. They recently ruled that prayers before high school football games are now illegal. In 1988 (according to the U.S. Justice Department), one out of every four households in America was the target of a violent crime or theft (in the U.S. West, it was 30.3 percent). This occurs as liberal judges release more and more criminals, or hand out minimal sentences. And it goes on and on.

But the prosperous, complacent, apathetic, well-entertained American people (*including most Christians*) barely take notice that their way of life, their traditions, and their freedoms are eroding out from under them so fast that before the 1990s are history, they will be slaves and will have lost it all.

It has happened in every major empire in history. They begin humble and poor, but strong in character and spiritual faith; they become prosperous; they forget their principles, values, and God; they lose their morality and vision; and they descend right back into slavery. That is where America finds itself today.

Chapter Two

Toward a Socialist America: The U.S. Political Plunge to the Left

The right side of the "perspective triangle" represents the social-political decline of Western civilization, and certainly America. As the moral and spiritual underpinnings of society grow more and more liberal and farther and farther away from biblical Christianity or even the Judeo/Christian heritage, one can expect the social and political realm to move as well. This is happening. Theological liberalism defines those who have left affirmation of scriptural authority and have allowed their belief systems to be open to anything. The political counterpart of the term liberalism invariably accompanies this change. This chapter concretely establishes this trend in America.

A political sickness dominates America today. Call it socialism, liberalism, or humanism; but whatever label you put on it, it is sapping our strength, our morality, our standard of living, and our freedoms. Every single plank in Norman Thomas' Socialist Party platform of 1932 had been adopted in the U.S. 20 years ago, and today the liberals who dominate both political parties, the Administration, Congress, the gargantuan government bureaucracy, the judiciary, academia, and the media are pushing

America into the socialist quagmire described by George Orwell in his novels *1984* and *Animal Farm*.

It has long been said that the communist system would move toward capitalism and democracy, while the capitalist, democratic countries of the West would move toward socialism and communism—with East and West meeting somewhere in the middle. Perhaps this is what the liberal Eastern Establishment means by their stated goal of "merging the common interests of America and Russia." John Strachey, a high official in the British Labor Party and also the British Communist Party said several decades ago:

> *"You cannot move directly from capitalism to communism. Socialism is a necessary stepping stone to communism and hence all communists should work for socialism."*

Mikhail Gorbachev refers to communism as "scientific socialism" and to himself as a socialist, while the old communists of Eastern Europe now call themselves socialists and have renamed their communist parties "Democratic Socialists," "Social Democrats," etc.

The U.S. government and power structure has been moving the country to the political left so gradually and for so long (like boiling the frog slowly in warm water) that most Americans don't even remember what America was like when it was truly free. Most Americans believe in free enterprise, not socialism, but our politicians are, in piecemeal fashion, imposing socialism on us. Most Americans are traditionalists, who are interested in their families, their country, their businesses, and their neighborhoods. In Washington, however, both Democrats and Republicans are fundamentally internationalists who view our traditional nationalism as old fashioned, out-dated, unsophisticated, and even reactionary.

These liberals tells us that we must be taxed more and our defenses cut because of our huge deficits, and yet they spend ever increasing billions of our money for foreign aid (to the Third World, Soviet bloc, Red China, etc.), for the World Bank, for 25 percent of the funding of the United Nations, and for dozens of other international boondoggles. The majority of Americans are hardworking citizens who don't approve of liberal wealth redistribution schemes whereby they are taxed to pay subsidies to those who don't want to work or to the impoverished Third World masses.

Most Americans are law-abiding citizens who don't approve of handing neighborhoods, cities, and housing projects over to criminals while social workers, lawyers, and judges debate the fine points of the criminal's rights and disadvantaged background. While our streets, our property, and even our schools are unsafe and insecure, our liberal government's response is not to punish the criminals, but to nurture them, to deny the victims any means of self-defense (especially via firearms), and to then send us the bill. In many instances, the criminal is treated better, given more rights, and pampered more than the victim.

Most Americans believe firmly in the principles of fairness and of equal opportunity, but Congress, the executive branch, and the federal judiciary have turned racist and are fanatically promoting quotas and reverse discrimination in favor of racial minorities, gays, womens libbers, AIDS victims, the poor, etc. Socialistic legislation is being passed that allegedly protects minorities, but in reality discriminates against the great majority of middle class Americans. Most Americans are heterosexual, and yet the government, the TV networks, the American political left, and our educational system, in their obsession with homosexuality, are trying to push homosexuality and the gay lifestyle down the American people's throats.

Today, no matter what business you are in, there are at least two or three federal agencies such as OSHA, EPA, SEC, IRS, BATF, etc. (and several state and local ones, as well) to regulate your business and to harass you with hundreds of bureaucratic regulations. The cost in extra paperwork, extra employees, time, money, and aggravation of adhering to this myriad of regulations is driving tens of thousands of small- to medium-sized U.S. businesses out of business. Only the largest companies, those staffed with dozens of accountants and lawyers, can survive this bureaucratic onslaught.

Furthermore, our government is now criminalizing (e.g., with heavy fines and jail sentences) what were formerly civil violations, so that if a businessman inadvertently violates one of the myriad of new regulations, he can go to jail. For example, if an employee of a bank, a stock brokerage firm, or a coin dealer gives any information to a client that can be "construed" as helping the investor to avoid the IRS reporting requirements emanating from the Bank Secrecy Act of 1986, the criminal penalty for that employee is *10 years in jail and a $500,000 dollar fine per violation*. The penalty is *less* for bank robbery, murder, rape, or drug dealing.

Violations of the Clean Air Act can result in a *450-year* jail sentence; S&L or bank fraud can result in a *100-year* jail term; and failure to register currently owned semi-automatic firearms can result in a one to eight-year prison term. Now, do you see why the Administration wants to double U.S. prison capacity? It's not for traditional criminals such as murderers, drug dealers, bank robbers, and rapists, but for middle-class Americans who fall victim to the new rash of socialist laws and regulations.

Crises of one sort or another (real or manufactured) are a great excuse for quantum jumps in socialistic legislation and government controls. Those planning the New World Order speak continually of *crises*—the population crisis, environmental crisis, social crisis, constitutional crisis, etc. Crises provide the rationale for *crisis management*. The primary issue with which the socialists are planning to socialize America in the 1990s and move us into a world government is environmentalism.

The Environmental Crisis: The Greening of America

On January 14, 1990, Mikhail Gorbachev addressed the "Global Forum of Spiritual and Parliamentary Leaders on Human Survival" (an international environmentalist group) in Moscow. The Soviet leader told the visiting delegates:

"We are in a world, and as a world we have an ecological imperative. We are approaching a point of no return in the environment. We are a human society and we are rational, and we will not let an ecological disaster happen. There is an environmental consciousness that now pervades Europe. In the past it was the nuclear threat. In the Nineties it will be the environmental crisis."

Gorbachev proposed a symbol for the worldwide environmental crusade—*a green cross.*

Don Bell wrote in his excellent *Don Bell Reports* on September 9, 1989:

*"Regardless of all other attempts and plans, including military conquest, if the New World Order and its world government are to succeed with **the necessary approval of the people of the world**, there had to be created a great cause of global dimensions, a cause great enough to overshadow all racial, cultural, ethnic, religious, economic, and monetary differences. There had to be created 'a religious revival to protect Mother Earth.' There had to be problems that could be expanded to crisis proportions, problems that individual nations couldn't resolve, problems that involved not the protection of the United States or of Mother Russia, but of **Mother Earth**. Therefore, the architects of the New World Order created three major dangers, not to any nation, or nations in particular, but to **Mother Earth**, which they call 'the planet that is the homeland to us all, regardless of race, creed, or national origin.' Interestingly enough, this 'Mother Earth' worship appears in ancient Bible times. Many of the nations that the children of Israel were to utterly annihilate in the Promised Land (after the exodus) had as part of their religious practices various forms of earth worship. Jehovah God found this so detestable He wanted it completely obliterated to avoid contamination of His people.*

"Those dangers upon which the global environmental crisis is based are: 1) the greenhouse effect; 2) the ozone hole; and 3) toxic pollution. The media and the political left have taken these three global environmental crises, presented them as a permanent crisis and a

threat to the 'global village,' which can only be remedied by 'global cooperation.' **Therefore, global authority with the power to overrule national governments must be established. 'A New World Order for a new age of cooperation is needed,' the globalists say.**"

This globalism certainly sounds like the Beast system of Revelation 13. As David Horowitz and Peter Collier (former 1960s radicals) said in their book, *The Destructive Generation*:

"The message has now gone out to all leftists: **'Substitute green for red'** *— that is,* **push socialism labeled as environmentalism as the new priority.**"

The media responded. *Time* magazine in December 1988 nominated earth as the Planet of the Year. *Fortune* magazine declared 1988 as "the year the earth spoke back." Then Gorbachev made a speech before the U.N. in which he said:

"Let us also think about setting up within the framework of the United Nations a center for emergency environmental assistance."

Then in March 1988, 24 nations met at the World Court (at the Hague) and called for a

"supranational agency within the framework of the U.N. that could impose sanctions against any country negatively impacting the environment."

Out of this came agreement by these nations to accept the binding jurisdiction of the World Court under "a large number of international treaties." The U.S. State Department and the Administration enthusiastically signed on (and signed away a large measure of U.S. sovereignty).

Meanwhile the Greens are organizing and increasing their power all over Europe. In 1989, the Ecologist Party (Greens) won over 1,800 city council seats across Europe. Similar Green parties virtually dominated the domestic political scene in West Germany and Sweden. Over two million voters opted for the Green Party in England in 1989. All over Europe the Green (environmental) parties are pushing the dissolution of NATO, the support for immediate and unconditional nuclear disarmament, the abolishment of private banking, the establishment of government control over the amount of goods people can buy, the imposition of heavy taxes for air and road travel, the revamping of educational curriculum to indoctrinate students with these Green issues, the promotion of homosexual rights, and the support of feminist issues.

These Green/socialist issues are catching on in America—many under the guise of environmentalism. Zbigniew Brzezinski, in the winter issue of the Council on Foreign Relations quarterly, *Foreign Affairs*, indicated that the environmental crisis is designed as a cover for the grand merger of East and West, of the Warsaw Pact nations and the nations of Europe. He wrote:

"The Council of Europe and the European Community could also make an important contribution by offering to assist in the creation of a central European program for ecological salvation."

The environmental crisis is the vehicle upon which the New Age movement, the New World Order, and the communists' plan to socialize Europe and America, and to move the world to global government before the close of this decade. *The environmental crisis is a cover for the grand merger of East and West, of the Soviet bloc, Western Europe, and America.*

The Administration, congressional liberals, and radical environmentalists have pushed the most horrendous environmentalist bill ever through both houses of Congress. The current cost of the 1970 and 1977 Clean Air laws is $31 billion per year (three times higher than anywhere else in the world) and the Bush Clean Air Act will cost American business between $50 billion and $100 billion per year (*that's $500 billion to $1 trillion for the decade of the 1990s*) according to economist Warren Brooks. It will drive millions of jobs to other countries where conditions and costs are more sensible. *It's the formula for the deindustrialization of the U.S. economy, which is already reeling due to lack of world competitiveness caused by high taxes and over-regulation.*

The Clean Air Act requires as many as 150,000 American businesses, from heavy manufacturing to small print shops and dry cleaners, to secure specific EPA permits for every one of more than 191 "air pollutants" if they emit more than 2.5 to 7 pounds per hour. Who will monitor and measure these emissions — the business? The EPA bureaucrats? In addition, every time a company changes any part of its process affecting any one of the permitted substances, even if that modification produces less toxicity, new permits are required. Every new product would have to pass through EPA filters. *Penalties would include up to 450 years in prison (that's right, 450 years) and unlimited fines at $25,000 per day, with company* *informants and competitors offered up to $10,000 in bounties for reporting suspected violators to the EPA.* (Remember, Big Brother is now *criminalizing* what were formerly civil violations of government regulations.)

The act requires production of vehicles using alternative fuels (ethanol or electricity) and drastically limits hydrocarbon and nitrogen oxide emissions, greatly increasing production costs. The highly flammable fuel will turn minor car wrecks into flaming torches. Methanol (another mandated fuel) is highly poisonous and can be expected to contribute to 100 to 300 poisoning deaths per year, while doing nothing for emissions on 1985 or later model cars. It is estimated by economist Brooks that the Clean Air Act will "force all Americans to pay $20 billion more a year for driving — primarily because of smog in the Los Angeles Basin, which serves as a model for the rest of the country."

The Clean Air Act phases out chlorofluorocarbons used in refrigeration, air conditioning, foam insulation, solvents, fire extinguishers, aerosol cans, and in the cleaning of electronic equipment. These CFCs are used by 5,000 companies (in equipment worth $135 billion dollars) to produce $28 billion in goods or services annually. American business and industry will lose tens of billions of dollars annually from the phase-out of chlorofluorocarbons and many companies will be forced to close down.

Under this act, tens of billions of dollars will be spent each year to cure *acid rain* (e.g. $100 billion over the next 20 years), in spite of the fact that an official 1987 federal government study on *acid rain* by the National Acid Precipitation Assessment Program reported that relatively few U.S. lakes and streams were acidified and damage to crops, forests, and human health were negligible. The study said $700,000 worth of annual liming of a handful of lakes would completely eliminate the problem. *Global warming* (the so-called "greenhouse effect") is another one of the "great crises" cited by the environmentalists (in spite of respected climatologists reports that the earth is actually cooling slightly). The Clean Air Act will cost tens of billions to lower atmospheric carbon dioxide levels (allegedly the cause of global warming) in spite of the fact that industrially generated carbon dioxide is a minor part of total global CO_2 levels (i.e. 18 billion tons out of 759 billion tons of CO_2 entering the atmosphere each year).

In summary, the environmental crisis is a phony crisis manufactured by the socialists to socialize America under another label. The Bush Clean Air Act will bankrupt thousands of U.S. companies, cost hundreds of thousands of U.S. jobs, cost hundreds of billions of dollars over the next 10 years, and cause the shutdown of U.S. industry in places like Detroit, Philadelphia, Baltimore, Pittsburgh, Chicago, Toledo, and St. Louis. *Human Events* says the act "threatens economic strangulation of the U.S. on the altar of ideological environmental madness." *It will, however, create a lot of new jobs and industry for Western Europe—because that is where the business will move when it shuts down here.*

The Clean Air Act could precipitate a U.S. recession/depression, but even more ominously, *it will deindustrialize America, help to make us a fourth-rate industrial power, and give us a quantum leap into socialism.*

The Hate Crimes Bill

Congress has passed and President Bush signed a Hate Crimes Bill which requires the Justice Department to collect and publish data on crimes motivated by prejudice against a race, religion, ethnic group, *or sexual*

orientation. Pushed through by the powerful gay/
homosexual lobby, National Gay and Lesbian Task
Force, this law authorizes federal and state authorities to
collect data on so-called hate crimes and to formulate
laws or regulations to prosecute perpetrators of same.
"Hate crimes" is then defined as an assault, intimidation,
or harassment against a minority group or homosexual
group—*in other words, unkind words or even thoughts
toward these groups can be construed as a "hate crime."*
Sen. Jesse Helms was one of the few vocal opponents
to this bill. Quoting Sen. Helms from the *Congressional
Record* (Feb. 8, 1990), the senator said:

> *"Let the Senate understand that this bill is the
> flagship of the homosexual, lesbian legislative
> agenda. Apparently there is a great deal of
> political clout in the homosexual community.
> With this legislation, the radical elements of the
> homosexual community have hoodwinked a lot
> of people into believing that this is not a homo-
> sexual right's bill. . . . The bill actually attempts
> to shift our focus away from criminal behavior
> and toward motivation behind the behavior."*

Sen. Helms goes on to point out in the *Record* that 80
percent of the statistics collected by the National Gay and
Lesbian Task Force since 1985 to support this legislation
are based primarily on verbal crimes (i.e., calling a gay a
"blankety blank queer") or some such other heinous crime.
As Helms pointed out in his losing fight against this legislation, a person will be guilty of a "hate crime" for simply
speaking out publicly (or having negative thoughts) against
a Jew, a Black, a Mexican, a lesbian, a homosexual, or their
political movements. Helms went on:

"We are now considering legislation based on statistics that include name-calling at public rallies as crimes. Are we going on to the school yards of this country and when two kids get angry with each other and call each other names—what are we going to do, cart them over to the reformatory or add them to the list of 'hate crimes' perpetrators. This is ridiculous!"

Helms went on to point out the hypocrisy of liberals who defend flag burning and pornographic art as "free speech," but want to jail someone for exercising their "free speech" by verbally expressing their disapproval of a gay, a Black, or some other minority group or organization. If a person verbally (or in writing) pointed out that the National Organization for Women is made up of leftists, lesbians, and men-haters, that person would be guilty of a "hate crime." Helms concluded:

"There is no doubt in my mind where the passage of this legislation will lead us. It will be the first time that sexual orientation—and that means homosexuality—will be marked out for protected status. The radical homosexuals know this, and this legislation is simply one step in their radical revolution. They make no bones about their ultimate goal in getting this Hate Crimes Act enacted. Mr. David Wertheimer of the Gay and Lesbian Anti-Violence Project, commenting on the need for this legislation, said: 'Our final goal should be nothing less than the expansion of the Civil Rights Act to include lesbians and gay men.' "

Other supporters of this Hate Crimes Act are rather interesting: American Bar Association, National Council of Churches, National Education Association, League of Women Voters, National Organization for Women, National Lawyers Guild, Presbyterian Church U.S.A., United Church of Christ, United Methodist Church, Unitarian Church, and a host of gay/lesbian organizations.

Homosexual inclusion in the Civil Rights Act means employers, churches, clubs, etc. will have to accept or employ gays in the same ratio as they claim to be in the population (i.e., 10 percent) whether they have AIDS or not. Discrimination against gays would become a criminal offense. But the broader implications of this Hate Crimes Act are really ominous. Free speech in America is now in grave danger. This legislation will be used against conservatives and Christians over the next few years as they speak out against groups who threaten our American way of life and freedoms, and will be used to silence, jail, or otherwise destroy the opponents of a socialist America. Subsequent legislation will undoubtedly criminalize such "hate crimes" so that one day in the not-too-distant future, a conservative or Christian could be jailed for speaking out against the Trilateral Commission, the Council on Foreign Relations, the State Department, or various leftist groups, etc.—all "minorities in need of protection."

America's Gun Control Juggernaut

". . . One of the basic conditions for the victory of socialism is the arming of the workers and the disarming of the bourgeoisie [the middle class]. *"*
—from *Lenin's Collected Works*

"Register all firearms, under any pretext, as a prelude to confiscating them."
—from *The Communist Rules of Revolution*

"Tell the American people never to lose their guns. As long as they keep their guns in their hands, whatever happened here will never happen there."
—a female student from Beijing, Red China,
describing her parent's last words to her

"Before a standing army can rule, the people must be disarmed, as they are in almost every kingdom in Europe. The supreme power in America cannot enforce unjust laws by the sword, because the whole body of the people are armed, and constitute a force superior to any band of regular troops that can be, on any pretense, raised in the United States."
—Noah Webster, *An Examination Into the Leading Principles of the Federal Constitution*, 1787

"Americans need never fear their government because of the advantage of being armed, which the Americans possess over the people of almost every other nation."
—James Madison, *The Federalist Papers*

The disarming of Americans is essential to converting the U.S. to a socialist America and merging it into a global government. Every communist leader from Lenin to Gorbachev to Gus Hall (chairman of the Communist Party U.S.A.) has reiterated that an important part of communist strategy is:

1. Arming the right people (e.g., the criminals, the terrorists, the revolutionaries, the communists); and

2. Disarming the reactionaries or nationalists who might meet violence with violence in any attempted communist takeover.

Communists, socialist bureaucrats, and criminals have no desire to be shot—they prefer to deal with an unarmed citizenry. And what is equally important is that both the communists and the criminal element have long proven that they can and will obtain firearms, no matter what the government restrictions to the contrary may be.

The communists have taken over nation after nation when the number of communists in that country numbered less than three percent of the population. How could that happen? Because they were the ones with the guns. It happened in Latvia, Estonia, Lithuania, China, the Balkans, and numerous countries in Europe and Asia. More recently, this happened in Cuba, Central America, and Africa. It is happening today in the Natal Province and Black townships of South Africa—where the revolutionary comrades have the guns (always of Soviet make) and the moderate Christian, anti-communist Blacks remain unarmed (by edict of South Africa's White liberal government). It is happening today in the Philippines, in the mountains of Peru, and in El Salvador where the communist revolutionaries have the guns and the people do not. And it could happen in a united Europe over the next five years as thousands of well-armed Spetsnaz commandos and KGB agents are pouring into Western Europe at this writing.

Many Americans are still not capable of understanding that the communists abroad and at home, aided and abetted by liberals, socialist politicians, and the media are working overtime to disarm the American people. Through media disinformation, they have confused the people and the issues. Many people still think that gun ownership has primarily to do with target shooting, squirrel hunting, match competition, going after doves or deer, or gun collecting. These are recreational uses, and are relatively unimportant.

A couple of years ago, the gun control movement coined the emotionally negative phrase "Saturday night special" to launch a campaign against handgun ownership (e.g., .357 magnums, .38 specials, .45 automatics, etc.). They were only partially successful in certain states and cities thanks to the efforts of several large pro-gun citizens' groups. Now, the anti-gun political left (led by Handgun Control, Inc. and the National Coalition to Ban Handguns) has coined a new emotional propaganda phrase with which to incite anti-gun hysteria—"the assault rifle."

In the immediate wake of the Stockton, California murder of five school children by a maniac with an AK-47, the political left across America began to scream in well-orchestrated unison—"assault rifles are evil and barbaric" and must be banned. After a week's national media blitz on this theme, they began to substitute for the phrase "assault rifles," the phrase "semi-automatic weapons"—*which includes most of the rifles and over half of the handguns and shotguns in America.* So the second phase was to launch a cry for the banning of ***all** semi-automatic firearms.*

Note: The only hunters' rifles which are not semi-automatic are the older bolt-action, lever-action, and pump-action models—a tiny minority of all U.S. rifles and revolvers. Even the popular World War II .45 automatic is a *semi*-automatic pistol. (Even bolt-action rifles and most shotguns are included in the new anti-gun legislation.) According to the U.S. Defense Department, "assault rifles" are by definition *"fully* automatic." None of the foreign-made rifles banned by the Administration are fully automatic (these have been illegal since the 1930s), nor are they "assault rifles." This was a scare/ propaganda phrase fabricated by the leftist gun control groups and latched onto by the media and the Bush Administration.

In March 1989, the Administration moved to ban the importation of certain foreign-made semi-automatic rifles (such as the Uzi, AK-47, etc.) and in April 1989 widened the ban on importation to *all* foreign-made semi-automatic rifles, including .22 calibre. They pressured Colt Industries, which has large military contracts with the government, to cancel production of the AR-15 (and it did) and they are pressuring other U.S. manufacturers to do the same. *The BATF has even been sent into gun stores across America since mid-1989 to photocopy Form 4473 records of anyone who has bought a semi-automatic weapon. (This is called the BATF Advanced Tracing Program.)* (The BATF is the "gestapo" of gun control, which is made up of rabidly anti-gun bureaucrats who have, for years, trounced on the rights of gun dealers, gun owners, hunters, etc. They will be the primary "enforcers.")

Meanwhile, the highly emotional anti-gun propaganda onslaught is accelerating all across the country, orchestrated by the political left. Stringent gun control legislation has been introduced in the House and Senate, in about 30 states, and dozens of cities—legislation ranging from registration of all handguns, rifles, and shotguns, confiscation of handguns and rifles, outlawing of the manufacture of firearms and ammunition, etc. This entire anti-gun onslaught is *too well orchestrated*, and moving too rapidly via hundreds of leftist groups, the press, congressional liberals, and almost identical legislation popping up all across America at one time, *to be spontaneous.* (In many ways, this onslaught closely resembles the highly emotional, brilliantly orchestrated leftist drive for South African sanctions.) The political left is making its great final drive to disarm America. And they have a weak, liberal, vacillating president who will help them facilitate their plan.

Note: The drug war has been an excuse for the government to massively invade America's financial privacy, under the guise that *all* Americans are "potential money launderers." Now the drug war is being used as an excuse for confiscating Americans' firearms under the pretext that drug runners use guns, so if we want to stop the drug war, we must disarm the American people. This, of course, is total nonsense, since the drug runners and criminals will never be disarmed. Furthermore, they use fully automatic weapons which are already illegal.

Why is gun control so dangerous? According to the American Federation of Police:

> *"There are many Americans who fear for their lives. They know that at some point, they will have to protect themselves, their own families, and their own property. Should these people be disarmed? No, we don't need to disarm our loyal citizens, our friends, and our neighbors."*

Gun control is unconstitutional. The Second Amendment guarantees, "The right of the people to keep and bear arms shall not be infringed."

Crime in America (including murder, rape, robbery, and drug-running) is at an all-time high today. According to respected Florida State University criminologist Gary Kleck, in a scholarly article in the February 1988 issue of

Social Problems: "Personal defense with firearms in America occurs more than 2,000 times per day." He estimates that "there are 645,000 defensive uses of handguns against criminals per year (*excluding* police and military uses)." Kleck concludes that "civilian ownership and use of guns has a deterrent and social control effect on violent crimes and burglary."

A high-ranking official in the Houston Police Department told this writer several years ago:

> *"The police cannot prevent most crimes. They cannot be everywhere at once, nor can they anticipate where a criminal will strike next. They can only pick up the pieces, or bodies, after the fact. . . . Armed citizens have to protect themselves. We cannot. It is the law of the jungle."*

If strict gun control laws are enacted, criminals will continue to get all the guns they want, while the citizens will be left unarmed and defenseless. In interviews with prison inmates, the majority of inmates have admitted that when mugging or breaking into a home, their main worry is that they may be facing a person who is armed.

A second danger of disarming Americans is the giant horde of illegal immigrants (10 to 20 million to date) who have entered America in recent years. There is an above-average criminal element in this group. Another problem is the vulnerability to an armed communist invasion from Central America through Mexico over the next five to ten years. A disarmed American citizenry is a much more vulnerable target.

As in the anti-South Africa, anti-apartheid movements, the anti-gun political left is extremely well organized, coordinated, and financed. The present onslaught has been planned for several years. Key elements of their strategy include:

1. *Rely on emotionalism and ignorance*—Capitalize on morbid events like the California schoolyard killing, or a vicious double murder in Denver, and then emotionally manipulate a vulnerable public with disinformation, semantic deception, and distortion to create an overnight anti-gun bandwagon. Emphasize the idea that *"guns* kill people," instead of the truth that *"people* kill people"—with knives, strangulation, hammers, poison, cars, *and guns.* Ted Bundy didn't need a gun to viciously kill 50 to 100 women.

2. *Utilize the Hegelian Principle*—This is a three-step process authored by Hegel and perfected by the Marxist/Leninists: thesis, antithesis, and synthesis. The *first step* (thesis) is to create (or fabricate) a problem. The *second step* (antithesis) is to generate opposition to the problem (fear, panic, hysteria). The *third step* (synthesis) is to offer the solution to the problem created in step one—*change which would have been impossible to impose on the people without the proper psychological conditioning achieved in stages one and two.*

3. *The propaganda onslaught*—Having created the problem (e.g., "guns kill people, and therefore, are evil"), step two is to create fear, panic, and hysteria. Since early 1989, we have seen the most concentrated, orchestrated media blitz against guns since the media and political left cranked up for the INF treaty and for South African sanctions. Thousands of articles in newspapers and news

magazines have appeared with titles such as: "Buyers Hoarding AK-47s"; "There's No Right to Bear Semi-Automatics"; "Assault Weapons: Death and Taxes" (an article claiming that the medical cost of treating gunshot wounds in America is $1 billion per year); "Pushers Best Friends, the NRA"; "Playing With Guns," etc. Nationwide polls (with questions such as "Do you think we should end bloodshed and massacres with assault rifles?") claim 80 percent of the public is for banning these "killing machines." In short, the media is creating the appearance of a "groundswell" of support for a gun ban, just as they did with South African sanctions. It is also tying the guns directly to the emotional issue of drugs, intimating that if you get rid of one, you'll get rid of the other.

4. *Attacking the pro-gun groups*—The political left and the media have launched a massive propaganda campaign against the 2.8 million-member National Rifle Association, gun dealers, gun magazines, and owners by depicting these pro-gunners as bloodthirsty, heartless, trigger-happy sleazeballs. The *New York Times* article ("Pushers' Best Friend, the NRA") by Ted Kennedy talked about how "*the unholy alliance between the NRA and the drug dealers* is slowly turning some urban neighborhoods into killing fields and transforming Washington and other cities into free fire zones."

5. *Extending the bans to handguns and ammunition*—It is noteworthy that the campaign to ban assault rifles and semi-automatic weapons is being spearheaded by Handgun Control Inc. and the National Coalition to Ban Handguns. The attack on semi-automatics is a backdoor attack on banning

handguns—their top priority. This is seen in a lot of the new legislation popping up in various states. Legislation has been introduced to ban the manufacture, transfer, and importation of .25 calibre and .32 calibre bullets, saying: "Without ammunition, a handgun is useless." Much more legislation on other calibres of ammunition will follow.

6. *Link guns to drugs and the drug war*—In a classic use of guilt by association, the left are equating guns with the drug war arguing that with a gun ban, the drug war would evaporate. Sen. James McClure (R-ID) has countered that the gun ban "has almost nothing to do with any real assault on drug trafficking and drugs in this country. . . . Can anyone believe that someone smuggling illegal drugs into this country will have any trouble smuggling illegal guns?"

7. *Split the gun owners off from the law enforcement community*—There are hundreds of liberal police chiefs (appointed by liberal mayors) around the country who have joined the political left in supporting gun control, and some of those are getting high media visibility. However, the great majority of law enforcement officers agree with the National Sheriffs Association, which has said: "There's no valid evidence whatsoever to indicate that depriving law-abiding American citizens of the right to own firearms would in any way lessen crime or criminal activity. . . . The National Sheriffs Association unequivocally opposes any legislation that has as its intent the confiscation of firearms . . . or the taking away from law-abiding American citizens their right to purchase, own, and keep arms."

There are numerous current anti-gun legislative initiatives. For example, one has been introduced which would ban nationally the sale of all new semi-automatic rifles and pistols capable of holding a ten-shot magazine (e.g., almost *all* of them), and shotguns and .22 rifles with tubular magazines holding more than six rounds. Every person who presently owns such an "assault weapon" would have to register it with the BATF within 30 days (e.g., fingerprints and the same kind of information now needed to get a machine gun license—including permission of the local police). All magazines holding ten rounds or more and fitting a semi-automatic rifle, pistol, or shotgun become illegal to possess after 60 days.

Another bill specifically names AR-15s, Ruger Mini-14s, and eight others, but says the attorney general and treasury secretary can ban all others. *A person who fails to register his .22 rifle (or other semi-automatic) or turn in his ten-round magazines is subject to a five-year jail sentence as a criminal felon. This bill calls for confiscation within 30 days after enactment into law with no compensation.*

In California, bills have passed both legislative houses (on April 17, 1989) making it *a felony to possess, sell, or manufacture* an "assault weapon" or semi-automatic rifle or pistol. *Failure to register these firearms in California will carry prison terms of up to eight years.* Similar legislation has been introduced in Florida, Colorado, Oregon, Washington, Minnesota, Massachusetts, Connecticut, Rhode Island, New York, New Jersey, Maryland, Illinois, Wisconsin, and about a dozen other states; as well as local legislation in Cleveland, New Orleans, Los Angeles, New York City, Denver, etc. One bill introduced in the Colorado legislature even calls for the police and highway patrol to set up roadblocks to stop cars and check them for firearms.

Still other legislation in the U.S. Congress calls for the following gun control measures (which will apply to gun stores, at gun shows, and in all private gun transactions):

1. The legislation *gives the secretary of the treasury full power to outlaw the possession, sale, or gift of any semi-automatic rifle* he deems not to be suitable for sports. The bill will ban specific semi-automatic firearms and within a short period of time all other semi-automatics will be included. The most dangerous aspect of the bill is that it gives a government bureaucrat the authority as to which guns he can arbitrarily ban.

2. This legislation *allows the secretary of the treasury to decide what reason is good enough to own a firearm.* He could, for instance, be free to rule that only hunting is a suitable reason, and as a practical matter, the BATF has already so ruled.

    Note: There is a quiet move on among environmentalists and liberal government bureaucrats to ban most public lands (i.e., national forests, wilderness areas, etc.) from hunting. So, if gun ownership is restricted to hunting, and hunting is banned in most areas, then the gun controllers will argue that guns are no longer needed.

3. This legislation requires that *before a rifle can be transferred by sale or gift, the recipient must undergo a comprehensive background check* (which will take a month or more) which includes a mug shot, fingerprints, and an interview with the local police.

    The local police chief has to sign off on the approval, and if he is liberal (as is the case in most of America's large cities today where the police chiefs are appointed by liberal mayors) he will probably refuse to approve the transfer. (In most large cities such as New York, Chicago, Denver, etc., it is already virtually impossible to get a gun permit from the police.)

4. This legislation outlaws *possession, sale, or gift of magazines with a capacity of more than seven rounds of ammunition.*

5. This legislation will *criminalize the possession of firearm springs, pins, screws,* etc., because the bill's wording says any part or combination of parts used in a restricted firearm is restricted as well.

6. This legislation *bans the manufacture of any firearm capable of receiving a bayonet without alteration of the gun.* Since a bayonet fits over virtually all gun barrels, virtually all guns are covered by this provision.

Failure to register firearms or adhere to all new gun transference procedures will render the gun owner a felon and render it illegal for him to ever again own a firearm.

The bottom line is that rifles, shotguns, and pistols will be covered by the above legislation. There are 200 million privately-owned firearms in the U.S. today, owned by about 70 million Americans (or about half of American households). There are 20 million handgun owners in the U.S. The lion's share of these owners are very emotional and possessive about their firearms—and see them as a way to protect their families. They will not take kindly to the government confiscating $25 to $50 billion worth of their firearms. Bloodshed and even a revolution could follow.

The political left has decided to declare war on 70 million American gun owners. This war is not against assault weapons, but against honest, law-abiding citizens. To take the guns out of the hands of American citizens at a time when criminal rage in America is exploding and our judges and courts are coddling and releasing dangerous felons (e.g., the Stockton murderer had been in jail and released by liberal judges seven times) is insane, unconstitutional, and, in itself, criminal. The U.S. cities like New York and Washington, which have stringent gun control bans, have the highest crime rates (including murder) in America *and* the highest incidence of the use of handguns in the perpetration of crimes against unarmed victims. (The criminal can always get a gun.)

Switzerland, on the other hand, insists that every male of military age must keep a powerful, *fully* automatic assault rifle in his home. Every home must be armed—by law—and some even keep mortars. Yet Switzerland has one of the most law-abiding citizenry, the lowest crime rate, and least violence of any country in the free world. And it has remained free for over a thousand years. Compare it to New York and Washington where handguns are completely banned. In fact, in Washington, Chief of Police Maurice Turner recently said that the District of Columbia gun ban law had completely failed, and he has called for an armed citizen's police auxiliary to help restore order.

Hard statistics have proven that armed citizens are far less likely to be crime victims than unarmed. Citizens acting in self-defense kill about three times more assailants and robbers than do police. But don't guns kill people? Yes they do—but in 1985, 45,901 Americans died in auto accidents; 12,001 died from falls; 4,938 died in fires; 4,407 drowned; 3,612 died from drugs or medication; 1,663 died by choking to death while eating; and 1,649 died from gunshot wounds. Undoubtedly all of these deaths were tragic, but should we now eliminate all autos, all high places, all fire, all water, all drugs/medication, and all food—as well as all guns? Get the point?!

The *Wall Street Journal* recently summed up the potential disaster if the anti-gunners from George Bush to Ted Kennedy, from Bill Bennett to Jane Fonda, from Howard Metzenbaum to Dan Rather get their way:

> *"What will happen if severe restrictions on semi-automatic rifles pass Congress or the state legislatures today? Millions of citizens who still believe in the Constitution will **not** forfeit or register their firearms; squads of federal and state agents will snoop; massive no-knock warrants will be issued; and both citizens and police will die in raids. While previously law-abiding citizens (now felons) and police battle each other, the drug lords will continue their nefarious trafficking. Adding firearms prohibition to drug prohibition means war on the innocent (and perhaps a police state), and by diverting police resources, will give armed pushers even more free reign."*

Thus perhaps the most dangerous of all the socialist attacks on America in the 1990s is the onslaught to register and confiscate America's firearms. America cannot be subjugated to communism or a socialist dictatorship until Americans are first disarmed. Poland has strict gun control; so does Cambodia, Russia, and Red China. Over 100 million people were brutally slaughtered in those countries, but first they were disarmed. The danger to people when they can't own guns is far greater than any danger gun ownership can ever create.

Conclusion

Gun control advocates, liberals, and the political left in America, armed with gun control endorsements from Presidents Nixon, Ford, Reagan, and Bush, are currently building gigantic momentum for a series of local, state, and national gun control initiatives aimed ultimately at banning the manufacture and sale of all firearms in the U.S. and registering and confiscating all firearms owned by honest, law-abiding Americans.

As crime and pillage increases all over America, honest, law-abiding citizens who wish to hunt, target practice, or, most importantly, defend their families, are being declared to be criminal felons for not registering or turning in their firearms. Hundreds have been jailed for so-called firearms felonies and tens of thousands more will be jailed if the plethora of new gun control legislation across the country is enacted.

Gun control in America is apparently to be a major cornerstone of the New World Order. It will be very difficult for the globalists to establish their world government under the United Nations without first disarming the American people.

The idea of an armed citizenry is as relevant today as it was 200 years ago. The British tried to keep firearms out of the hands of the colonists before the War for Independence. They said that the colonists did not need their guns because they had the British army to protect them from French and Indian attacks. Hostilities erupted near Boston on the road from Concord to Lexington when the Red Coats tried to confiscate a magazine of colonial muskets.

Today's "red coats," the Kennedys and those from Handgun Control, Inc., tell us the same thing the British tried to tell our forefathers—that private people do not need their guns.

Well, we need our guns as much as the American colonists needed theirs. While we enjoy peace with the French and the Indians today, America is a battleground in a drug war. Americans are being held hostage in their homes because they do not dare go out on the streets. There are not nearly enough police to protect the citizens. After all, there are only 150,000 police on duty at any one time in the whole country trying to protect a quarter of a billion Americans.

There are over 100 million firearms in private hands in this country, yet only a tiny fraction of one percent are ever used in crime. Private citizens are able to kill over 3,000 attackers in justifiable self-defense each year, and they wound and apprehend over 15,000 each year as well.

On average, over 2,700 Americans each day use a handgun, or a rifle, or a shotgun, to resist a criminal attack. While the advocates of gun control talk of it being more dangerous to use a gun in self-defense, Dr. Gary Kleck, a criminologist at Florida State University in Gainesville, has found that in fact, one is nearly twice as likely to be harmed when failing to resist a criminal as when resisting.

Gun control only has implications for law-abiding citizens. They will lose the ability to defend themselves and become more vulnerable in our crime-ridden society.

Surveys of felons have shown that their proclivity to commit criminal acts is more constrained by fear of encountering an armed victim than by fear of police and courts. *In 1990, about 645,000 citizens used their handguns to protect themselves from robbers, rapists, and murderers.* Hard statistics have proved that armed citizens are far less likely to become crime victims than those who are unarmed. Citizens acting in self-defense kill about three times more assailants and robbers than do police.

The gun controller's war on semi-automatic rifles is a subtle attack on the ownership of *all* rifles and shotguns (since about two-thirds of those in existence are semi-automatic), just as the gun controller's campaign to ban "Saturday night specials" was a disguised attack on ownership of *all* handguns. By calling these semi-automatic rifles and shotguns "assault weapons" or "para-military weapons," they have persuaded liberals in the national, state, and city governments and in the media that they are inherently evil and should be banned. (These rifles are actually no different than regular hunting rifles except for larger magazines. They just look different.)

They claim that semi-automatic weapons are the weapon of choice of drug dealers and organized crime. This is a lie. Police statistics show that the lion's share of gun-related crime in America is committed with shotguns (e.g., 60 percent), .38 specials, and machine guns (which are already illegal). So-called "assault rifles" are used in less than one percent of homicides in America.

The ultimate goal of the gun controllers is registration and confiscation of *all* handguns (semi-automatic or not) and *all* rifles and shotguns. They believe that they can accomplish this within five years. The trend in gun control legislation (local, state, and national) is accelerating dramatically. By the mid-1990s, if this momentum is not blocked, the American public will be disarmed. The tyranny of a Soviet-style police state will follow.

The liberal Eastern Establishment wants total gun registration and confiscation in America and believes they can slam-dunk this on the American people over the next few years. George Bush hails from the hierarchy of that Establishment and three more of the Establishment's men (former Presidents Ford, Nixon, and Reagan) have all jumped onto the gun-control bandwagon as well.

Bush and the Establishment believe that the American public must be disarmed before they can merge America into the New World Order under the United Nations. The best armed populace in the world will be very difficult to subjugate under a Soviet-style police state (*a la* Russia, China, Cuba, etc.) until it has first been disarmed. The big push for disarming Americans will come between 1993 and '96.

The implications of America's present gun control juggernaut are:

1. *Millions of law-abiding U.S. citizens who simply want to protect themselves are about to become criminals as Bush, the Congress, and the political left criminalize non-criminal acts. Tens of thousands of these individuals will be jailed.* Perhaps this is why Bush is doubling the size of the U.S. prison system.
2. The Bush Crime Bill and the gun control legislation described above will destroy Americans' civil rights, their Constitutional rights, and their freedom, and usher in a police state. The powers of the FBI, DEA, CID, BATF, etc., are about to be expanded dramatically, with an all-powerful police emerging by 1993 or '94. *In the very near future, gun owners and other Americans are going to have to fear that knock on the door in the middle of the night. The American version of the KGB is Beginning to emerge.*
3. The present gun control legislation will drive a

wedge between honest, law-abiding citizens and the local police—who will be forced to divert their energies from fighting real crime to harassing non-criminals who are about to be called criminals by "Big Brother." This legislation will turn the police against the citizenry, and the citizenry against the police.

4. This gun control juggernaut is just part of a larger plunge into socialism by America. *The Bank Secrecy Act of 1986, the Clean Air Act of 1990, the Hate Crimes Bill of 1990, are all part of a thrust to criminalize non-criminal activity, to control the American people, and to transform them into slaves by the end of the decade.*

5. America is becoming more like Russia every day. You can go to jail for owning a gun, for dealing in cash, for advocating financial privacy, for polluting the environment, for having unpopular thoughts, etc.

The Second Amendment to the U.S. Constitution was enacted not to protect hunters and sportsmen, but to insure that the government never had a monopoly of force it could use to oppress the citizenry with a police state. Recent events in China, the Baltics, and Russia should remind us once again that when a government has a monopoly on firearms, there is no check on its lust for power or oppression.

Alexander Solzhenitsyn wrote in his Nobel Prize-winning book, *Gulag Archipelago*, after 11 years in communist concentration camps:

"... At what exact point, then should one resist the communists? ... How we burned in the *prison camps later thinking: what would things have been like if every security operative, when he went out at night to make an arrest, had been uncertain whether he would return alive and had to say good-bye to his family?*

"Or if during periods of mass arrests people had not simply sat there in their lairs, paling with terror at every step on the staircase, but had understood they had nothing to lose and had boldly set up in the downstairs hall an ambush of half a dozen people with axes, hammers, pokers, or whatever else was at hand. . . . The Organs [police] would very quickly have suffered a shortage of officers . . . and notwithstanding all of Stalin's thirst, the cursed machine would have ground to a halt."

Car Searches/Sobriety Checks to Begin

The key words in the Bill of Rights which protect individuals from government harassment are "freedom from unreasonable search and seizure." The Fourth Amendment to the U.S. Constitutions says:

"The right of the people to be secure in their persons, houses, papers, and effects, against unreasonable searches and seizures, shall not be violated."

In early June of 1990, the U.S. Supreme Court (the same group of nine persons who ruled that flag burning is legal) ruled six to three that police checkpoints to apprehend drunks are legal. Police roadblocks to stop cars and interrogate drivers, give sobriety tests, and search the car if the police choose to do so seem far more in line with East bloc police state tactics than the America we have known.

Roadblocks, auto searches, and the running of sobriety checks on all drivers (99 percent of whom are not drinking) has a current parallel in the government's monitoring all of our bank accounts, our deposits and withdrawals to find that very occasional money launderer or drug dealer. *In both instances honest, law-abiding citizens are assumed to be guilty until they can prove themselves innocent.*

A few years hence, after we have gotten used to roadblocks, sobriety interrogations, and searches (just as we have come to take airport searches for granted), what if Big Brother decides he wants to search our cars and our homes for "illegal" firearms, or for cash, or "for some yet-to-be-declared illegal suspicious activity," or "wants to check your papers," as they do at East bloc checkpoints. *The Constitution says there first has to be reasonable cause before we're pulled over and searched. A Soviet-style police state will give us no such protection and neither will our present Supreme Court.*

Red Dawn Over Memphis

Big Brother and his agents are harassing more and more U.S. citizens and businesses, churches, etc., using gestapo-type tactics of intimidation, interrogation, formerly illegal search and seizure techniques, and imprisonment. A case in point is Franklin Sanders, a Christian, a coin dealer, a newsletter writer (he writes *The Money Changer*), and a patriot who has long warned his clients, readers, and friends about the growing abuse of government power, especially by the IRS.

In January 1990, Sander's home was raided at dawn by ten IRS revenue agents and seven SWAT team members carrying automatic weapons, who proceeded to hold him, his pregnant wife, and seven children captive for eight hours while the agents waited for a search warrant. The interview which follows between Sanders and former Congressman Ron Paul is frightening—it's right out of Orwell's *1984* or East Germany, Russia, or Red China. But it's America 1992, and it could happen to you!

Q. Why were you abused?

A. In 1985, I was the first person to publish an interview with an IRS whistle-blower showing that the IRS intended to have a computer dossier on everybody in the country. The dossier would include everything you did with your money. About two weeks later, the IRS's Criminal Investigation Division (CID) told me I was the subject of a criminal investigation. I wrote a letter to the agent, who claimed he was a Christian, and rebuked him on scriptural grounds. That is one of the overt acts I am charged with. They say it was a threatening letter. Well, if one Christian can't tell another when he is violating Scripture, then put me in jail.

Q. What else are you charged with?

A. They said I am operating a secret banking business. In 1984 my partner and I started a gold and silver bank, a warehouse exchange system. I have written about the dangers of our shaky banking system for ten years. I sent thousands of announcements to people and went up and down the country making speeches promoting the bank. That's hardly secret. Also, the indictment cites as overt acts the fact that customers of mine closed their regular bank accounts. The government must now consider it a crime to close your bank account.

Q. *The IRS has also harassed your wife?*

A. *Yes. In May 1986, while I was out of town, a Vietnam vet, a man I barely knew, sent a threatening letter to the agent. The IRS-CID followed my wife around with two carloads of armed men. She had three children with her and was two months pregnant at the time, and I wasn't in town to protect her. When I got back, they hauled me into court. They arranged with the Tennessee Revenue Department to raid my office. They sent two armed men and held me hostage for four hours. They went through my files and took records.*

Q. *And they have harassed members of your church?*

A. *I'm a member of the Presbyterian Church of America. In April 1989 they subpoenaed nine members of my congregation to appear before a grand jury and asked them all sorts of crazy questions, such as: Do you have a paramilitary group ready to overthrow the U.S. government? Did anybody in your church teach or preach that you should not file tax returns? Did anybody preach that you can avoid filing tax returns? Well, my pastor has never preached about taxes, except to once say the property tax is ungodly.*

Q. *But so what if he did?*

A. *Exactly. The IRS wanted the church to turn over all its records. The church has a 2,000-year-old history of not doing that. The General Assembly of the PCA stuck by us even though they indicted 11 members of the church, four of them women.*

Q. *What was the January assault?*

A. *They arrested us in the middle of the night on*

January 9, and to do so sent seven SWAT team members and ten revenue agents. They were wearing black ninja suits and carried automatic weapons. My seven children were in the house. These men were cowboys. They only had a search warrant for me and my wife, and yet they kept the children captive. They stole my computer and my records. They have my bond set at $100,000.

Q. *How are you holding up?*

A. *The biggest problem is financial. I have been reduced to charity. As you know, justice in the United States is for the rich. Lawyers want $25,000 to $100,000 to defend my case. But it is either that or get a Soviet-style court-appointed attorney who is paid a pittance by the government. And even if I'm exonerated, I won't get reimbursement.*

Note: Thousands of U.S. citizens are similarly being harassed, persecuted, and jailed today by various agencies of the U.S. government in what is rapidly becoming the United Socialist States of America. New government regulations, and old ones which carried civil penalties, are being criminalized, with stiffer prison terms handed out than for murder, rape, burglarly, and drug dealing. It's being done to intimidate the masses into compliance. Violaters of new gun registration laws will become the next group to come under attack.

The American Political Left Helps Establish Communism In South Africa

Nowhere is America's plunge toward the political left and socialism more evident than in its efforts to overthrow the pro-Western government of South Africa and establish in its place a communist government under the ANC and its Marxist/Leninist revolutionary leader, Nelson Mandela. For over a decade the U.S. political left has held a gun to the head of the South African government, blackmailing and intimidating the South Africans to surrender their government to the communist ANC.

That the African National Congress is a Soviet-backed terrorist organization; armed, trained, and financed by the KGB since the 1950s, *is well known* to George Bush (former head of the CIA), our State Department, our intelligence services, and our Congress.

That the South African Communist Party (a surrogate of the U.S.S.R. headed by a White Lithuanian communist and colonel in the KGB, Joe Slovo), totally dominates the ANC *is well known* to our American leaders.

That the ANC has brutally butchered thousands of moderate, non-communist, Christian South African Blacks via the "necklace" treatment and other horrific methods of slaughter *is also well known* to American leaders.

That Nelson Mandela and his murderous wife, Winnie, are hardcore communist revolutionaries who have paid 100 percent allegiance to Russia, and to communist revolution in South Africa for the past 40 years *is well known* to Bush, our congressional leaders, and our intelligence services.

That Mandela has promised a communist-style confiscation of virtually all private property when he comes to power, that he consistently gives the communist clenched-fist salute in public, that he constantly marches and speaks before the Soviet flag, all in plain sight before the television and newspaper reporters of America and the West, *is also well known* to our leaders.

That U.S. economic sanctions against South Africa

(far more draconian than any ever directed at any communist dictatorship in the world) have pushed millions of moderate South African Blacks out of work, impoverishing them and preparing them for conquest by the "necklace"/AK-47 wielding ANC comrades, *is well known* to the Administration, the State Department, congressional leaders, and our intelligence services.

That Nelson Mandela pledged his comradeship, loyalty, and allegiance to his allies, Fidel Castro, Colonel Kadafy, and Yassar Arafat (and the PLO) on national television before millions of American viewers during his American tour in June 1990 *is well known* to the American people and the liberal leadership of America.

That Mandela and his murderous ANC terrorists have been in bed with, armed by, and allied to the Cubans, Libyans, and PLO (America's sworn enemies) for over 20 years *is well known* by our socialist leadership, as is Mandela's televised statement that the enemies of Castro, Kadafy, and Arafat are Mandela's enemies as well.

That Mandela publicly offered to return to America after his visit in the summer of 1990 and help stir up a revolution among American Indians on behalf of the far-left American Indian Movement (AIM) *is well known* to the Administration, the congressional leaders, and our liberal media.

That the far political left, the Communist Party U.S.A., and hundreds of communist front organizations across America went into a feeding frenzy of celebration as the world's most popular communist (after Gorbachev) —Nelson Mandela—was given his triumphant entry into America in mid-1990 is *well understood* by our Establishment leaders.

That America is totally dependent on the vast treasure chest of strategic minerals found in South Africa that are *absolutely essential* to the running of our defense, auto, space, and heavy manufacturing industries; and *that* if these minerals were to fall into the hands of a hostile, pro-Soviet, Marxist/Leninist government, America would be brought to its economic knees almost overnight, *is well known* to the Administration and America's liberal leadership.

If these things are known and understood by the Administration, the CIA, and Congress (*and they are*) then *why* are our leaders deliberately handing our most valuable and strategic allies over to the communists? *Why* did Nelson Mandela receive a ticker tape parade in New York (which cost millions) normally reserved for great American or foreign heroes? *Why* was Mandela wined and dined in our White House by our president and his State Department? *Why* was he allowed to speak before a joint session of the U.S. Congress (an honor only accorded to three civilians in U.S. history)? *Why* was he given the greatest television and newspaper coverage of any foreign leadership (including Churchill, de Gaulle, and Gorbachev) in U.S. history?

The answer to these questions is that America and its leaders have plunged so far to the political left, have become so socialist and one-world oriented that we can accept evil as good, we can accept our enemies as friends, and we can accept the false as truth. Lenin once said:

> *"We will spit in their face* [e.g., the faces of the Western capitalist leaders] *and they will call it dew."*

Surely Mandela was spitting in the faces of our congressional leaders and in the faces of the American people as he publicly pledged his allegiance and friendship to Castro, Kadafy, Arafat, and the world communist revolution. And our leaders smiled in joy and said: "It doesn't get any better than this."

Conclusion

If the liberal political and media leadership of America can sell Mikhail Gorbachev and Nelson Mandela (two of history's bloodiest Marxist/Leninist revolutionaries, avowed atheists, and evil men) to the American people as great leaders and men of peace, then selling socialism, the environmental crisis, gun control, world government, or even the Antichrist to the American people should be an easy task indeed.

The American people have been gradually prepared for socialism and world government by our leaders, our educational system, and the media for decades. The 1990s is the decade of destiny—the decade in which the forces of evil plan to converge and establish their global government. Whether it's the New World Order, the New Age movement, the massive Soviet military juggernaut, or a combination of all three, a socialist dictatorship is to be imposed on the people of America and the West before the year 2000.

But first America, the last great bastion of freedom and capitalism, must be socialized, must be mediocratized, must be weakened, and made into a second-class power, and its people turned into passive, non-aggressive, intimidated, obedient serfs. How can such a transformation of a formerly great nation and people take place? Socialize, centralize, and mediocratize the country, its people, and its institutions. This writer has observed a very similar process taking place in South Africa over the past ten years, and the majority of their people are now passively awaiting their government's handover of power to the communists.

The process of socializing America has been so gradual that most Americans haven't even noticed the transition. A few new freedoms taken away every few weeks or months, a few new controls or restrictions added, and over a period of a few decades, the freedom is gone. Now that the globalists have their target in sight, however, they are beginning to accelerate the process.

Environmentalism will be one of the primary vehicles for accelerating the socialization of America and Europe (hence the Clean Air Act and a host of other environmentalist absurdities). People control, especially of dissidents or reactionaries who will not accept the new system, is essential. Hence, the Hate Crimes bill, gun control and confiscation, new search and seizure powers, elimination of financial privacy and computerization of people's lives and financial affairs, arrest and imprisonment of tax protestors, conservatives, Christian anti-abortion protestors, and other maverick patriots who will not adapt to, or who may potentially lead opposition to the new system.

Weakening America is essential to merging America into a one-world socialist system where a dominant superpower would just not fit. That weakening has come and is coming via massive disarmament; undermining America's financial strength via massive debt financing; diluting American business with massive imports produced with cheap Third World (or communist bloc slave) labor; selling off our national assets to foreigners made possible by a weak and declining dollar; transferring our high technology, our food surpluses, and our industrial strength to communist bloc countries; squeezing the American free enterprise system to death with an avalanche of socialistic regulations, red tape, taxes, and bureaucratic controls, and opening the floodgates of pornography, abortion, and pro-homosexual initiatives.

The three watershed events that will signal that the end of a free America is near and that a socialist America has arrived are:

1. *The collapse of South Africa into a communist revolution*—prosperous industrial America cannot survive without those strategic minerals.
2. *Gun control and confiscation in America*—a socialist dictatorship will be imposed immediately after the American people are disarmed.
3. *The merger of America with a united Europe*—it will be called the Atlantic Community.

Chapter Three

Toward a Cashless Society: The U.S. Government's Attack On Financial Privacy

---

Revelation 13 describes a one-world economic system where no one can buy or sell without special identification numbers on their hand or forehead. This system is controlled by the Beast, or the Antichrist. The decline of Western society in both the social/political and economic/financial arenas is bringing such a system into greater likelihood at an accelerating pace.

George Orwell's classic novel, *1984*, described a drab, depressing world in which an all-powerful, socialist government, called Big Brother, enslaved the people by controlling every aspect of their lives: their movements, their finances, and even their thinking. Big Brother regulated every aspect of the peoples' lives to protect them from themselves. He changed or reversed the meanings of key words and concepts so that slavery was called freedom, war was called peace, hate was called love, etc. Big Brother entertained the masses constantly with his own brand of mediocre entertainment, which brainwashed them with leftist political propaganda. He distracted the masses with periodic regional wars. He became the conscience of the people, he rewrote history, and he controlled the minds and thoughts of his subjects.

But most importantly, Big Brother watched the people. He kept them and every aspect of their lives under constant surveillance, 24 hours a day. Big Brother totally abolished all aspects of privacy.

Uncle Sam is becoming the Big Brother of George Orwell's *1984*. Big Brother is alive and well in Washington, and in some of our state capitals and city governments as well. A movement is under way in this country under the guise of various crises of one kind or another that is trying to take away an immense amount of our privacy and freedoms. People in our giant, faceless bureaucracy are working overtime to achieve these aims. In a day when communist regimes all over Eastern Europe that have practiced Big Brother techniques for decades are beginning to disintegrate, it is ironic that the United States of America is moving to institute many of these same techniques, all in the name of protecting the people from a series of society-threatening crises. Some of these crises are the drug crisis, the money-laundering crisis, the environmental crisis, the global warming crisis (even though some scientists report that the earth is growing colder), the terrorist crisis, and the crime crisis. Big Brother must protect us from these countless crises. Each of these crises seems to be an excuse for a clique of liberal politicians and bureaucrats to place draconian socialist controls on every aspect of American's lives.

In the socialist America which seems to be emerging in the 1990s, Big Brother wants to scrutinize every single American's movements, monitor our transactions, and ultimately regulate our decisions. He wants to control *how* we spend our money, *where* we spend our money, and *how* we monitor and keep track of our money. There is a very real danger that George Orwell's *1984* is descending on America in the 1990s. It is happening so slowly that most people don't realize it.

We all know the story of putting a frog in a pan of boiling water, and he hops out very quickly. But if the frog is put in a pan of warm water, he is content to stay in the pan. The heat is increased gradually, and it's just a matter of time before he is boiled. Our government is increasing the heat so gradually that we don't realize that the United States is nearly as socialistic at the present time as some countries in the Eastern bloc are.

What is happening is really our own fault. We are looking to good old Uncle Sam to protect us, to provide for us, and to make sure we are safe and secure. For every ounce of benefits we receive from the government, we lose another ounce of freedom. Do we actually need more and more government bureaucracy to protect us from ourselves?

In the good old days of yore, Americans took care of themselves. We didn't have to have the government come into our homes and make sure we were taking care of our children, to dictate to us whether we could or could not spank them, and that we needed a government-run daycare center. The government didn't dictate curriculum. The government didn't dictate how many people with different religious persuasions, sexual proclivities, or racial backgrounds we had to hire. Somehow in the past, we managed to muddle through without all of this government "protection."

The government didn't promise security from the cradle to the grave; we recognized that we needed to take care of ourselves. With the help of God and a lot of hard work and sweat, we could take care of ourselves. When we became old, we knew our children would take care of us, just as we took care of our parents. Americans were a highly-independent, self-sufficient, well-motivated people. But if you do things long enough for people, they become incapable of doing things for themselves.

For example, take a rat or any untamed animal out of the wild, put him in a cage, and feed him consistently over a period of time. When you release him three years later, he can't fend for himself. The government is trying to make Americans dependent upon it for everything. We can't suffer pain, so anything that threatens to give us any pain will be taken care of with a government program. But each program that keeps us from suffering pain or discomfort takes more and more of our freedoms away. If it continues, before this decade is over we may well be a very, very unfree country.

Words like surveillance, regulation, monitoring, control, restriction, and scrutiny conjure up what looks to be a very gloomy future. But there are ways you can protect yourself if the government bureaucracy gets out of hand, as many believe it already has.

First, we need to understand as much as possible about this subject. Action without knowledge leads to confusion and chaos. Hosea 4:6 says, *"My people are destroyed for lack of knowledge. . . ."*

The government has already gone to great lengths to monitor, for instance, your financial transactions. Many things the government is doing today would have been technologically impossible 20 years ago, 15 years ago, perhaps even 10 or 5 years ago. The advent of advanced technology and computers has enabled the government to monitor its people more closely than ever before. Government agencies are employing laser-listening devices that can pick up conversations through walls or from 100 yards away. They can radio monitor a conversation on a cellular telephone, intercept faxes, and monitor you in a hundred different ways.

This writer personally knows of coin dealers who

have had people enter their offices and try to do trades with them using cash. When they have taken the cash, they discovered they were dealing with an undercover IRS agent running a sting on them. (Some would call it entrapment.) The agent was covered with body mikes, recording everything that was said.

The government doesn't have to eavesdrop on most of us, however. They can obtain most personal information about individuals through computers. When the Social Security number was first introduced, it was only to be used for Social Security and couldn't be used for anything else. Now it's being used for identification for everything. If you want to buy tires for a car, if you go to a doctor, if you go almost anyplace, they want your Social Security number. (Incidentally, the government is taking the money from the Social Security fund and is using the money to cover the deficit. Social Security wasn't supposed to be a tax, but now it's one of the largest taxes we pay.)

It is common knowledge that the IRS uses Social Security numbers, but there are also dozens of computerized data banks that use them too. If they have your Social Security number, they can key you into their data bank. They used to call them files, but that's a rather antiquated word. Today, most people would discover that they are in at least a few dozen government data banks. Some of these are hooked up to MasterCard/Visa and consumer credit bureaus which readily give out the information.

For example, there are now computer-readable passports. Most people who have applied for passports within the last four or five years have been issued these. They are placed in a machine, and within seconds, thousands of items of information about you from numerous government data bases are available. A stranger can be reading about where you traveled, your credit, and all kinds of information you thought heretofore was private.

Why should we have privacy? Is privacy important? Privacy is one of the most fundamental rights that we have. The idea that I can go behind closed doors with my family and talk, laugh, pray, or argue; the idea that I can be in my bedroom with the door closed with my wife; the idea that I can have financial privacy without someone looking over my shoulder and second-guessing what I'm doing is an inherent, constitutional right given in the Fourth Amendment. The concept of privacy is a God-given right. If you want, if you crave privacy today, it's as if the government assumes you must be a criminal. You must be a drug dealer, you must be a thief, and you must have something to hide. (Isn't it ironic that the right to privacy is a key principle used by liberals to justify abortion?) Our founding fathers didn't view privacy that way. They thought it was absolutely essential, that it was one of the essentials of freedom.

In Russia and Soviet bloc countries, the KGB spends two-thirds of their time on surveillance of their own people and intruding upon their privacy. The Iron Curtain countries are not turning into democracies and what is happening in Russia and Eastern Europe is one of the greatest strategic deceptions in modern history. But at the same time they are "allegedly" becoming free, the U.S. government is beginning to scrutinize its people the way the Iron Curtain countries have always done.

The present goal of Big Brother is the abolition of all financial privacy, first in America, and then all over the world. Attorney General Thornberg, speaking recently to a group of bankers in New York, said the crackdown on international drug money launderers will mean less bank privacy in the U.S., and urged the banks to closely screen their customers. Many banks now require a photo to open an account, and treat the depositor as a criminal if he asks whether government reports are required for particular transactions.

Many (eventually most) banks commonly provide information on your account without your approval or knowledge to government agencies, businesses, and creditors. The American Bankers Association, in a training film called *Dirty Money*, says: "The only people concerned about currency transaction reports are drug traffickers."

When the Establishment wants to brainwash the American people, it repeats a concept over and over thousands of times *a la* Adolf Hitler, who said: "Tell a lie, tell it often enough, and the people will believe it."

In this vein, we have been inundated with media disinformation about "*glasnost/perestroika*," "the death of communism," "the end of the Cold War," etc. We are also being inundated with the concept that "money laundering is the lifeblood of drug dealers."

One would think from listening to the Administration and the media that "money laundering" is the greatest threat to the survival of mankind, far more dangerous than AIDS, nuclear war, or perhaps even than the drugs themselves. And anyone who would even contemplate money laundering is an evil person, who must be severely dealt with to protect society. The December 18, 1989 *Time* magazine cover story, "A Torrent of Dirty Dollars," talked about the scandalous ability of the coke kingpins to launder billions of dollars in drug proceeds using many of the financial services available to the Fortune 500.

"In a wash cycle that often takes less than 48 hours, the drug smugglers can turn coke-tinged $20 and $100 bills into such untraceable, squeaky

*clean assets as money market deposits, car
dealerships, and resort hotels."*

The article went on to quote liberal Massachusetts
Democractic Sen. John Kerry, who said:

*"It is hard to understand why we failed so long to
institute adequate controls. The state of regulations is so lackadaisical, it is almost damnable."*

The entire article (as does an avalanche of current
government propaganda) concluded that cash is evil;
bank secrecy or privacy is evil; Swiss banking, and anyone
who uses a Swiss bank or offshore trust, is a money
launderer and is evil; and that the only way to halt the
incredible evil of money laundering is to abolish all cash
transactions and financial privacy in America and abroad.
Drug dealers are no longer the target. The target is money
launderers who are defined as "people who use cash or
seek financial privacy" and who can all be assumed to be
guilty of drug dealing until proven innocent.

So, "money laundering" is being used as an excuse by
Big Brother to eliminate cash transactions, monitor all
financial transactions, eliminate Swiss banking privacy,
and neutralize all offshore tax havens. It would seem that
if there hadn't been a drug war, one would have had to
have been invented. Ron Paul very succinctly describes
the concept:

*"The new federal felony of money laundering is
the crime of using your own cash, honestly
earned and voraciously taxed, without filling
out a federal form. The money laundering law
says nothing about drug profits. **Their real***

purpose is to stamp out the use of cash for reasons of government control and taxation."

Our Administration, Congress, and bureaucracy have a formidable bag of tricks to use against the American people to eliminate financial privacy and cash.

The New Currency

In September 1989, former Treasury Secretary Donald Regan was used as a point man by the Establishment to float the idea of a new currency—multi-colored $50 and $100 bills to replace greenbacks already in circulation. People would only have 10 days to make the switch, and anyone with more than $1,000 would have to file a treasury form. The forms would be used for selecting IRS audit victims, he suggested. This trial balloon brought little public reaction, so later they began talking about including $5, $10, and $20 bills. The idea is to flush out hundreds of billions of dollars from the underground economy.

An amendment to bar code the new currency passed the U.S. Senate unanimously on October 3, 1989, 100 to 0. The bill empowers the treasury to use the latest optical scanning technology to trace cash denominations of $10 or more. The serial numbers of $100, $50, and $20 bills would also be read by optical scanning devices like those used at grocery store check-out counters. The new currency will have a computer-readable strip linking it to its bank of issue *and to the individual receiving it*. The senator introducing the amendment, John Kerry (D-MA), defended this by saying: "This is necessary because money laundering is not isolated to drug use." Regarding the bar code measure, he said:

"It provides a mechanism by which our government, our law enforcement agencies, our financial institutions, and foreign institutions as well, can efficiently track U.S. currency —bill by bill—without any undue administrative burdens."

Cash Reporting Requirements

The Bank Secrecy Act of 1986 called for cash reporting by banks or other financial institutions of all cash deposits or withdrawals of $10,000 or more (or a combination of transactions over several days totalling $10,000). The amount for cash transaction reports (CTRs) to be filed has since dropped to $3,000, and the the new threshold appears to be $2,000. Most banks fill out CTRs on their clients without telling them, as per IRS instructions. Eventually the amounts to be reported may fall to $500.

Banks have also been ordered by the treasury to report "suspicious transactions" of any amount to the IRS. The Administration says transactions are "suspicious if they are a break in the account holder's usual pattern of deposits and withdrawals." So, if you normally make three or four deposits in a month, and then you make six or eight, you can be turned in.

Over 7 million CTRs have been filed with the IRS since the legislation passed in 1986. There are 450 IRS agents at the Detroit Data Center processing CTRs (and the IRS has another 500 special agents doing criminal investigations on money laundering). People with a "suspicious" number of CTRs are likely to receive an IRS audit.

If any bank employee fails to fill out a CTR or a financial advisor advises a client on how to avoid the reporting requirements, the criminal penalty is 10 years in jail and a $500,000 fine per offense. Do you think Big Brother is serious about abolishing financial privacy? The penalty is far less if you simply commit a minor "non-reportable" crime, such as drug dealing, rape, murder, burglary, or bank robbery.

Big Brother also wants to discourage the use of cash in retail stores. The primary tool is the 8300 form, a retail CTR that asks for the amount, occupation, address, and Social Security number. Originally to be used for cash purchases of $10,000 or more, the amount has been lowered to $3,000. Congress has made it a felony if retailers fail to fill out 8300. The most frequent retail outlets filing these forms are jewelry, appliances, furniture stores, and car dealerships. If you have the 8300 form filled out on you, there is a 100 percent likelihood that an IRS audit will follow.

Structuring

As former Congressman Ron Paul likes to point out: "The government loves vague laws. They are essential to tyranny and executive discretion." *Examples of this include the U.S. RICO laws and the U.S.S.R. hooliganism laws. The Bank Secrecy Act prohibits "structuring," which is defined as an attempt to evade financial reporting requirements.* But this law makes obeying the law against the law, *a la* Orwell's "double think."

A federal district court in Indiana recently convicted a man who made several bank withdrawals under $10,000 of "structuring." The court proved *no* criminal intent, it found *no* evidence of *any* crime being committed by the accused, and it set *no* time limit on the "structuring" (the withdrawals could have been over a day or a year).

A Tulsa, Oklahoma man was indicted for "structuring" cash transactions to keep them under the $10,000 limit in buying a motor home and an airplane. He won in court, and all charges were dismissed, but *The Daily Oklahoman* reported, in describing the case:

> *"Under federal law the government is allowed to seize a person's assets and distribute them, even if the accused is acquitted, or the charges eventually dropped, those assets may be transferred to state law enforcement agencies."*

The Tulsa man did *not* get back his stolen airplane, motor home, or $37,200 in cash.

These incredible "structuring" convictions have set ominous legal precedents. Big Brother can convict, fine, or jail anyone he doesn't like in the future, for "structuring" violations if he has deposited or withdrawn various amounts of cash *under* the reporting requirements from his bank over an unspecified period of time (e.g., days, weeks, or months). This includes almost everyone who banks in America.

This sounds more like Russia than America, doesn't it? Can we really call ourselves a free country? Does this really have anything to do with catching drug dealers?

Targeting

Empowered by the Anti-Drug Abuse Act of 1988, the treasury can now target a specific area of the country and require every bank, S&L, coin dealer, and stock broker to report *all* cash transactions, theoretically from one dollar up. Under the "targeting" blitz, all laws protecting financial privacy are wiped out. Without notice, treasury agents invade the banks or other financial institutions one morning to install a surveillance operation. Tellers are trained to think of the customers as potential criminals, and the treasury even has its own tellers if needed.

Employees are told they now work for the government and must cooperate with the treasury in documenting every transaction. This secret financial raid (or "targeting" blitz) can go on for several weeks, and the treasury can even restrict cash withdrawals during the exercise if it chooses. One such "targeting" has already occurred, and if it yields good post-blitz audit results, many more will be staged.

Wire Transfers

In October 1989, the Administration began to monitor all international wire transfers of funds, saying they were "trying to halt the extensive laundering of drug profits earned illegally in the U.S. and sent abroad." U.S. banks and money managers are now forced to report on computer tape to the treasury *all* incoming and outgoing international bank wires.

Cash Confiscation

If large amounts of cash (e.g., $5,000 to $10,000 or more) are found on an individual, regardless of whether he is suspected of drug dealing or any crime, the cash will be confiscated by the government and, in most instances, not returned. In 1989, a Denver restauranteur had $10,000 in cash confiscated as he was leaving Stapleton International Airport, and a Florida man, en route to New York City, had $639,578 in cash confiscated while on an Amtrak train. In both instances, sniffer dogs smelled out the money. Both individuals had no police records, were suspected of no crime (although the latter was charged with criminal racketeering [under RICO], because he had the cash). Both men were released (with the charges dropped), but the IRS ultimately kept *half* of the Denver man's cash and *all* $639,578 of the Florida man's cash.

Targeting Swiss Bank Secrecy and Tax Havens

The Administration is putting massive pressure on Switzerland and Swiss banks to abolish Swiss bank secrecy and reveal the names of U.S. depositors. Two Swiss banks have closed their U.S. offices due to worry over having their assets frozen by U.S. authorities. The Administration has accused Switzerland of being "an international turntable for concealing the origin of criminally-gotten funds" and "a partner to drug dealers and money launderers." Switzerland and Swiss banks are beginning to knuckle under to the colossal U.S. pressure—Switzerland is now in the process of passing a money laundering law, and cracks are now beginning to spread in Swiss bank secrecy. U.S. businessmen and investors returning from Switzerland have recently been strip-searched, had their bags gone through with a fine tooth comb, and papers photocopied. It's called "operation harassment."

Big Brother is beginning to break Swiss bank secrecy and is now targeting tax havens such as the Cayman Islands, the Channel Islands, Hong Kong, Liechtenstein, Luxembourg, Mexico, Panama, the Bahamas, Singapore, the United Arab Emirates, and Uruguay. Americans travelling to and from these destinations with any regularity can expect to come under surveillance and perhaps even harassment.

The United Nations Convention Against Illicit Traffic in Narcotic Drugs and Psychotrophic Substances

The Administration (according to former Congressman Ron Paul) is pushing for the passage of this U.N. treaty and

> *". . . urging governments to attack the financial aspects of the drug trade by adopting strong measures to criminalize money laundering, and by imposing sanctions on those who use the international financial system to disguise and move criminally derived funds across national borders."*

The original treaty had nothing in it about money laundering, but the U.S. government succeeded in making the attack on money laundering and bank secrecy the central point of the treaty.

Under this treaty, *money laundering will now be a global crime, bank confidentiality will be outlawed, the easy seizure of property under U.N. authority anywhere in the world will be possible, and quick extraditions of persons suspected of financial crimes will be the norm.* President Bush said, "We will handcuff these money launderers, and jail them . . . just like any street dealers." Yes, and anyone else who believes in financial privacy, offshore banking, etc.!

Putting the U.N. in charge of "financial" crimes, "property seizure," and "bank confidentiality" is an interesting twist for the New World Order clique!

The Convention on Mutual Administrative Assistance in Tax Matters

This treaty has been signed by the U.S., Norway, and Sweden. Five nations must sign it for it to go into effect. The treaty calls for international cooperation between the tax collection agencies of the signatory countries. The U.K., West Germany, Australia, and Switzerland have all refused to sign it to date.

Customs Service Seizures

The Customs Service is getting more and more involved in the war on cash and privacy. Customs officials are seizing more currency and private property from Americans returning from abroad than ever before. Customs official William Rosenblatt recently expressed great pride over the loot his agency was confiscating from U.S. citizens:

> *"Back in fiscal year 1985, U.S. Customs, working with other federal and state and local agencies, only seized $95 million. We are now seizing almost $200 million, but we won't be satisfied until we can come up here and say that we are getting billions."*

This writer recently went to the Pacific Rim on a speaking tour. Upon returning to the U.S., another person who had also been on the tour had his bags searched by U.S. Customs. This individual had brought back 10 relatively inexpensive watches and 10 shirts as gifts for employees. All were confiscated by U.S. Customs with no explanation. The items weren't cash, and they weren't illegal, but the incident did illustrate the raw, arbitrary power of Big Brother.

Non-Banks Targeted

There are a myriad of small check-cashing stores in big cities for people who can't afford, or don't want to use checking accounts. Now the Feds are targeting them. Sen. Kerry is bothered that these businesses sometimes ignore the CTR filing requirement. At a recent hearing, a treasury official promised that the IRS is "taking initiatives" to crack down on these small businesses.

Other private businesses are also under attack. Wealth that the government considers "excessive" is reason enough for investigation. As a top DEA official said, "if agents know of a small restaurant whose owner banks $10,000 [in cash], something has to be suspicious."

National ID Smart Card

The Justice Department is pushing for a national gun registration card which would include each American's fingerprints, a retina scan, and a lot of the computer-linked technology that the Treasury Department is proposing for the new money. The 1988 drug bill called for such a card, and the Justice Department, the IRS, the FBI, and Immigration and Naturalization Service have long pushed for one. A hologram, called a "wiggle picture," which the treasury is pushing for use on the new money, will also be used on this biometric ID card.

Conclusion

George Orwell's *1984* is rapidly emerging in America

in the early 1990s, ushered in by George Bush and his socialist, New World Order associates in the Administration, the Congress, and the government bureaucracy. As America and Russia move toward a "merger of our common interests," America is becoming more like Russia every day. The socialists in control of America (both Republicans and Democrats), if they continue their current thrust, will deprive Americans of virtually all of our freedoms (financial and otherwise) and turn us into slaves before the decade of the 1990s is over. And they will do it all in the name of good, in the name of protecting us from the drug crisis, the financial crisis, etc. There are a few things that people can do:

1. *Guard your Social Security number*—Avoid giving it to anyone unless you're required by law to do so. You don't have to give it to most businesses, doctors, and many people who routinely ask for it.

2. *Keep your tax returns private*—Avoid giving them to banks or mortgage lenders. They often give the information out or sell it. If applying for a mortgage, you can often get a "no disclosure" form, provided you make a down payment of 25 to 30 percent, and have a good credit history.

3. *Use cash, cashiers checks, money orders, and travellers checks* whenever possible.

4. *Buy low profile investments*—which you hold in your own possession, such as gold, silver, semi-numismatic coins, and rare coins.

5. *Utilize postal money orders*—They are very private and come in amounts up to $700. (However, if you buy these money orders in amounts up to $3,000, you will now be reported to the U.S. Treasury.)

6. *Review your public credit records*—Get printouts of your files from the credit agencies and clear up any problems that might arouse the interest of unfriendly parties.

7. *Never break any tax laws or privacy laws*—Even in the face of the growing encroachments against our privacy, it is not a good idea to knowingly break any laws. If you disagree with the laws, work to have them repealed. One should not get involved in any form of tax evasion or tax revolt. Legitimate deductions are fine, but elaborate tax avoidance schemes are presently landing a growing number of tax protestors and conservatives in jail. "Tax crimes" will be among the most vigorously pursued, aggressively prosecuted, and severely penalized in the 1990s. As the Bible says, ". . . *Render therefore unto Caesar the things which are Caesar's; and unto God the things that are God's"* (Matt. 22:21).

If one backs away from the details and looks at the big picture, at America's current urge to disarm and merge, at the gun control juggernaut, at the move toward a cashless society, abolition of financial privacy, and socialistic controls over most aspects of our lives, a very ominous picture is emerging with respect to freedom in America. Are we destined to enter the next century as slaves? Is Jesus' return near? Is there prophetic significance to these incredible developments?

Chapter Four

The Computerization of the American People

"And he causeth all, both small and great, rich and poor, free and bond, to receive a mark in their right hand, or in their foreheads: And that no man might buy or sell, save he that had the mark, or the name of the beast, or the number of his name. . . his number is Six hundred three-score and six."

—Revelation 13:16-18

Cash Is Out—Computers Are In

The U.S. government, the social planners, and the New World Order/New Age crowd hate cash because it represents freedom, privacy, decentralization, and independence—just the opposite of their goals for a global collectivist society. Cash makes it difficult to control people, and therefore it must be abolished. Today, we are moving rapidly toward a cashless society and the globalists intend to accelerate that trend. Very few people carry significant amounts of cash anymore. When this writer was a boy (in the 1940s and '50s), people carried cash and used it for most everyday purchases and personal transactions. Today, most of us use checks and credit cards, rather than cash. A person is considered weird or anachronistic

93

today if he uses cash to any great extent. The police and government authorities look at people who use (or possess) a great deal of cash today with great suspicion (e.g., they must be doing something wrong, or have something to hide).

The *New York Times* carried an article by Harvey E. Wachsman, president of the American Board of Professional Liability Attorneys, on January 31, 1991, advocating the total elimination of cash:

> *"First the government would change the color of the currency and require old money to be exchanged at the treasury. Then all the new currency would be returned by its owners to the bank of their choice. All banks would be required to open accounts free of charge to all depositors. . . In place of paper money, we would all receive new cards—called Americards —each biometrically impregnated with the owner's hand and retina prints to insure virtually foolproof identification.*
>
> *"The government would supply all homes and businesses free of charge with machines to read the card, certify the holder's identity, and make instantaneous electronic debits and credits. Regardless of what such machines would cost, the government, with $100 billion in new tax revenues, and no more printing and minting costs, would come out ahead.*
>
> *"think of the benefits to the average American. No one would have to write a check ever again. Bills could be paid electronically from home."*

And what about the benefits to the government?

"Individuals and businesses would no longer be able to conceal income. All transactions would be recorded in a computerized bank file and would be easy for the IRS to check."

One hundred billion dollars in additional taxes could be squeezed out of the U.S. taxpayers each year. Wachsman says this cashless scheme will smash the underground economy, eliminate most robberies since no one would have any cash to steal, and make it difficult to sell stolen property because there would be records of all transactions. *This Utopian scheme has several glaring shortcomings: it would eliminate freedom for those serfs living under it; it would eliminate all financial privacy; and it would give Big Brother the chance to keep track of, tax, and control every dime we earn, save, and spend.*
Is the Wachsman scenario for a cashless society realistic? Is it something the Establishment would ever try to install? *The liberal Eastern Establishment and New World Order crowd are already trying to put this system (or some variation of it) in place and believe that it will be up and running by the latter half of the 1990s.* One wonders if they had the Wachsman scenario inserted in the *New York Times* as a trial balloon.

Cashless Society Experiments

Indeed, a number of experiments for the cashless society are being run around the world at this writing:

1. *Maryland* will be the first state to distribute welfare and food stamp benefits electronically through cash cards and automatic teller machines. Seen as a test for national welfare distribution

across the country, the program is designed to make it more difficult for recipients to exchange their benefits for drugs or other illicit transactions. Called the Independence Card (a name straight out of Orwellian "double think"), it is praised as "empowering the poor by lessening the stigma of welfare." The Independence Card is a "smart card" designed for the purchase of all food and other small items. Eventually it will be used for all purchases. It is a trial run for the cashless society for all Americans all across the country.

2. *Denmark* is set to become the world's first cashless society. A new "smart card," called Denmart, will replace small change and will be used in telephones, buses, parking meters, launderettes, cafeterias, and in shops for small purchases. Denmark will be the first country with a general card to make coinage obsolete. The Denmart Card, with a built-in microprocessor, will be able to calculate credit and even store information such as telephone numbers.

3. *Taiwan* began experimenting in July 1990 with a cashless electronic system which replaces currency in many common transactions by the use of integrated circuit cards. The integrated circuit cards have replaced functions done by credit cards, telephone calling cards, gasoline charge cards, and employee time cards, and will soon be used in Taiwan for payment of telephone bills, on inner-city rail systems, and in settling accounts between various government agencies. (Similar experiments have been run in Singapore and Australia for several years.)

4. *Germany*—In 1985-86, a "point-of-sale" cashless economy was experimented with in Munich and

West Berlin. This system was developed by the Nixdorf Computer firm, with bank bookkeeping of transactions done by an electronic terminal, Eurocheque card, and a personal PIN code. Purchases made by consumers in stores would be debited within three seconds directly from their bank accounts. This cashless experiment was initially used in textile stores, gas stations, grocery stores, and banks. In addition to Germany, Nixdorf Computer has installed similar systems in Austria, Norway, Great Britain, and Spain.

5. *Paris Island, South Carolina*—The U.S. government is running a cashless society test at the giant U.S. Marine base on Paris Island, whereby no cash can be used. Each Marine is issued a "smart card" and his pay is electronically entered on it. He must use the card to pay for everything he buys, from haircuts, to magazines, to movies. On its computers, the government can thus track every cent, and maintain a **T**otal **F**inancial **P**rofile of each Marine. Paris Island is, in fact, a small cashless economy—even the telephone lines take "smart cards." The TFP will be used on each of us within a few years, according to the cashless society planners.

6. *Electronic Banking*—In 1988, only 37 percent of bank transactions were authorized directly by computer. By 1990, the number was 78 percent and rising. The banks are making it easy for retailers to process cards at the counter with automatic recording of payment details and portable hand-held terminals.

7. *The Day of the "Smart Card"*—"Smart cards" are the next leap in technology for the cashless society.

"Smart cards" are the size of a conventional credit card, but most contain tiny computer memory chips capable of storing up to 1,000 pages of data, and have tiny metal contacts on the cards, connecting the chip to the outside world, like plugging in a cable. "Smart cards" are already being used for making phone calls, paying parking meters, buying lottery tickets, doing electronic banking, buying groceries, etc.

"Smart cards" were used for buying almost everything at the 1992 Olympic games at Barcelona, Spain. By 1995, computer industry experts predict over half of the people in America, Europe, Japan, Australia, and throughout the free world will be using these cards. A few years later, it will be almost everyone. Linking "smart cards" and the worldwide telecommunications network will open the door to universal electronic transactions in all walks of life. *The era of paper money and coinage is rapidly drawing to a close and the new age of a cashless society is dawning.*

The path to 100 percent electronic money, and total government financial control of citizens, as Harvey Wachsman explained in the *New York Times* article, is Americard—a "smart card" that does it all. Cash is freedom! A man without money is free to do very little. *If modern electronic credit and debit cards can be substituted for cash, then every financial transaction of your life can be catalogued and stored for future reference and those with the power to cut off your access to electronic money can strangle you in a heartbeat. The potential for totalitarian blackmail and control is incredible—but most Americans don't even seem to notice.*

The Day of the Computer

We live in the day of the computer. Computer knowledge, speed of processing, and technology is now doubling every two years. This tremendous explosion in computer technology and gathering of information has set the stage where all sensitive personal and financial information about you will be centralized and available for review.

For years, the government collected vast amounts of sensitive information about you but was not able to make full use of the information because managing and correlating this material was impossible. All that has changed with the computerization of virtually all government files. This process happened at a rapid speed in all levels of government and in the private sector over the past 10 years. The banks, credit agencies, insurance companies, all types of stores and businesses, and general employers now have access to these records which, within seconds, can give massive quantities of sensitive information about you.

Part and parcel of this total computerization of all information is the cashless society, whereby computers will electronically transfer credits and debits. As credits and debits are electronically transferred to and from your different financial accounts, no "real money" will change hands—there will be no need for cash because computers will electronically conduct the transactions. The need for cash and checks will evaporate. Today, upward of three-fourths of all banking is done electronically. The U.S. government electronically deposits most payroll, welfare, and Social Security checks, as do many businesses.

Each American has dozens (if not hundreds) of computer data files on him—with the government now maintaining between two and three dozen separate files on each American. *The key for the government's managing, merging, integrating, and using all of this miscellaneous computerized data is a single, universal number—to tie all the various data bases together. Your Social Security number has become that universal key to merging and releasing all that computerized information.*

It is virtually impossible to live in America without your Social Security number. If you have any contact with the government, you must have the number. It is required for federal, state, and local tax forms; for all medical plans; for passports; to receive welfare, unemployment benefits, medicare payments, food stamps, or any government check for any purpose; to open a bank account or a securities account, etc. Most businesses and retail stores have begun asking for Social Security numbers on transactions as do most doctors, dentists, and medical practitioners. (No one is legally bound to give the number to these latter groups and it seems unwise to this writer to do so.)

The Government's National Computer Network

Out of this explosion in computer technology and tying together of dozens (or hundreds) of data bases via the Social Security number has come a national computer network where government agencies can almost instantaneously call up any or all information on you or your family, covering your life, finances, and activities literally from the cradle to the grave. (Social Security numbers are now required for two years old and up.)

Since 1985, the IRS has been computerizing all Americans and that project is now virtually complete. A computer profile now exists on virtually every American family or individual, which will enable the government to monitor virtually all of your activities by computers: trace, track, and watch your financial, business, or personal dealings, locate you in very short order, and perhaps eventually directly access your taxes based on your computerized financial profile—electronically debiting your bank account for the taxes due.

The computerization of the American people will enable the government to watch and control you from the cradle to the grave. *If this sounds a lot like George Orwell's 1984, Nicolae Ceaucescu's Romania, Hitler's Third Reich, or Yeltsin's or Deng Xiaoping's communist "paradise"—that is because it is!* The New World Order/ New Age government of the future will be able to watch and control its subjects more completely and efficiently than any totalitarian power in the past. The computer will help them to do so!

As a sample of the kind of people-tracking information which is now being amassed on computers by the U.S. government, the following government memo was sent to employees of one large government agency charged with tracking and monitoring Americans and their finances:

> *"We now have available to us a new source of background information called METRONET which provides information on over 111 million people in 80 million households across the country. Not only does it eliminate the need for ATLAS, since ATLAS was originally purchased from METRONET by the credit bureau, but it also allows for the following variety of searches:*
> *"**Phone Search**—provides a complete name and address report which is provided in accordance with U.S. Postal Service standards. As*

mentioned above, it is the same as ATLAS except that the record search can continue further once the name and address of the subject has been determined.

"*Address Search*—requires that the zip code, street address, and last name be entered in order to verify an address and receive the subject's current phone number. If it is a single family dwelling and your subject has moved, METRONET lists the current resident.

"*Household Profiles*—provides the time at current residence, type of dwelling, the subject's age and year of birth. It also provides the names, ages, and year of birth of up to four additional family members.

"*Neighbor Search*—requires only the address to obtain details on up to 30 neighbors at new or old addresses. These details include names, addresses, phone numbers, dwelling types, and length of residence. It also provides the current resident at the subject's last-known address.

"*Change of Address Alert*—automatically searches the U.S. Postal Service's National Change of Address files which is updated every two weeks. With 20 percent of the population moving to a new residence annually and the fact that 30 percent of these people never notify the postal service of their new address, METRONET also checks for any change of address that a subject has provided to a publisher or marketing company to make sure that their magazines or other products will be forwarded.

"*Street Name Scanning*—helps obtain the

*correct street name abbreviations by checking
an alphabetical table of all street names in any
given zip code that begins with a specified letter.*

*"**Surname Search**—allows the investigator
to search an entire geographic region (e.g., state,
county, city, zip code, etc.) when the only
information known is the last name of the
subject."*

The Financial Crime Enforcement Network

As part of the thrust to monitor and control the
American people, the Bush Administration has established
the financial crime center (FINCEN) in Arlington,
Virginia, whereby through the use of sophisticated
computers, the government has combined more than 100
data bases on bank records, criminal suspects, driving
records, census data, and myriads of business and financial
activities of millions of honest, law-abiding citizens.

*FINCEN is the largest government-run artificial
intelligence data base ever established.* FINCEN has over
200 employees from the IRS, the FBI, the Secret Service,
and the FDIC and works closely with the BATF, the CIA,
and the Defense Intelligence Agency. FINCEN acts as a
collection point, clearing and distribution center of
computerized data for virtually all other government
agencies. Data which it receives and redistributes comes
from: bank deposits, Fed bank reports, comptroller of the
currency bank reports, FDIC bank reports, census income
figures, Customs monetary reports, Secret Service credit
reports, and FBI and DEA drug data.

FINCEN currently has access to over 35 financial
data bases, and they will create another 100, including

computerized land records, real estate records, credit reports, CTRs, 8300 forms, bank reports, etc. The models, data, financial patterns, and individual names generated by FINCEN are being shared with the IRS, its Criminal Investigation Division, and state and local governments. Before a recent amendment to the "Right to Financial Privacy Act" passed, these activities were illegal. Virtually all of the activities of FINCEN violate the U.S. Constitution's Fourth Amendment guarantee to the right of privacy.

FINCEN and U.S. government officials admit that FINCEN is a trial run for a world system of financial tracking, surveillance, and control. FINCEN is an essential element of George Bush's New World Order and of the coming New Age.

A Computerized California Driver's License

California is now issuing new driver's licenses that contain more high-tech security devices than our currency. Bar codes, holograms, magnetic strips, and digitized images of the driver are now incorporated into the new licenses. High-tech driver's licenses and identification cards are now a part of the ever-expanding wave of technological changes that allow computers to dominate more and more aspects of our lives. By issuing these new driver's licenses (and similar non-driving California identification cards), California makes it easier for personal information to be incorporated into many government and non-government computer data bases.

The new California driver's license has triple-track magnetic strips on the back to enable storage of large amounts of personal, financial, and driving data—for use by the police or retailers with the equipment to read the strips. The California driver's license also has computer bar codes for the storage of additional data. The computerized California driver's license is a trial run—other states are about to adopt this license format and within a few years, all of them will.

As of March 31, 1992, there are no more state-issued commercial driver's licenses—one national commercial driver's license is issued instead. The single license will be linked with a national computer network. *A national driver's license for individuals will follow a year or so later, with all of the characteristics of the new California driver's license. This license will, in effect, be a national computerized ID card.*

A National Debit Card System

A dozen of the largest regional automated teller machine (ATM) networks are discussing the start-up of a national debit card system that would allow consumers to deduct purchases instantly from their checking accounts. The network would use small card-reading machines in each of the participating retail stores. The consumer at a grocery store, for example, would slip an ATM card through a terminal, punch in a personal identification number (PIN), and the amount of the purchase would be deducted instantly.

So far, the debit card has been confined largely to regional grocery store chains and gas stations. If the newest efforts progress, a nationwide debit card network could be on stream by 1993 or '94.

The Singapore Test Case: Monitoring an Entire Population

New identity cards were issued in June 1991 to every

citizen of Singapore over the age of 18. They will enable
the government to keep electronic tabs on most of
Singapore's 2.7 million people. The "smart" devices, the
size of a credit card, have machine-readable bar codes
that keep the owner's number and other personal information ready for official inspection. A photograph, thumb-
print, and personal details are recorded electronically.

When the details of the new cards were announced,
parliament was told an electronic grid was being established to link the police, immigration, and income tax
department, vehicle registry, housing authority, pension
fund, and other agencies. If a person is wanted by any of
these agencies, the system will allow instant sharing of all
information. Since the new computer identity card must
be used for virtually everything, each person will be more
or less continuously plugged into the electronic grid.

By the mid-1990s, every motor vehicle in Singapore is
to have electronic number plates and a small black box on
the undercarriage. Sensors will be imbedded in street sur-
faces and motorists will be charged for road use, just as they
are for water or electricity, with bills rendered monthly.

Singapore has run experiments with "smart cards"
and cashless shopping for several years. Now it is
experimenting with electronic "tagging" of released
offenders (already used in America). It involves strapping
a tamper-proof beeper to the body, which alerts authorities
when it is moved more than a specified distance from a
receiver in the person's home. From cashless shopping to
electronic surveillance, the tiny prosperous island of
Singapore is becoming a laboratory for the New World
Order, for a cashless society, and computerized/electronic
surveillance and control of an entire population.

It seems that Singapore could teach the Russians and
Red Chinese—and perhaps even George Bush—a thing

or two about people control and surveillance. George Orwell . . . take note!

Computer Chips In People

The February 12, 1992 issue of *Time* magazine carried an article entitled, "The Soldier of the Future," which stated:

> *"Dog tags . . . will be replaced by a microchip embedded in a molar. . . . Scanners will read bar code data off the tooth, such as blood type, allergies, medical history."*

Already (according to the *Washington Times* on August 30, 1990) tiny computer chips are being injected into animals, including pets, so they can be identified, traced if they are lost, etc. A glass capsule the size of a rice kernel, containing a microchip and a tiny antenna is the essence of the system. The capsule can be injected into the animal with a veterinary syringe. When activated by radio frequency signals from outside scanners in hand-held boxes or fence gates, the devices transmit a 10-digit ID code.

If technology has advanced so a bar-coded microchip can be contained in a molar, it can just as easily be inserted under the skin—as the ultimate form of people control. It causes one to ponder Revelation 13:17: *"And that no man might buy or sell, save he that had the mark. . . ."*

Conclusion

The explosion in computer technology over the past 10 or 15 years is a mixed blessing. It has made our lives more efficient, organized, and fast-tracked, but it has also opened up Pandora's box as far as Big Brother's scrutinizing, tracking, and one day controlling every aspect of our lives. American children two years old and up must now have a Social Security number (their universal number tying them to the government's myriad of data bases) so they can literally be tracked from the cradle to the grave.

With a benevolent, free market, freedom-oriented government (the kind Americans have enjoyed for 200 years), this computer technology would be no threat. But with a Hitler, Yeltsin, or Deng Xiaoping in power, or a New World Order/New Age-oriented leadership, this computer technology could be a dangerous vehicle for enslaving America and the world.

Chapter Five

America's Accelerating Economic Crisis

The left side of the "perspective triangle," depicting America's decline, is the realm of the economic and financial. Alexander Tyler, a British historian who warned democracies of the impact of financial irresponsibility, said that:

> *"Democracies cannot exist as a permanent form of government; they will only exist until the people find that they can vote money for themselves from the treasury and until the politicians find that they can distribute that money in order to buy votes and perpetuate themselves in power. Hence, democracies always collapse over weak fiscal policy to be followed by a dictatorship."*

There are many examples of this throughout history. The terrible financial policies of Germany in the 1920s and '30s led to the rise of Hitler and his dictatorship, and ultimately to World War II.

Debt is the Achilles' heel of a democracy, no matter how great that democracy is. The United States has relied on debt very heavily. We have violated biblical principles about debt, such as owing no man (Rom. 13:8) and the borrower becoming the servant of the lender (Prov. 22:7). In the last 15 to 20 years, this country has gone on the most incredible debt binge in the history of the world. We are not the kind of people who will deny ourselves anything. Tightening our belts and cutting back is not something to which we are accustomed. According to recent government reports from Congress, the standard of living of the average American has dropped almost 25 percent in the last 15 years. Haven't people noticed? No, they have taken up the slack by simply borrowing more money. They whipped out the Visa or MasterCard, or they went to the bank and borrowed money or took out a home equity loan. We have superficially maintained our standard of living by going into debt.

The people have done this, but the government has done it as well. The United States has a total internal debt of $16 trillion; that includes private debt, corporate debt, and governmental debt. That's not all. The United States also has Eurodollar debt of another $1.5 trillion, and U.S. international debt of $700 billion, which brings the total to $18.2 trillion. We maintained the facade of prosperity during the 1980s by borrowing $750 billion from abroad. We financed the federal deficits by allowing the Japanese, Taiwanese, Europeans, and others to buy a third of the treasury debt floated to cover these deficits.

As the cost to service these debts has risen in recent years, we have seen a record number of defaults in different parts of the country as well. It's a two-fold problem. The number of defaults in this country multiplies daily. At this very moment, 1.2 million Americans are in bankruptcy court, with over 900,000 Americans going bankrupt in 1991 alone (this includes many Christians). More corporations are also filing for bankruptcy now than at any time since the peak of the Great Depression (e.g., over 100,000 in 1991). Many of these are large companies that are going under, and a lot more are going to go under because of the huge debt load they are carrying. Record numbers of banks and savings and loans have been failing in recent years (resetting post-Depression records). The consequence of this explosion of debt, this $16 trillion debt pyramid, is that cracks are beginning to spread throughout the entire American financial system. You can blow up a balloon, and continue blowing and blowing, but sooner or later, it's going to pop. Our country's financial structure resembles the balloon.

The government is not alone in overspending. The problem is prevalent across the spectrum. We have been inundated with the concept that prosperity is equivalent to the usage of debt. Over the past decade, consumer debt has tripled to $3.5 trillion. How many credit cards do each of us have in our wallets or purses? Credit card debt increased from $50 billion to $185 billion over the past decade. Real estate and mortgage debt rose to $6.5 trillion over the past decade. In 1929, debt service was 10 percent of the American people's total income. Today, that figure is 25 percent, more than twice what it was during the 1920s.

Corporate Debt

Because of falling prices and rising debt, the corporate sector is going to suffer, and that means bankruptcy for many of America's largest corporations. In January 1990, Federated department stores, Allied department stores, and Bloomingdale's department stores went broke. Revco drug stores and Circle K convenience stores have filed for bankruptcy, and 7-11 stores, on the verge of financial disaster, sold out to the Japanese. Eastern Airlines, Pan

Am, TWA, Continental Airlines, and America West all declared bankruptcy in 1991 and 1992. Corporate America has tripled its debt in the past 10 years from $700 billion to $2.5 trillion. They have retired a large amount of equity as they have floated $310 billion in junk bonds to pay for leveraged buyouts. The leveraged buyout craze that hit Wall Street was the most speculative craze since the late 1920s. They floated over 3,000 junk bond issues to finance the debt binge. In 1989, $12 billion of those same bonds went into default, with $25 billion in junk bonds going into default in 1990.

In the 1930s, corporations had 70 cents cash for every dollar in short-term debt (i.e., debt that comes due within 12 months). Today, corporations only have nine cents cash to cover each dollar in short-term debt. That's an 87 percent drop in short-term debt coverage. As America sinks into recession or depression, many companies will be in serious financial trouble. The debt load of American corporations is four to five times greater than it was in the late 1920s. During the 1920s, many corporations floated seven to eight percent non-rated bonds, and these were more than enough to bankrupt many of those companies. By 1931, 44 percent of all the corporate bonds issued during the 1920s had gone into default. The corporate debt burden is far heavier today in the early 1990s, and a very similar disaster could befall corporate America and our bond markets. Today's corporate bond market has become a giant time bomb which is ticking. The leveraged buyout (LBO) craze has magnified the problem.

Who owns corporate junk bonds? Many individuals have bought them. There are over 100 mutual funds which are concentrated in junk bonds, so, numerous small investors indirectly bought them. Many were bought by banks and the savings and loan industry.

Insurance companies and pension funds have also bought a lot of junk bonds (e.g., in early 1992, life insurance companies owned $85 billion in junk bonds—equivalent to the entire net worth of the industry). Financial institutions, viewed by most as being very conservative, have been loading themselves up with these junk bonds.

When it comes to debt, our American government is bigger and has done it "better" than anyone else. Through U.S. government debt alone, the United States has become the largest debtor nation in the world. In 1981, the United States was the largest creditor nation in the world. Other countries owed us more money than we owed all other countries (e.g., $141 billion). Just 10 years later, we owe other countries more money than they owe us (e.g., $400 billion). It took from George Washington through Jimmy Carter, 205 years, to go from $0 to $1 trillion in debt. It took 12 more years (1981-1992), the so-called conservative Reagan/Bush years, to go from $1 trillion to $4 trillion. In other words, the United States government accumulated four times more debt during the Reagan/Bush years than in all the prior years of U.S. history.

Federal Debt

The government officially says the debt is $4 trillion. In 1991, the government paid over $300 billion in interest on the debt, but that's not the whole story. They are practicing internal borrowing by slipping in and taking away from the pension funds in order to pay the day-to-day bills of running the government. Most people who are recipients of these pension funds have no idea that this is taking place. Because of this, the actual federal debt is $4.5 trillion. There are federal agencies which handle Fanniemae's, Ginniemae's, farm loans, and student loans, and that debt, which is $720 billion, is not counted as part of the deficit. It's as if they have set up a second set of books. There are also implied guarantees to banks and savings and loans of $3.7 trillion. If all of that is added together, the total government debt is actually $9 trillion.

U.S. federal government debt growth (the true measure of the budget deficit) first hit $1 trillion on October 1, 1981 (it took *205* years). It took only 12 more years to grow to $4 trillion by mid-1992. The average federal deficit was $50 billion per year in the Carter years, $200 billion per year in the Reagan years, and $400 billion per year in the Bush years. The deficit for fiscal year 1992 will be almost $600 billion.

Fudging on the Statistics

The government distorts most economic statistics, whether it's unemployment, gross national product, inflation, or the federal and trade deficits. For example, you can be unemployed and appear on the unemployment rolls for a year, but you will be removed from the unemployment rolls after one year. You may roll onto the welfare rolls and still be unemployed, but you are no longer counted as unemployed by the government. You may be a middle manager who has lost a $60,000-a-year job. Unable to find good work, you end up delivering pizzas at night for minimum wage. You are considered just as employed by the statistics as when you made $60,000 a year.

A financial newsletter writer in the Pacific Northwest attended a meeting held by the leaders of the timber industry at which an economist from the Reagan Administration was speaking. The economist was asked how high unemployment was in the Pacific Northwest timber industry, and he said, "We've done a great job;

we've brought unemployment down to eight percent."
The newsletter writer knew the speaker because they had
been roommates in college. Later, he asked the speaker
how much unemployment really was. The economist
winked at him and said, "It's actually 25 percent." That's
fudging quite a bit. In mid-1992, the Bush Administration
said U.S. unemployment was 7.3 percent. Private studies
indicated that the true unemployment rate was closer to
14 percent.

We have been taught for years that the gross
domestic product (GDP) is the combined goods and
services of America, the production capacity of America.
In actuality, the government counts government spending
as part of the GDP. What's productive about that? They
take taxes from us, they run it through the government
filter, dissipate 80 to 90 percent of it, and give us back a
little. If government spending is subtracted, then the GDP
is about half of what the government reports it to be.

The government claims inflation is between four and
six percent. Almost everyone knows that their cost of
living is increasing more than that. Ten to fifteen years
ago, you could buy a Chevrolet for $4,000 to $5,000.
Today, this same car is $15,000 to $18,000. The government does not count that as a price increase. The rationale
is used that it's a better car because the model has been
changed and improved—even though the old Chevrolet
for $4,000 was made out of steel, and the new one is made
out of cheaper metal and plastic. If the price on an item is
increasing rapidly, the government takes it out of the
market basket of goods and services used to calculate the
inflation statistics (CPI). In the "real world," the official
government inflation numbers need to be doubled (e.g., if
they say 6 to 7 percent, it's really 12 to 14 percent).

What about the federal and trade deficits? In 1988,

the federal deficit reportedly was $155 billion. The real deficit was $252 billion. The government borrowed $100 billion from Social Security and various retirement funds while claiming a surplus of $20 to $30 billion in the Social Security Trust Fund. They raided the retirement funds so they could say the deficit was only $155 billion. The 1990 deficit was $276 billion according to the Congressional Budget Office, but the Administration claimed it to be about $150 billion. They "fudged" by $127 billion while expropriating that amount from Social Security and other pension/trust funds. They are deceiving the American people and telling them they are cutting the budget deficit.

They also did this with the trade deficit in 1988. The trade deficit was supposed to be $118.7 billion, and the real deficit was $141.7 billion. The Reagan Administration fudged by dropping $23 billion in freight, port charges, and insurance. The government continually understates these statistics in order to make the politicians look better. All this makes it very hard to plan and to know what is really going on.

The Banking and S&L Crises

The failings in the banking and S&L industries are another consequence of the huge accumulation of debt in the United States. Between 1987 and 1988, 700 banks failed, a post-Depression record. Ten percent of the country's 13,000 banks are on the FDIC's problem list. Since 1981, 1,700 out of 4,000 S&Ls have closed, and another 500 are expected to close from 1992 to 1994. In 1991, withdrawals of over $100 billion were made from S&Ls alone, with the withdrawals growing to the $120 billion rate in 1992. By 1995, only 1,000 savings and loan institutions will be left, if that many.

The government is talking about bailing out the S&Ls. Bailouts are paid for by U.S. taxpayers, or else the printing presses are run and inflation is created to accomplish the bailout. The bailout for the savings and loan institutions is likely to ultimately reach $1 to $1.5 trillion. That's 20 to 30 times greater than the Marshall Plan for rebuilding Western Europe after five years of World War II and is actually greater than the cost (in present dollars) of all U.S. wars from the Civil War through Operation Desert Storm. These are enormous numbers for papering over only one of the cracks in our financial system.

There is a run on the savings and loans. Quietly, but on an accelerating basis, more and more money is being withdrawn from savings and loans. Investors are beginning to realize that many (if not most) savings and loans are shaky. The FDIC is now technically insolvent—the Federal Deposit Insurance Corporation actually covers the deposits in banks, and now savings and loans. The Federal Savings and Loan Insurance Corporation (FSLIC) used to insure savings and loan institutions, but it went bankrupt in 1988. The FDIC took over insuring $1 trillion in deposits in the savings and loans and $3 trillion in banks, or $4 trillion total. But the FDIC has less than $10 billion to insure $4 trillion—one-half of one percent.

What is ominous is that if more banks fail (remember that banks have been defaulting at a rate of 200 or more per year for six years—record failures since the Great Depression), where is the money going to come from to cover the bailouts? When Continental Illinois Bank went under in the spring of 1984, it took 25 percent of the total FDIC insurance funds just for that one bank. When Franklin National Bank failed in the spring of 1974, it took 40 percent of the FDIC's total funds. The comptroller of the currency, Charles Bowsher, has said that the FDIC is insolvent and that the failure of one large money center will push it over the edge. The savings and loan crisis is much larger than the Latin American debt crisis, a $400 billion plight, and both are erupting at exactly the same time.

There is a connection between the savings and loan industry crisis and the real estate market. Real estate has been dropping in 85 to 90 percent of the country. Real estate loans held by the banks total $700 billion, and real estate loans held by the savings and loans total $2.8 trillion. Yes, there has been mismanagement and fraud in some savings and loans, but 95 percent of the savings and loan problem has been the dramatic plunge in real estate prices in many areas throughout the United States. Real estate dropped 30 percent in value in Colorado in the late 1980s. In 1989 alone, it dropped 30 percent in Arizona, and Texas and New England have seen real estate prices falling by 50 percent or more. The northeast, the southeast, the midwest, California, and even Hawaii have seen sharp drops in real estate prices. People have leveraged themselves to the hilt. They have borrowed large amounts of money against real estate property, and as real estate values decrease, many people are losing their property, and the savings and loans and banks are left holding these properties.

In the 1980s, over $1 trillion in new commercial real estate loans were floated. Most of these were for large high-rise commercial office buildings. Most of them had no prior lessees and many of them were financed 100 percent, with nothing down. They are now called "see through" office buildings because they are empty and most of them are in default. U.S. banks loaned over $100 billion for commercial real estate in the past 10 years; insurance companies loaned $260 billion, and pension funds loaned several hundred billion. These financial institutions, along with the savings and loans, are caught in the downward spiral with defaulting real estate. It is called by some the "death spiral."

The Resolution Trust Corporation (part of the FDIC) will dump $400 to $500 billion of real estate on the market in the next four or five years. It is planning on dumping the defaulted real estate in blocks of $500 million. That is putting incredible pressure on existing real estate, pushing down the value of the existing real estate holdings, and of properties lent on or controlled by the banks, savings and loans, insurance companies, and pension funds. So, many more banks, savings and loans, and insurance companies will fail as real estate prices continue to drop.

Despite the spreading cracks in the U.S. financial system, from Wall Street to Washington we are being told that "Everything is fine; we've never had it so good. Happy days are here again, and lie ahead as far as the eye can see." Actually, America is rolling over into a depression which could be even more severe than the Great Depression of the 1930s.

However, there are a number of things the conservative investor or saver can do. These will be developed in depth in Chapter Seven. The common denominator between the bank failures, personal failures, and business failures is too much debt. You need to reduce your debt and reduce it as quickly as possible. Become liquid and get out of debt. Be careful of savings and loan deposits. Check and continually monitor your savings and loan or bank very closely. If your financial institution is not strong, you may want to withdraw your funds and move them elsewhere. Liquidate all real estate except for your home prior to the great FDIC "fire sale." They have already begun dumping billions and billions in real estate. Avoid the stock market. It is a ticking time bomb.

Keep a couple of months expenses in cash at home for bank closures or other emergencies. Avoid corporate bonds because of corporate America's tremendous indebtedness. Thousands more corporate bankruptcies are coming. Approximately 20 to 30 percent of a portfolio should be in precious metals, which perform extremely well in times of financial chaos and/or inflation. Precious metals mining stocks did very well during the Great Depression—up to 10 percent of a portfolio could be invested in these. Store a year's supply of food reserves—enough for each member of the family. The United States' food reserves are almost depleted. They're down to a surplus of only 30 to 45 days, because we have been shipping our food to Russia. Also develop a second source of income. Set up a small cottage business in which your whole family can be involved, a business which can produce a product or service which people will need in good times or bad.

The most important thing is to pray for wisdom and guidance. James 1:5 says that God will give us wisdom if we ask Him for it, and Isaiah 58:11 says the Lord will guide you continually. The Word of God talks more about finances than it does about salvation. God knew that finances would be a very important (and problematic) area for His people. We need to seek God's wisdom and guidance as to what to do with our finances and how to be a good steward of what He has provided us in the chaotic decade of the 1990s.

The Insurance Crisis

The speculative debt binge of the 1980s has caught up

with the insurance industry. The junk bond/LBO craze of the 1980s, as well as the stampede into overpriced real estate, has set the stage for a major crisis in the insurance industry in the early 1990s. In 1990 and 1991, 65 insurance companies collapsed, including four majors, and more seem likely to follow.

The 1980s saw a switch from a very conservative life insurance industry which primarily sold life insurance, collected premiums, invested them in safe, interest-bearing securities, and then paid out occasional death benefits, to an industry which began to come up with innovative new non-life products to compete with banks, savings and loans, stock brokerage firms, and money market funds.

In a search for higher investment returns, more investor dollars, and greater competitiveness, the industry created and sold universal life policies, single premium annuities, variable life policies with stock and bond mutual funds, guaranteed investment contracts, and money market portfolios. In 1970, life insurance companies earned 94 percent of their income from premiums and 6 percent from other products. By 1990, insurance premiums represented only 34 percent of life insurance company income, high-risk investments—60 percent, and other sources—6 percent.

In the latter half of the 1980s, insurance companies (especially life) began to load up their portfolios with the same kind of high-risk, speculative investments that have caused record post-Depression bank and savings and loan failures—junk bonds and real estate. Had the U.S. economy continued to expand in the late 1980s and early 1990s, as it had for several decades, the banks, savings and loans, insurance companies, pensions funds, and credit unions might have escaped unscathed. But the economy did not continue to expand—it is now in the throes of a major contraction and these speculative investments are rapidly contracting as well.

Today, the life insurance industry holds 6.4 percent of its total assets in junk bonds (actually the number may be much higher) versus total industry capital (or net worth) of 6.5 percent of assets. So, almost 100 percent of industry capital is invested in junk bonds and 20 percent of total assets (or over three times industry net worth) is invested in real estate or real estate mortgages.

The May 3, 1991 issue of *The Holt Advisory* said the following regarding the crisis of confidence which has developed in the insurance industry:

> *"The insurance industry is on the brink of a disaster which could shake it to its very foundation. The cause of this disaster is not limited to a handful of junk bonds. And its consequences are not limited to the failure of a few weak companies. Rather, the disaster we see ahead stems from many years of high-risk investing. And it could result in many **decades** of hardship for millions of Americans. It is a looming crisis of confidence, of lost credibility, of spreading fear among the public and ultimately, of a 'run on the bank' as policyholders pull their money out of the insurance industry.*
>
> *"The Holt Advisory and its publisher, Weiss Research, rates over 1,700 life, health, and annuity insurers. And in the **majority** of companies, we find weaknesses which most other analysts have underestimated or overlooked.*
>
> *"**Weakness #1: Low-Quality Bonds**—Industry defenders will tell you that only a few*

companies have excessive holdings in junk bonds, that Executive Life's failure was an isolated case, and that the problem will soon go away. This is not true. The new classification of junk bonds adopted by the state insurance commissioners reveals that many large companies have more than double the holdings in junk bonds than previously believed.

"In addition, many life and health insurers have disproportionately large holdings in the lowest quality investment grade bonds—those with a classification equivalent to S&P's triple-B ratings. If you consider that Dun & Bradstreet is reporting a surge in business failures and that Wall Street rating agencies are announcing record numbers of downgrades, it is very likely that a larger-than-normal percentage of these triple-B bonds will be downgraded, bloating still further the junk holdings of insurance companies.

"**Weakness #2: Mortgages and the Underlying Real Estate**—Many insurance companies carry assets similar to those which have caused severe losses to banks and S&Ls. But because the regulators assume that insurance companies are unlikely to have liquidity problems, there is no serious effort to re-evaluate (e.g., mark to the market) these assets despite surging mortgage default rates. The recent runs on Executive Life and some other companies in trouble should dissuade regulators of the notion that liquidity problems are unlikely in this industry.

"**Weakness #3: Insufficient Capital**—For each company we rate, we calculate how much *capital would be needed in various economic scenarios. And we are sorry to say that only a small minority have all the resources we believe they need to cover their investment and business risks in a severe recession.*

"The Surge in Failures—Already, we are seeing a surge in failures. Until Executive Life's demise, however, the insolvencies were mostly small firms, easily covered by the state guaranty system. Now we are entering a new chapter in the crisis. Why? Because the failure of Executive Life alone is many times larger than the sum of all the failures during 1989 or 1990 and it cannot be covered by the guaranty associations.

"Why It Could Be Worse Than Just a Shake-out—Normally, the shake-out can be a positive development. The weak companies shrink in size, and they shrink in number. Only the stronger companies remain. But today, by failing to disclose these problems, the insurance industry is inadvertently risking the possibility that this flight to quality could degenerate into a wholesale panic. In the case of Executive Life, for example, regulators deliberately told the public not to worry; all the rating agencies, except for Weiss Research, gave Executive Life excellent grades; and the sales representatives of the company itself had no legal requirement to disclose the risks to the consumer.

"Now, the newest data reveals that there are other companies with exposures similar to that of Executive Life. Will millions more consumers be kept in the dark? Will more companies which currently have A+ ratings

*from other services fail? If so—if the industry
continues to downplay and cover up its problems—public confidence will be badly shaken.
Policyholders will be driven not by reason but
by emotion. They will no longer trust the word
of the insurance agent, the insurance commis-
sioner, or the insurance rating agency. They will
shy away from buying new insurance policies,
surrender old policies, and rush to take their
money out through policy loans. And, worst of
all, they will have no means—and no desire—to
discriminate between good and bad, weak or
strong.*

    *"Make sure you don't get caught in this
panic. Avoid companies with low ratings and
companies that have large junk bond holdings."*

Junk bonds are not the major Achilles' heel in U.S
financial markets—real estate is! There are between $300
and $400 billion junk bonds in existence depending on
how you count them and how many bonds are downgraded
to junk status. There are $6.5 trillion in real estate
mortgages—20 times the size of the junk bond market.

The savings and loan industry has loaned almost 100
percent of its $1 trillion in deposits into the real estate
market—primarily residential. Of 12,247 U.S. banks,
11,000 with assets under $1 billion have 50 percent of their
outstanding loans in real estate. The remaining 1,247
banks, with assets over $1 billion, have one-third of their
assets in real estate. The insurance industry has 20 percent
of its assets (or over three times its capital) tied up in real
estate investments or mortgages. And many pension funds
have up to a quarter (or more) of their assets in mortgages.

Most insurance companies do not hold single family

mortgages, but rather commercial real estate and real estate paper, which is even less stable and more vulnerable to decline than residential real estate.

The problem is that real estate prices are falling in 85 to 90 percent of the U.S., with $75 to $100 billion in new real estate defaults in 1991, as over 900,000 Americans and 100,000 corporations went bankrupt. With 900,000 personal bankruptcies and 100,000 business failures in 1991, and a million personal bankruptcies and a comparable number of business closures expected in 1992, another $150 to $200 billion in real estate defaults can be expected in 1991 and 1992.

As bankruptcies, unemployment, and defaults proliferate, the value of the real estate holdings and mortgage paper of U.S. banks, savings and loans, insurance companies, and pension funds will continue to deteriorate— maybe even plunge. As investors, depositors, and policyholders begin to understand this, hundreds of such runs could develop. The FDIC, the Federal Reserve, and state insurance regulators couldn't beg, borrow, print, or steal money fast enough to cover that sort of financial panic.

So, it is worth considering the interlock between the banks, the savings and loans, the insurance companies, the pension funds, and the real estate market. All could be in an incredible self-feeding downward spiral over the next two to five years. Indeed, the downward spiral has already begun.

Chapter Six

The Financial and Political Parallels Between the 1920s and '30s and the 1980s and '90s

In the previous chapter, the accelerating financial decline of the United States was examined. A large number of banks, savings and loans, businesses, and individuals have collapsed into bankruptcy over the last five years. The number of failed banks and businesses are setting records not seen since the Great Depression. In this chapter, we will discuss some of the financial and political parallels between the 1920s and '30s and the 1980s and '90s, and the so-called supercycle, or longwave.

A bleak economic future for America is very possible, even though the great majority, from Wall Street to Washington and all across the country, are bullish on America. Washington politicians have a vested interest in telling people what they want to hear so that Americans will continue to vote for them, election after election. Wall Street has a vested interest in giving people good news so they can continue to sell securities and to ring Wall Street's cash registers. The Establishment, from Washington to Wall Street, through the press, will tell people the good news they want to hear. Americans are Pollyanna people: we like good news, and we love to have people tell us exactly what we want to hear.

But there are certain realities you cannot run away from. As discussed in the previous chapter, the United States has gone on a massive debt binge, and the debt pyramid is beginning to unravel. There are record numbers of bank and savings and loan failures. More individuals and businesses are filing bankruptcy than at any time since the peak of the Great Depression. There is also the $400 billion Latin debt pyramid. We have a spastic economy, with major parts of the economy already in recession or depression. Over 85 percent of the country is seeing real estate prices fall. The first regions of the country to feel the recession (or depression) were Texas, Oklahoma, and the oil states, the agricultural states, and some of the heavy manufacturing states. They've been feeling the crunch for several years. A giant financial contraction is coming, and all of this is leading to the rollover of our financial system into a massive depression.

The Supercycle

A Russian economist, Kondratieff, was employed by the Soviet government in the 1920s to develop a model or scenario for when Western capitalism would collapse. Kondratieff examined long-term interest rates, commodities prices, and many economic indicators. When Kondratieff finished his study, he saw not the collapse of Western-style capitalism, but rather a supercycle, 50 to 60 years in duration, that exists throughout the Western economies. There will be two peaks (a primary peak, a plateau period at the top, then a secondary peak), followed by a drop into a massive depression. That depression will last 10 to 15 years and then the economies will rebound for 15 to 20 years. Then there will be a blow-off phase, and everything will occur all over again. The professor said there would even be wars interspersed along the way. Kondratieff was very excited to identify the supercycle. Unfortunately, his bosses, the Soviet Kremlin leaders, were not. That was the wrong answer. They wanted Kondratieff to tell them when Western capitalism would collapse, not when it would go into a down cycle. They threw the poor professor into a Soviet slave labor camp, where he died a few years later.

People in the Institute for the Study of Cycles and other students of cycle theory believe there is another 50-year cycle, a biblical cycle, capped off with the year of Jubilee. In the Old Testament, the Hebrews were told every fiftieth year to allow their land to lay fallow, to get out of debt, clear the books, let any slaves have their freedom, and start over from scratch. Students of longwave cycle theory believe that the Kondratieff longwave (or supercycle) and the biblical 50-year cycle are probably one and the same.

The rationale behind this theory is that people repeat their mistakes—history is replete with examples of this. Hegel said: "We learn from history, we'learn nothing from history." People repeating their mistakes is true in economic history, as well as in other areas, and major mistakes tend to be repeated every two or three generations.

Let's turn to the Great Depression. Those who lived through the worst of it saw the bread lines and the soup lines. They saw people jump out of buildings on Wall Street, the collapse of the banks, and the collapse of speculation. They were extremely conservative with their finances for the rest of their lives; they no longer went into debt; they would no longer speculate.

Their children were a little less conservative. They saw the depression, they heard about it from their parents, but they didn't completely understand it. They always had a little soup and a little bread on the table. But they were still fairly conservative in how they handled their finances.

Then the third generation comes along, the grandchildren. Their attitude is, "The depression is ancient history. We're too smart for something like that to happen again. We have computer models, new economic models, and we've learned from past mistakes." But they haven't, and they repeat the same mistakes. They forget history. Every two to three generations, which fits into the 50-year biblical cycle as well as the Kondratieff longwave cycle, we tend to repeat our mistakes.

There were four major supercycles over the past 200 years. They bottomed in 1787, 1842, 1896, and 1949. They peaked in 1814, 1864, 1920—an important year—and 1980 was probably the last peak. There are actually two peaks, a primary peak and a secondary peak. After the secondary peak, the economy falls into the great abyss. There is also a supercycle plateau, and the two most important ones for the purpose of our discussion are the plateaus in 1920 to 1929, and 1980 to 1989. There are extraordinary parallels and similarities between the Roaring Twenties and the Roaring Eighties. There are also dramatic parallels between the declining 1930s and the declining 1990s.

Supercycles have a number of characteristics. First, let's examine the last supercycle bottom in 1949, after World War II. World War II actually began to pull us out of the depression, and that fits into the Kondratieff supercycle model. After the war, in 1949, we had very low interest rates and high financial liquidity. People had a lot of money; they had saved during the war and had not spent their savings. Speculative activity was virtually nonexistent. Business activity was at very low levels. Try to picture 1949. There was gross pessimism about future economic growth. No one was looking for a boom, and many people were looking for a depression. That's what the last supercycle bottom looked like.

A supercycle peak occurred in 1920, and again in 1980. Most of us can remember what it looked like in 1980. At a supercycle top, or peak, interest rates are surging to all-time new highs. Remember what was happening in 1980. Interest rates rose to over 21 percent; it was an insane period. Wage and price inflation rates were at double-digit levels. In 1980, we saw annualized inflation rates of up to 19 percent. There are also high levels of speculation at a supercycle top and very high levels of debt. Frantic business activity is also characteristic of a supercycle top. Everyone thinks that the good times are going to roll on forever. There is enormous optimism about the future price levels of commodities, real estate, and other speculative investments.

A supercycle top usually ends with a credit crunch, which began to take place in 1980-1981. That suddenly chokes the business boom and the commodity price inflation which has been fueled by easy credit which took place a few years earlier. The business boom collapses shortly after the supercycle top. This was seen in 1981 and 1982. Commodity prices crash, and a relatively brief but severe economic depression follows.

In the peak year, such as 1980, interest rates and commodity prices go into exponential blow-offs. The gold market in 1979 and 1980 went into a full vertical blow-off, with a vertically-rising chart. Examples of vertically-rising markets are the stock market in August through October of 1987, the stock market in October of 1929, and the gold market in the fall of 1979 and early 1980. A vertically-rising market is always followed by a vertically-collapsing market. In 1980, the commodities markets soared into an exponential blow-off and then crashed, and this was followed by a brief business depression.

Students of the supercycle believe that the last plateau, prior to the one we're in right now, was from 1920 to 1929. The most recent plateau was from 1980 to 1990 or 1991. The plateau period usually lasts eight to ten years. It's bracketed at the beginning and the end by a primary and a secondary peak which happened in 1920 and 1929, and again in 1980 and 1990-1991. Some economic recovery is experienced during this plateau period but with neither interest rates nor commodities reaching their previous highs. There is a major effort to restore liquidity which results in a lot of money pumping during this period. We saw this in the 1920s and certainly again in the 1980s. Credit standards are dramatically lowered which is why we are presently experiencing the major crises in the banks and savings and loans. Everyone is encouraged to borrow more during the plateau period. Who can't remember in the last few years having someone send you an application for another credit card? This is being encouraged from the government on down. A classic example is the farmers, who were encouraged by the government in the 1970s and early 1980s to borrow money. Many of them had to file for bankruptcy as a result.

During the plateau periods of the 1920s and again in the 1980s, large foreign and domestic loans were made. These were encouraged by the Federal Reserves' "easy money" policies, and that's how the United States was able to borrow $750 billion from abroad. Just like any near-bankrupt debtor, the government had to keep up the facade of financial health by borrowing from abroad. During the 1920s and the 1980s, the government reduced taxes and granted incentives to stimulate further expansion. There was credit hype to stimulate speculative mania, but it concentrated in securities rather than in commodities. A speculative boom occurred on Wall Street but not in the commodities market. The stock market became the center of attention, and trading volume broke all prior records. The end of the plateau period is usually marked by a violent stock market crash followed by a collapse in real estate prices and a severe economic depression.

Some thought the present plateau period was about to end when the stock market crashed in October of 1987. It is more likely that the plateau period of the 1980s was capped with the pre-election stock market blow-off of 1992. Real estate prices are dropping almost all over the country, having dropped 30 percent in Denver, 30 percent in Phoenix, and 50 percent in Texas and the northeast. These are some of the characteristics of the end of the plateau period.

The cracks now appearing in the real estate markets, the banks, and the savings and loans, along with record bankruptcies by businesses and individuals, are all symptoms of a rollover of the supercycle into another great depression. After the crash of 1929, Herbert Hoover maintained that this was simply an aberration (a temporary correction), and that the economy was fundamentally sound. Our politicians are saying the same thing today. The politicians of the Hoover era didn't understand for another year and a half that the country was in a depression. It was midway through 1931 before they would acknowledge that this was a depression. In the early 1990s some will say that the country seems to be sinking into a recession, then yes, it really is in a recession. Then before it's all over, they will realize that the country is not in a recession, but a depression. The stage is set for a depression that could last through much, if not all, of the 1990s.

It is very important to realize that before the Great Depression some people saw it coming. They were a minority and were probably ridiculed as gloom-and-doomers. They saw the handwriting on the wall. They got out of debt and became liquid, and 10,000 of them became millionaires in the midst of the Great Depression.

The financial parallels between the 1920s and 1930s and the 1980s and 1990s are astonishing. First, there was a huge amount of speculation on Wall Street during the 1920s. People were putting together pyramided trusts, there was a massive amount of margin trading, and all of that fell apart in October 1929. Similar things have been happening in the 1980s and early 1990s, only on a larger scale and much more excessive. There has been options trading and large commodities trading, all highly margined. The 1980s saw the advent of the junk bond market which floated almost $310 billion in junk bonds, and over the past three years, we have seen over $40 billion of those go into default. Hundreds of leveraged buyouts emanated from Wall Streets deals on which Wall Street firms made billions of dollars. But hundreds of companies cashed in equity and went heavily into debt, and now many of those companies are failing. There was an enormous amount of speculative mania on Wall Street in the 1920s, and there has been even more in the 1980s and early 1990s.

The 1920s had speculative banking practices, and the 1980s and early 1990s have had even more as banks have gone all out to try to increase the profitability of their loan portfolios, loaning into shakier and shakier deals. Commodity prices fell in the latter part of the 1920s, and this also happened in the late 1980s, as most farmers can attest to. There was an agricultural depression in the late 1920s, and the same thing recurred between 1985 and 1990. The farm sector has again been completely decimated.

The 1920s saw a rising tide of trade protectionism. In late 1929 and early 1930, Congress passed the Smoot-Hawley Protective Tariff. Supposedly, this bill was to protect the country from the Japanese who were dumping all kinds of products into the United States. But many believe that the passage of that bill helped trigger the Great Depression, provoking an international trade war, with other countries retaliating against the U.S. Look at what has again been happening in Washington in the late 1980s and early 1990s. Protective tariff and protective trade legislation is again being introduced into Congress to strike back against the Japanese and the Taiwanese to stop the influx of Sonys and Toyotas and the many products that are coming from the Pacific Rim. The U.S. is heading for another trade war, exactly as we were in the late 1920s.

An explosion of consumer installment debt occurred in the latter part of the 1920s, and consumer installment debt has risen to $3.5 trillion in the last few years in this country. There was a large mountain of mortgage debt in the late 1920s; it's much, much larger today. Today, there are $6.5 trillion in real estate mortgages. Remember, the tax laws were changed in 1986, and hundreds of thousands of Americans borrowed against the equity in their homes and made the mortgages even larger so they could buy "essentials" such as speed boats, trips to Las Vegas, and invest in the stock market before the crash in 1987. There was extensive mortgage debt in the 1920s, and there's even more now. Another characteristic of the 1920s was a giant pyramid of business debt accompanied by a sharp drop in corporate liquidity. The corporate debt today is five times greater than it was during the 1920s, and tripled during the decade of the 1980s.

The latter part of the 1920s saw a shaky banking system, and the banking system is even more shaky today. Ten percent of American banks are on the FDIC's problem list, 1,700 banks have failed in the past nine years, and FDIC bank account insurance is almost nonexistent. The 1920s also saw a record government debt, but government debt quadrupled under Ronald Reagan and George Bush from $1 trillion to $4 trillion. The 1920s also saw a psychological climate of official and consumer optimism and complacency. President Herbert Hoover, Washington, the politicians, and Wall Street told Americans, "We've never had it so good." After the crash in 1929, they said, "It's just a hiccup. Don't worry, things will be fine. The economy is fundamentally sound." The same things are being said today. There are some extraordinary parallels between today and the 1920s and early 1930s.

The political parallels between the 1920s and the 1980s are very intriguing as well. Let's take a look at the 1920s first. The supercycle peak was in 1920. The United States had just had a 20-year progressive, or liberal, period in government which was characterized by very heavy governmental intervention in domestic and foreign affairs, and was capped by Woodrow Wilson's push for the League of Nations. Three years before 1920, an unpopular war came to an end, World War I. A shift in conservatism appeared in 1920, along with a desire for a return to what was called "the good old days" with less government interference.

With a campaign slogan of "A Return To Normalcy," Republican Warren Harding was swept into office in 1920, only to die in office in 1923. Harding was replaced by

Calvin Coolidge, who was elected in 1924, and could have easily been re-elected in 1928. Coolidge was replaced by Herbert Hoover who, with a lot of conservative rhetoric, won a landslide victory against Democrat Al Smith with an electoral vote of 444 to 87. In the fall of 1928, Wall Street insiders became very nervous, and the Fed (Federal Reserve System) began to be hostile toward the boom. In the summer of 1929, the Fed raised the discount rate to 6 percent, and within 60 days the crash of October 1929 and the beginning of the Great Depression was under way.

In analyzing how the 1980s look politically, there are amazing similarities. The 1980 supercycle peak saw a shift from 20 years of liberal politics (called the New Frontier, the Great Society, New Economics) with the Kennedys, Johnsons, and Carters. This period was characterized by heavy governmental interference in domestic and foreign affairs. Six years earlier, another unpopular war, the Vietnam War, came to an end. A shift to conservatism began in 1980 and a desire for a return to "the good old days" with less government interference.

With a campaign slogan of "Let's Get the Government Off Our Backs," Republican Ronald Reagan was swept into office in 1980. Reagan was re-elected by a large margin in 1984 and could have easily been re-elected in 1988 if he could have run. The very popular Reagan was replaced by George Bush, who again, with much conservative rhetoric, won a landslide against the leftist Democrat Michael Dukakis, with an electoral vote of 426 to 112. Since Bush assumed office in 1989, U.S. debt, deficits, unemployment, bank, savings and loan, corporate, and personal failures have exploded even as the U.S. stock market was manipulated into a 1992 pre-election blow-off.

All this suggests that if we do not prepare for the tough times that are coming, many more Americans (including many Christians) will go bankrupt in the early to mid 1990s. The common denominator between the 1.2 million Americans who are in bankruptcy court today and the record number of business, bank, and savings and loan failures is too much debt. If Americans don't see the handwriting on the wall, reduce their debt, reduce their exposure to real estate and the stock market, and get liquid, many millions more will "go to the wall."

The great majority from Wall Street to Washington and across the country think that happy days are here again, that we have never had it so good. They don't want to look at the cracks that are spreading throughout the system. It's similar to what happens before an earthquake. The animals begin to get nervous, and there are small tremors and small signs before the big earthquake comes. But most people don't want to look at the small signs. Most ignore them because we're the Pollyanna people; give us good news, don't give us bad news. However, there will be a prudent few, like there were before other recessions and before the Great Depression, who will take defensive action and begin to be ready for the very, very tough times ahead.

There are many things you can do to prepare for the coming financial crisis. God warned Pharaoh (via His servant, Joseph) of the famine and economic crunch which would hit Egypt and all of the ancient world. Pharaoh heeded the warning and used Joseph as his administrator to prepare for the crisis. Undoubtedly some called Joseph a "gloom-and-doomer" and a pessimist, but when the crisis arrived, Egypt and Israel were saved. In the present circumstances, there are a number of things which you can do to prepare economically for the crisis. These will be discussed in Chapter Seven.

How to Prepare
for the
Coming Financial Crisis

"A prudent man foreseeth the evil, and hideth himself; but the simple pass on, and are punished."
—Proverbs 27:12

Today, there are basically three major scenarios on the economy. One is that happy days are here again, we've never had it so good, and the future is going to be better than what we have right now. The second major scenario on the economy today is that there will soon be a major deflationary depression similar to 1929 or worse. With accelerating bankruptcies and failures in the business and banking sectors, prices will fall and people will be out of work to an even greater extent in the 1990s than in the 1930s. The third major economic scenario is that of a financial crisis occurring with the government running the monetary printing presses and accelerating inflationary pressure by trying to bail out themselves, the banks, the savings and loans, and the Third World debtors, etc. Before discussing specifics of how to prepare for the coming financial upheaval, we will share some principles that you need to consider and to use, and that should be helpful in understanding and facing the future.

Principles to Consider

First of all, we need to understand that there is a huge gap between reality and the public perception of reality. What people perceive is happening and what is really happening are quite different indeed. The public is fed what they are supposed to know and to do by the Establishment press, by Washington, and by Wall Street. The reality of what is happening in the financial system with the widespread collapse of banks and savings and loans, the accelerating bankruptcies, the rising unemployment, and the declining real estate prices around the country, and the perception of what is happening, that everything is fine, are quite different.

Webster's Dictionary defines complacency as "self-satisfaction accompanied by unawareness of actual dangers or deficiencies." Individuals who have been in the investment business for decades have never seen a time when there is so much complacency and apathy among most investors as there is today. They don't seem to have the slightest idea that they could be sitting on a railroad track with a freight train headed toward them; they're very complacent. Although the stock market could crash again as it did in October 1987 when the market dropped $500 billion in one day, many investors may sleep right through it the next time.

This apathy and complacency is affecting most investment markets today. If you talk to the average stockbroker today, he'll say that he's never seen his business this quiet. Even in talking to many gold coin dealers, most are simply doing nothing. People are sound asleep. It's as if someone has dumped a sleeping fog over the United States.

The next principle is that in the short run, markets move on the public perception of the facts; in the long run, markets move on the reality or actual fundamentals. For example, the gold market was not very exciting prior to the Iraqi invasion of Kuwait—it had been flat to down for several years. On the other hand, the economic fundamentals for the gold market haven't been as strong in 20 years.

Also, you will probably find that politicians, bankers, and monetary authorities will do anything to postpone or disguise a financial crisis, even if the postponement compounds the problem. We should mistrust most public pronouncements by politicians, bankers, and monetary authorities. This may sound skeptical, but many will lie without hesitation to protect their own interests. We need to have a realistic perspective and a global perspective on monetary, economic, and geopolitical events. It is also important to keep in mind the three sides of the perspective triangle. Again, one side of the triangle is the monetary and economic decline of the United States. The social and political decline, which is the move toward a one-world government and socialism, is the second side. The base of the triangle is the spiritual and moral decline. It is vital to see all three sides of the world situation and how they relate to one another to get a perspective on these developments and to see the big picture. Then you can understand the specifics of these areas, and after that, you can understand what course of action to take to protect yourself and your family.

There are two Achilles' heels for investors in this country today: heavy debt and high illiquidity. Over the next five years, people need to invest primarily in assets which are very liquid and which will perform very well in both good and bad times.

Another principle is that the majority is always wrong. Most people were brought up to believe that the majority is right, but if you study the Bible, history, markets, or virtually any human endeavor, you will learn that most people are going the wrong direction at the wrong time. Wall Street calls this the Theory of Contrary Opinion, and it simply says that the majority will rush in to buy at the top of the market, and they'll rush to sell at the bottom of the market. This is not the old-time formula for making money, but it is the American way.

The last principle is that Americans are perpetual optimists. Psychologists call this the Pollyanna Principle which, again, is something like this: Whisper sweet nothings in my ears, tickle my ears, or tell me nothing at all. This perpetual optimism makes it very difficult for most Americans to anticipate problems. We usually only react to problems after we're up to our eyeballs in alligators. It is best not to be a perpetual optimist, or a perpetual pessimist, but to be a realist, and to adjust to things the way they really are.

Getting Out of Harm's Way: How to Prepare for the Coming Financial Crisis

Surviving and prospering in difficult, trying times is a function of proper mental attitude and proper preparation. Daryl Royal, the former coach of the University of Texas national champion Longhorn football team used to say, "When the going gets tough, the tough get going." Proverbs 23:7 says, *"As a man thinketh in his heart, so is he."* History is replete with examples of individuals and peoples who overcome great and difficult odds because of a vision of victory, an indomitable spirit, the will to survive, and the instincts of survival.

King Hezekiah rallied the Israelites against a wicked and powerful Assyrian king and vastly superior army;

Sam Houston rallied a rag-tag, numerically inferior army against a vastly superior Mexican army at the Battle of San Jacinto to win the war of Texas independence in 1836; Winston Churchill rallied the people of England against a vastly superior Nazi war machine in the Battle of Britain in one of the bravest stands a people has ever made; and there are hundreds more examples in history of people and individuals surviving difficult situations against overwhelming odds.

The narrow margin between victory or defeat, between honor or dishonor, between survival or death or slavery is mental attitude—having a stubborn vision of victory, a courage, a tenaciousness, an instinct for survival that says, as Winston Churchill encouraged the British people, "Never, never, never, never, never give up!" The difference between survival or death for many terminally diagnosed people is that tenacious instinct for survival.

But, in addition to the instinct for survival and a vision of overcoming difficult, seemingly insurmountable circumstances, proper preparation for difficult times is an important ingredient to survival. Most people will not prepare in advance for difficult economic or political times. And many only react to a crisis (e.g., Pearl Harbor) after they're up to their eyeballs in alligators. Someone once wrote about the four G's of survival, *God, Guns, Gold*, and *Groceries*. While these are all essential elements of survival, there are even more elements which should be considered in the period which lies ahead and for the balance of the 1990s.

Elements of Survival Preparation for the Coming Crunch

1. *Change Your Mindset*—Begin to look at every-

thing differently.

2. *Begin to Develop Discernment About People*—
Train yourself to watch what people do, not what
they say. We live in a day of great deception and
we need to become sensitive about what is true or
false in people.

3. *When You Invest, Invest First in the Right
People*—An investment can be great, and the
people untrustworthy, or incompetent, and it will
fail. Find like-minded, trustworthy people to
invest in, or with. Invest with or in people who
share your world view.

4. *Honestly Look at Yourself—Your Strengths and
Weaknesses*—The Bible says to know yourself.
Discover what in your life is not working. Work
on, or moderate, the weaknesses.

5. *Seek the Counsel of Others You Trust*—Seek wise
and godly counsel of people whose lives are
working well.

6. *Find Like-Minded People*—who understand where
this country is going, who have the instincts for
survival, and who are taking steps to get prepared
for the difficult times which lie ahead.

7. *Find Alternate Methods of Doing Everything*—
Develop other methods outside the system (e.g.,
bartering, growing your own food, swapping a
product or service you have with a farmer for food
he grows, etc.).

8. *Develop an Instinct for What Doesn't Feel Right*
—Become sensitive to what you have a hesitation
to doing.

9. *Begin to Eliminate Non-Essentials from Your
Life*—Eliminate time or money wasters. Buy only
what you really need, not what you want. Live

below your means. Develop habits of life to eliminate waste.

10. *Develop Physical, Mental, and Spiritual Disciplines*—before a crisis arrives—so they can be used naturally and without effort during the crisis.

11. *Learn to Treat Everything As If It Is Irreplaceable* – Treat everything as if it is the last one you can ever get (e.g., your car, tools, boots, guns, etc.).

12. *Buy Things That Will Last—Even If They Cost More*—Something mechanical that does not need power is better than something that needs power.

Reduce Your Debt

There are many things you can do to prepare for an imminent financial collapse. The first thing to do has been mentioned earlier: reduce your debts as quickly as possible. The common denominator for the large number of bankruptcies in this country (corporate and private) is too much debt. At the present time, almost one million people per year are filing for bankruptcy, with 1.2 million in bankruptcy court today. The Bible very clearly says that if you become a borrower, you become the servant of the lender. America has become a debtor nation, after being the largest creditor nation as recently as 1981.

One example of what happens to countries when they borrow heavily is South America. South American countries went into very heavy debt (e.g., $400 billion) in the late 1970s and early 1980s, and today they are the servants of the International Monetary Fund (IMF), the World Bank, and the New York bankers who now dictate economic policy to the Latin debtor nations.

This is also true for individuals. Your banker loves you when you deposit money in the bank, and when you borrow money from the bank. But if anything should go wrong; for example, if the price of your farm property should drop, you will discover that your banker doesn't love you as much as you thought, and he will begin to dictate to you and may ultimately own what you now have.

How do you reduce your debt quickly? There are two ways to do that: you can sell off some of your assets and pay down the debt, or you can begin to budget and save money on a monthly basis and accelerate mortgage payments. Another way to save is by cutting back on your standard of living and spending, which also enables you to pay down your debt. Some will use one route, some another. One very important note: if you want to survive a financial crunch, you should not be leveraged (e.g., have investments with a small or medium amount of equity and a large portion of debt). People in the real estate business used to say, "Real estate will rise forever. Don't you know that they're not making any more land?" But what they forgot was that over all that land, or bricks and mortar, was a gargantuan debt load (e.g., leverage). When a market is on the way up (e.g., rising), and you are leveraged (e.g., in the real estate or the commodities markets), it's a lot of fun and you make money quickly. But when the market is on a rollercoaster, or it's declining, then you have reverse leverage, which is very painful. You lose money just as quickly as you made it on the way up.

Reducing one's debt to as close to zero as possible is essential in the coming financial crunch. That may involve selling off some property to reduce your debt, moving to a smaller home as this writer did about two years ago, accelerating your mortgage payments with two half payments every 14 days, refinancing your home at the present lower interest rates, and perhaps shifting to a 15-year mortgage from a 25 or 30-year mortgage. Most people should get rid of their credit cards. (This writer uses them for business purposes only.) Use plastic only to the extent that it can be easily paid off each month.

If you are drowning in debt, consider debt consolidation where you reduce your overall interest rate and consolidate all of your debt into one payment, perhaps stretching out the repayment term. In any case, take on *no new debt* from this time forward. If you can't buy it for cash, don't buy it! Your sense of financial freedom will go up in direct proportion to how little debt you have.

Budgeting

Most Americans live *above* their means. Learn to live *below* your means. Apply Principle No. 9 above. Make yourself save at least 10 percent per month. (Some people can save 20 to 25 percent—the more the better.) Larry Burkett has developed an excellent study course on how to budget, called "The Financial Planning Organizer." A workbook, audio and video tapes, and kits are available. For more information, see the Appendix. Budgeting takes goal setting and discipline. The savings can be used to pay down debt if necessary. Investment alternatives for savings will be discussed below.

Use one of the methods discussed above to begin to pay down your debt, and certainly *assume no new debt*. As we sink into a major recession (or depression), you can survive it and prosper if you are not in debt. Or you can go into default and bankruptcy, as so many Americans already have in recent years and did during the Great Depression, if you have a lot of debt.

Monitor Your Bank or S&L Closely

The problems in the savings and loans are very

serious, and the numbers speak for themselves. As stated in Chapter Four, almost 50 percent of the savings and loans in the United States (e.g., about 1,700) have failed. It is projected that within five years, only 1,000 savings and loans will be left. There is no real savings and loan insurance because the FSLIC went broke and out of business in late 1988. Responsibility for insuring the savings and loan deposits was taken over by the FDIC, which now insures $4 trillion in deposits at banks and savings and loans, with a few billion dollars in insurance funds, or less than two cents per $100 in deposits. Savings and loans are a problem! They are tied into the real estate market, and as real estate declines, that will pull down more savings and loans. As more savings and loans fail, they will pull down real estate, which will cause more savings and loans to fail. Be very careful of savings and loans deposits! It may be advisable to put no money in savings and loans.

Another concern is Certificates of Deposit (CDs) of over $100,000 in banks. Banks will not insure any single account of over $100,000. One example is what happened at a savings and loan in Denver which failed in late 1989. One couple had $269,000 in the savings and loan, spread out over five different accounts. They asked the savings and loan manager if each of those accounts was insured up to $100,000, and he replied, "Absolutely." He was completely wrong. The combined savings and loan deposits were only insured up to $100,000, and the couple lost $169,000. Be very careful in buying large CDs in banks, because you are not insured over $100,000. Because the FDIC insurance fund is obviously insufficient, the government is presently talking of reducing total insurance coverage on the banks to $50,000 for all of your bank accounts.

Note: When you buy a money market fund, you

should understand that those funds are invested in large, multimillion-dollar uninsured CDs, commercial paper which is lowly rated or non-rated, and a lot of foreign paper. Therefore, be very cautious about deposits in money market funds, as well, because you're really investing in large, uninsured bank CDs.

Avoid Weak Financial Institutions

Thousands more banks, savings and loans, and insurance companies will collapse in the coming financial collapse and depression. *In spite of the perception to the contrary, there is no substantive insurance safety net under these institutions.* Over two million people have their assets frozen at present in financial institutions which have failed over the past two years. Millions more are likely to suffer their fate and have tens of billions in assets either lost or frozen.

It is essential that you obtain a Weiss Research rating on your bank, savings and loan, or insurance company and quickly evaluate your risk and alternatives if it is rated C-, D, E, or F. An instant telephone rating is $15 per institution and a detailed 18-page written report (which should be obtained for any institution rated B or less by Weiss) is $45. Weiss also has a new monitoring service whereby they will monitor your financial institution on an ongoing basis. For any of these Weiss services, call 1-800-525-9556.

Insurance Company Exposure—Many of the largest insurance companies in America have substantial high risk exposure to faltering real estate and junk bonds and are rated D, E, or F by Weiss Research. These companies should be quickly evaluated for risk exposure and alternative action. Millions of Americans have their life savings, their pension funds, or their life insurance death benefits tied up in life companies that can and will go down in the coming financial crisis. The following case, written by Martin Weiss in his newsletter, *Money and Markets*, illustrates the point:

> *"I am a widow and I have most of my life savings in Executive Life Insurance Company. I called Weiss Research to get a rating earlier this year. Your people told me it was a D+ and that it was in trouble. My agent was out of town, so I wrote to Executive Life asking them to cancel my policy and send me my money back. But after waiting for a long time, all I got was a letter from the company's president telling me there was* **nothing to worry about.** *By the time I finally got in touch with my agent, it was too late. The insurance commissioner of California declared a moratorium and my money was frozen.*
>
> *"A few weeks later I received a notice from the company telling me that I had the right to cancel the policy if I wanted to. My agent explained that it meant my money would be set aside for me, even though it would still be frozen. This sounded better than just letting it sit in a frozen policy. But then my agent said that the company changed its mind."*

This is typical of the runaround hundreds of thousands of policyholders have gotten from 66 failed insurance companies over the past two years. Neither a failing company nor its salesmen will tell you in advance that the company is in trouble. They will give you assurances that everything is fine right up to the collapse or forced closure. This writer had a client who had a $1 million annuity with Mutual Benefit. The policyholder refused to spend $15 for a Weiss rating, was given assurances that all was well ("not to fear") by his agent, and now has $1 million frozen, with its disposition up in the air.

This writer recommends Weiss A-rated insurance companies with respect to their financial strength and conservatism. For information or assistance in evaluating your insurance portfolio, call David Ritchie at 1-800-525-9556.

An Alternative to a Bank or Savings and Loan—The entire U.S. banking system, not just the C-, D, E, or F Weiss-rated banks and savings and loans, could be in harm's way if the U.S. financial system hits the wall over the next 6 to 18 months. A bank holiday, financial panic, or bank run could hit *all* banks—even the healthy ones. Many risk-adverse, conservative savers have moved the lion's share of their assets out of the banks and savings and loans, and into U.S. Treasury bill money market funds or U.S. or foreign government bond funds. Large foreign governments are not likely to default on their own paper since they keep floating more and more debt to cover their ongoing deficits. U.S. Treasury bills currently yield about 5 percent, U.S. government bonds up to 8 or 9 percent, and foreign government bonds up to 10 to 13 percent. Some excellent foreign government bond funds are available. For information on same, call International Collectors Associates at 1-800-525-9556.

Reduce Your Real Estate Holdings

Real estate is in a strong downtrend, but not just because of the liquidation of defaulted-on properties. Several studies have come from respected organizations on Wall Street recently that indicate that the baby boom that took place after World War II has turned into a baby bust. This bust is due to a combination of aborting 25 million babies who could have grown up to be home buyers in the 1990s and beyond, but are not alive now because of abortion, along with couples simply having fewer children. These reports indicate that because of the declining population, there will be an average 3 percent per year drop in residential real estate between now and A.D. 2007, a 50 percent drop in residential real estate over the next 15 years. This was analyzed in detail in *Barron's* magazine (October 1989).

Another reason the price of real estate is dropping in many parts of the country is because of overpricing and overbuilding. For example, California has incredibly high prices for real estate. This is also true of the Washington, D.C. area, and other parts of the East Coast and Florida. California real estate has topped, and the price of real estate in the northeastern United States has gone into a sharp downtrend. Again, in Denver, Colorado the price of residential real estate has dropped 30 percent. If the average homeowner in Denver, Colorado had 20 percent equity in their home, and real estate dropped in Denver an average of 30 percent, the equity of the average home throughout Denver has been completely wiped out. Many who have liquidated homes recently have had to write a difference check to the savings and loan or to the mortgage company.

Real estate dropped 30 percent in Phoenix and all over Arizona in 1989. The Resolution Trust Corporation, the government agency which is supposed to liquidate $400 to $500 billion of bad real estate coming from the savings and loans and banks, say they have $16 billion in bad real estate properties in the Phoenix, Arizona area alone. They have almost $1 billion in Denver. When they unload billions of dollars worth of real estate in the next few years, it will drive down the price of residential property another 10 to 20 percent or more. This is happening all over the country, not just in Phoenix and Denver. People have deluded themselves into believing that real estate always increases. No market increases forever, not real estate, not gold, not anything. Markets rise and fall. There is a 19-1/3-year cycle in real estate, and most of the country is beginning to experience the downturn of that cycle right now. Real estate will likely be on a long downtrend for the next four or five years.

It is not advisable to be making new real estate purchases anywhere in the country for the next few years. This is not a recommendation to rush out and sell your home. But, on the other hand, if you do not own a home at this time, it is best to rent for the next few years. In most parts of the country, you'll have a chance in two or three years to buy a home for less than today—perhaps 20 to 40 percent less.

Let's say, though, that you not only have a home, but other properties as well, such as a beach or mountain condominium. Sell down to where you have no more than 25 percent of your total assets in real estate. There will be a time to buy real estate again aggressively, but that time is three to six years away, on the other side of the emerging financial crunch. In the meantime, keep as much of your assets liquid and conservatively positioned as possible.

The Stock Market Is Only for Speculators

The early to mid 1990s are likely to see much lower stock prices—with a bear market which could take the Dow Jones Industrial Averages down to 1,000 or lower. Deteriorating financial fundamentals in corporate America and the unraveling of America's gargantuan debt pyramid are the key factors in the emerging bear market. The stock market is for speculators only, and it is recommended that conservative investors avoid the market.

Avoid Corporate Bonds

Some may find they have invested in a high-yield bond fund, or what turns out to be a high-yield corporate bond fund. You should get out of all corporate bonds. Bonds will have a problem, not just because of interest rates rising and falling. Bonds will have problems because of the depression and the crunch on corporate earnings. Many corporations have too much debt burden with too much of it in junk bonds, and the junk bond market is falling apart. Over $40 billion have been lost in defaulting junk bonds in recent years. U.S. Treasury money market funds are a good short-term place to park funds and foreign government bond funds are an excellent place to invest conservative, risk-adverse funds for a 10 to 13 percent return.

Note: Government and municipal bonds are not a good hedge against inflation. In fact, they are a guaranteed loss of purchasing power *vis'-a-vis'* inflation. So, any government bonds owned should be counter-balanced with an inflation hedge such as gold.

Acquire Precious Metals as Financial Insurance

Gold and silver (especially gold) are a traditional hedge against chaos. In times of political chaos, gold performs very well. When the Soviets invaded Afghanistan in late 1979-early 1980, gold was at $400 an ounce, and it more than doubled to $850 an ounce in six weeks. Financial crises and banking crises are very bullish for gold. When people lose faith in financial institutions, whether it's banks, savings and loans, or bonds, they run to something that's more than just a paper promise to pay, and they turn to gold. Gold does extremely well in inflationary times as well.

In the early 1970s, gold moved from $35 dollars an ounce to $197.50 an ounce. In the latter part of the 1970s, gold did extremely well, rising from $102 an ounce in August 1976, to $850 an ounce in January 1980. Gold is moving into its third major up-leg in the early 1990s, after having built a base between $300 and $400 for seven years (from 1985-1992). Up to 30 percent of an individual's portfolio ought to be in a combination of gold and silver. The metals rose sharply in the 1970s, they did almost nothing in the 1980s, but they should do extremely well in the 1990s. In addition to precious metals, people should probably have 5 to 10 percent of their portfolio invested in precious metals stock, especially North American gold mining stocks. Gold and gold stocks rose sharply during the Great Depression— while most assets were dropping sharply in value. The 1990s could even be better for the metals.

What Precious Metals to Buy—Precious metals should be bought and held primarily in the following forms:

1. $20 AU (almost uncirculated) U.S. Liberty or St. Gaudens;
2. Morgan or Peace silver dollars (graded MS 60); and
3. Junk silver coins (pre-1965 U.S. dimes, quarters, and half dollars).

This writer would hold about two-thirds of that metals

position in gold and one-third in silver. The junk silver coins are for survival or barter, the St. Gaudens, Liberty, and silver dollars are for a storehouse of wealth and for price appreciation. All of these gold and silver coins are very liquid and at present metal prices (e.g., the $300 to $350 range for gold and $4 range for silver) are historically very cheap (e.g., near 10 to 15 year lows, or, in inflation-adjusted terms are selling at prices not seen since 1933).

A Better Way to Own Gold—The $20 AU Liberty coin is this writer's favorite gold coin. It is a blend of a bullion and a semi-numismatic coin—trading presently at about a 20 to 25 percent premium above the gold spot price. Above 15 percent, the U.S. government defines a coin as a collectible (as of 1983)—below 15 percent as a bullion coin. The latter is reportable on a form 1099 upon liquidation—the former is not. In addition, if the U.S. government should ever move to confiscate gold again (remember, it was illegal to hold from 1933 to 1975, and has only been legal to own for 17 years) *a collectable coin such as the $20 AU Liberty is far more likely to not be confiscated and to remain legally tradeable.*

This writer does not like rare coins because of their illiquidity and high commissions, and because they seem unlikely to appreciate in a depression. On the other hand, bullion coins are very liquid and have low commissions but are also reportable upon liquidation and more likely to be confiscated. In between the two extremes is the $20 AU Liberty—with high liquidity, low commission, no reporting requirements by dealers upon liquidation, and far less chance for confiscation.

From 1984 to 1986, the premium on the AU Liberty was 60 percent—today the premium is 20 to 25 percent. In a rising gold market, that premium has historically expanded. If gold should rise from its present $350 range to $550, that is a $200 gain on bullion or a bullion coin. On the other hand, if an AU Liberty can be bought today at a 20 percent premium at about $430, and gold rises $200 to $550, the premium on that coin is likely to increase to at least 50 percent, as it did in the 1980s. That would price the $20 AU Liberty at about $840—a $410 increase or more than twice the upside dollar move of a bullion coin.

Investors should immediately switch from their bullion (e.g., Krugerands, Maple Leaf, Austrian 100 Coronas, etc.) to the $20 AU Liberty coin because of the *greater likelihood of legal tradeability in a future period of crisis and the greater upside potential.* Call International Collectors Associates at 1-800-525-9556 (one of the largest dealers in the world of the $20 AU Liberty) to make the swap.

A Second Source of Income

It is prudent for a family to develop a second source of income. Start a cottage business of some sort in which you can involve not only yourself but also your family. Produce a product or provide a service which people have to have in good times or bad. Make it a fun, family-type thing, but there's also a purpose: making additional income on the side which you could fall back on if your primary source of income should dry up.

Legal Protection

America today is the most litigious country in the world. We have more lawyers and more lawsuits than the rest of the world put together (e.g., *700,000 practicing lawyers and 187 million new civil lawsuits per year*). Millions of Americans sue millions of other Americans every year at the drop of a hat. Some of these lawsuits are legitimate—many are frivolous or for the purpose of legal plunder of the suee's assets by the suer. Some of these lawsuits have political motivation by the political left against conservatives (as when the Christic Institute sued General Jack Singlaub several years ago because of his "alleged" assistance to the Nicaraguan freedom fighters) and also against Christians or Christian ministries.

Every doctor, professional, businessman, or business owner has nightmares about being sued literally out of existence. Over the past two years, this writer has researched the concept of *legal bullet proofing*—the act of building a legal structure of trusts around oneself, one's business, medical practice, etc., that makes it almost impossible to have large legal judgments rendered against the target of the lawsuit.

There are two internationally-recognized law firms which this writer knows of which specialize in creating legal bullet proofing structures for individuals or businesses with a high risk of lawsuit. These structures are *not* designed to protect from bankruptcy or IRS judgments— just lawsuits. They are appropriate only for individuals with a net worth of $1 million or more.

If you have a high risk of lawsuits, legal bullet proofing is something you should probably investigate. For information or specifics on this concept, call 1-800-525-9556.

Preparations for Greater Self-Sufficiency

Food Reserves—Americans are totally dependent on the system for their food, water, electricity, etc. What happens when an Oakland firestorm, a San Francisco earthquake, a Hurricane Hugo, or a Los Angeles riot hits? The system and its infrastructure comes to a screeching halt—at least in the area so affected. But what happens to a family in the coming depression when the breadwinner loses his job? How do they eat—especially if he cannot find another job? These are reasons *this writer feels strongly that every family should have at least one year's supply of food reserves (dehydrated or freeze-dried).*

This writer began to acquire such reserves in the 1970s—before President Reagan and President Bush sold down our food surpluses (to the Russians) to only 30 to 45 days of supplies. This writer continues to add to his own food reserves and is offering them via his company to mavericks or contrarians who see the need for same. A key element of preparation for the coming financial/ political upheaval is having at least a year's supply of such reserves. Call 1-800-525-9556 for information on how to acquire same. Developing skills in gardening (preferably organic) is also very important.

Firearms—America is the most crime-ridden country in the world today and urban social unrest and rioting are now spreading at an alarming rate. At a time when the U.S. government is moving toward registration and eventually confiscation of firearms, Americans need them more than ever to protect their homes and families (not to mention for hunting). This writer strongly believes that every family should have at least one handgun, one rifle, one shotgun, and several hundred (preferably thousand) rounds of ammunition for each. Supplies of ammunition are presently being choked off by the U.S. government, and by early 1993 both ammunition and firearms could become very difficult to acquire. A handgun could include a .45 semi-automatic or a 9mm, such as the Browning, Glock, or CZ-75; a rifle could include a Ruger Mini-14, a 30-06 deer rifle, or a 30-30; a shotgun should include a 20-gauge pump. *These items can still be* *purchased legally on a low profile basis from individuals via newspaper ads or at gun shows. With the present economic squeeze, many such firearms are becoming available—often at bargain prices.*

This writer expects to receive some criticism from some Christians to whom the concepts of preparedness, food reserves, gun ownership, etc., are either foreign or anathema. This writer can find nothing in the Scriptures, however, that seems in conflict with protecting one's family if one discerns an approaching period of political, financial, or social upheaval. As the Bible says in 1 Timothy 5:8, *"But if any provide not for his own, and specially for those of his own house, he hath denied the faith and is worse than an infidel."*

Country Living—A Retreat—America's major cities are becoming cesspools of crime, drugs, and social upheaval—*and the major economic crisis has not even arrived—yet!* Urban lifestyles are definitely in a major decline in America. If a family can live in a small town or a more rural or country setting, not only can they lower their risk from crime, but they can live a far more basic, self-sufficient lifestyle. Many people must work in a major city for employment, but they can live 25 to 75 miles out in the country and commute to work if they choose to do so. (A small town or rural setting 200 to 300 miles from a major city is the most ideal situation.)

Not only is it a more basic, self-sufficient lifestyle, it will prove to be far safer in the coming period of political, social, and economic upheaval. The concept of a survival retreat is foreign to most Americans today, but if one should feel so inclined, there are a number of excellent books on the subject: *Tappan On Survival* by Mel Tappan; *Live Off the Land In the City and Country* by Ragnor Benson; *The Survival Retreat* by Ragnor Benson, etc.

A **Nuclear Bomb Shelter**—Not one in a million Americans thinks of protection from nuclear war today— especially with "the death of communism, the end of the Cold War, and the dawn of 'peace on earth.' " But this writer has begun to think about such things of late, especially in light of the September/October 1991 *McAlvany Intelligence Advisor* newsletter on Soviet deception and war preparations. It is "curious" that all of the Swiss population are required by law to have a nuclear bomb shelter in their homes, and that most of the Soviet population have been so protected over the past decade or so. What do they know that we don't?

Art Robinson co-authored a book in 1986 with Dr. Gary North entitled *Fighting Chance*—about nuclear war survival, how to build a bomb shelter for $10,000 or less out of an obsolete filling station gas tank, and how to survive a Pearl Harbor-type surprise nuclear attack by the Russians. This writer has a few hundred copies of that book available for $5 each. (All proceeds will go to Art Robinson and his Fighting Chance Foundation—see the Appendix for more information.) Bruce Clayton's book, *Life After Doomsday*, and *Nuclear War Survival Skills* by Cresson H. Kearny are also classics on the subject. A Romanian pastor named Dumitru Duduman has also written an interesting book related to this subject entitled *Through the Fire*, which can be obtained for a $6 donation (see Appendix).

Self-Sufficiency Skills—There are a number of skills which most city dwellers who have grown up over the past generation or two do not have, such as hunting; backpacking; cross-country skiing; carpentry; gunsmithing; auto mechanics; organic gardening; canning; a knowledge of emergency medicine including herbology, homeopathics, and other alternate methods of healing; ham radio operation, etc. These skills can be fun, but all are directly related to greater self-sufficiency from the system and could be very useful in a time of financial or political upheaval such as this writer believes is likely for the balance of this decade.

Home Schooling Your Children—Almost a million children in America from hundreds of thousands of families are now being home schooled by parents who have become fed up with the awful situation in the public schools; the sex, drugs, violence, and liberal secular humanist education which has become the norm in the government schools in America today; and which is graduating many high school seniors as almost functional illiterates. Practiced primarily by conservative/Christian families, home schooling has become a viable alternative for such families. There are dozens of curricula available to such families based on conservative, constitutional, free market, biblical principles. Home schooled children usually test one to three years ahead of public or private school children, grow up without most of the incredibly negative peer pressure in public schools today, and are bonded much closer to siblings and their entire families. Teenage rebellion is almost unheard of among home schoolers.

Home schooling is one of the greatest and most positive breakthroughs in America in the past 50 years— and is a major step toward self-sufficiency. Highly recommended!

Keeping Healthy—Understanding Nutrition and Alternate Medicine—Americans are not by and large a healthy people today. Our nutritional and health habits are poor, and degenerative diseases and a host of viruses with no real cures in conventional medicine are proliferating in America. This writer has studied over the past decade and been fascinated with a number of alternative approaches to medicine, such as nutritional therapy, herbology, homeopathy, bio-magnetic therapy, etc. which seem to have real merit in both preventative medicine and the treatment of many degenerative diseases which continue to stymie traditional medicine in America.

In a more basic, self-sufficient situation, understanding and being able to apply alternate medicinal skills not dependent on the medical system as we know it could become very important in maintaining the health of one's family. Ultimately it is *you* who are responsible for the health of your family and yourself. Books on this subject abound. A few worth reading are: *Elementary Treatise in Herbology* by Dr. Edward E. Shook (Trinity Center Press); *Advanced Treatise in Herbology* (same author and publisher); *School of Natural Healing* by Dr. John R. Christopher (Bi-World Publishers); *Third Opinion*, an international directory to alternative therapy centers for the treatment and prevention of cancer by John Fink (Avery Publishing Group, Garden City Park, NY, $12.95); and *You Can Live* by Lindsey Williams, a guide to natural health centers in America and Mexico (Life and Health Publications, Portland, OR, $7).

Toward a State of National Emergency: How to Prepare

The possibility of a state of national emergency being triggered over the next two years (e.g., to fight the depression, to fight the drug war, to put down urban rioting or social unrest, or to install the New World Order) is very high. In late 1991, the Gingrich Anti-Crime Bill (HR-4079) proposed such a state of emergency—*for five years* (giving the president World War II-type powers). The coming depression or urban rioting could be the excuse for the triggering of the executive orders which were signed into law by Congress in the Kennedy and Nixon era.

The executive orders listed below were combined by Richard Nixon into Executive Order (EO) 11490, which puts all of them into effect if a national emergency is declared: *EO 10996*—provides for control of the communications media; *EO 10997*—provides for control of all power, fuels, and minerals; *EO 10998*—provides for control of all food and farms; *EO 10999*—provides for control of all transportation, highways, etc.; *EO 11000*—provides for the mobilization of all civilians into work brigades under government supervision; *EO 11001*—provides for control of all health, education, and welfare; *EO 11002*—designates the postmaster to operate a national registration of all persons; *EO 11003*—provides for control of all airports and aircraft; *EO 11004*—provides for relocation of any populations; and *EO 11005*—provides for control of railroads, waterways, and public storage facilities.

The federal government would use the National Guard or military to implement these orders and the Constitution and Bill of Rights would, of course, be suspended for the duration of the emergency. Gun control (e.g., confiscation) would be strictly enforced under these orders.

Former Congressman Ron Paul recently wrote a thought provoking article about the potential for such a state of emergency. His observations are sobering food for thought:

"What might trigger such a state of emergency? One real possibility is the threat of a nationwide bank run. Shortly after Congress authorized

the most recent $70 billion 'loan' to the Federal Deposit Insurance Commission, a treasury spokesman admitted that the collapse of a single large U.S. bank could exhaust these funds. The most recent analysis from banking watchdog Veribanc is that more than 400 banks will fail in 1992 alone.

"If, in the president's judgment, a bank run, or the prospect of one, constitutes a national emergency or even an 'emergency type situation,' he can immediately assume the powers granted him in executive orders such as Emergency Banking Regulation Number 1.

"This regulation provides the government with a wide range of unconstitutional powers, including strict restriction on your right to draw on your banking accounts in times of crisis. **Cash withdrawals would be restricted,** *according to the regulation, 'except for those purposes, and not in excess of those amounts, for which cash is customarily used.'* **Moreover, 'banking institutions shall prohibit withdrawals of cash in any case where there is reason to believe that such withdrawal is sought for the purpose of hoarding.'**

"In other words, assuming your bank remained open, you would be able to draw upon it to make regular payments for mortgages, utilities, etc. If your bank were closed, you'd have to beg a bureaucrat for access to your own money.

"Naturally, there would be widespread opposition to such measures—demonstrations, and perhaps even riots. To deal with them, the

president could next invoke Executive Order 11921, 'Emergency Preparedness Functions.' EO 11921 begins with total censorship—not just press censorship, but the total control of all 'devices capable of emitting electromagnetic radiation.' Translated into English, this means regulation, perhaps even confiscation of—for example—CB radios, cellular phones, and computers.

*"Continuing, **the order authorizes 'utilization of excess and surplus real and personal property.' Property owned by 'hoarders' can be confiscated and sold. Who is a 'hoarder'? Perhaps anyone with the foresight to prepare for an extended bout of emergency controls."***

How to Prepare for a State of National Emergency

Ron Paul's article then includes a brief "what to do" list by Mark Nestmann (editor of *Low Profile: Your Monthly Guide to Privacy and Asset Protection*):

"If a full-blown emergency is declared, there is no effective defense short of holing up in an extremely remote area or leaving the United States entirely, assuming travel beyond U.S. borders has not already been banned (another EO provides for such a prohibition).

"You can prepare yourself for lesser emergencies, however, such as the imposition of Emergency Banking Regulation Number 1, rationing, etc.:

1. *Keep your money in a strong bank. Even if you keep your money in a federally-insured bank, and the funds are available to pay off depositors, you may not recover your funds quickly if the banks fail.*

2. *Keep at least a 90-day supply of food, water, and heating fuel in your home. Begin acquiring these supplies now. If you try to purchase them after a crisis begins, you may be considered a 'hoarder' and subject to arrest.*

3. *Keep a supply of small denomination gold and silver coins at home. A national emergency could be declared in the event of hyperinflation or depression, and gold and silver may replace currency as the most widely accepted trading medium in the underground economy.*

4. *Purchase an electrical generator for use during periods when outside power is not available. If you live in a sunny area of the country, you might even consider purchasing a photo-voltaic (solar-powered) electrical backup system. Solar water heating is also viable in some areas, and is usually considerably less expensive to purchase and install than a photo-voltaic system.*

5. *Purchase a good shortwave radio. Once an emergency is imposed, you'll want to avoid transmitting (if such transmission is banned), but you'll at least be able to listen in on what is occurring in other parts of the nation and the world. (President Roosevelt banned ownership of shortwave radios in World War II, but prohibition was difficult to enforce.)*

6. *Purchase items that you could barter in an*

emergency. After World War II, Germany existed on a barter economy with cigarettes being the most common medium of exchange. Other barterable items include those that might be rationed. The potential list is almost endless: batteries, tires, kerosene, toilet paper, coffee, sugar, bullets, etc.

7. **Talk to people who have lived under emergency controls to see how they adapted.** *Any American who lived through World War II has first-hand experience of government by emergency. So does any immigrant from the Soviet Union, Eastern Europe, or Communist China. Or go to a library and look for issues of local newspapers that date back to the World War II era.*

8. **Two good books on preparing for government by emergency are:** *Gary North's* **Government by Emergency** *and John Pugsley's* **The Alpha Strategy.***"*

Note: Given the likelihood of a coming depression, the Bush push for a New World Order, and the potential for a state of emergency, this writer believes *readers should begin to think seriously about increasing their own self-sufficiency, and reducing their dependence on the system.*

Conclusion

America is headed for difficult times—whether the great majority recognize it at this point or not—*and they do not!* But one does not have a feeling of helplessness or despair if one is prepared or preparing for these times.

There is a great deal one can do to protect oneself and one's family—financially and physically if one chooses to do so. But first one must acknowledge that we have a gigantic looming financial/political problem in America, that the government will not solve these problems (e.g., government *is* the problem, not the solution), and that *we (with the help of the God of the Bible) must be responsible for the health, wealth, and welfare of our own families.*

Survival preparedness is 65 percent mental and 35 percent physical/financial preparation. The Bible says in James 1:5, *"If any of you lack wisdom, let him ask God, that given to all men liberally, and upbraideth not; and it shall be giveth him."* And Isaiah 58:11 says, *"And the Lord shall guide thee continually, and satisfy thy soul in drought, and make fat thy bones: and thou shalt he like a watered garden, and like a spring of water, whose waters fail not."*

This writer personally believes that the single most important aspect of survival preparation is spiritual— having a close personal relationship with God; knowing the Bible and its instructions and blueprint for living; seeking and receiving God's guidance and direction daily as to what to do, and not to do, who to trust, and who not to trust, etc. As this writer has said on numerous occasions—what is coming in America is a *financial* battle for survival, a *political* battle for survival, and a *spiritual* battle for survival—which must be fought on all three levels.

Note: For information or assistance on accelerated mortgage payment plans, evaluation of your bank or savings and loan, or precious metals, government bonds or food reserves, call International Collectors Associates in Durango, Colorado, at 1-800-525-9556 (in Colorado, 303-259-4100).

For an in-depth, monthly source of information on the topics analyzed in this book, this writer publishes the *McAlvany Intelligence Advisor*. This newsletter analyzes global monetary, economic, political, and geo-political developments from a conservative and Christian perspective and offers ongoing strategies on how to survive and prosper in the turbulent 1990s. To obtain sample copies or to subscribe, call 1-800-525-9556.

Chapter Eight

The Communist Onslaught Against South Africa

South Africa is the most strategic country in the world, as far as the United States is concerned. For some reason, many years ago the Lord saw fit to put most of the world's strategic metals reserves in South Africa and Russia. Ninety percent of those reserves are located in those two countries. Magnesium, platinum, vanadium, gold, diamonds, and chromium are strategic metals without which we cannot build automobiles, jet aircraft, and many other things.

The Russians understand the importance of taking South Africa and denying these strategic minerals to the United States. For example, Soviet President Brezhnev said in 1973 in his so-called "Brezhnev doctrine":

"We will take the two treasure chests upon which the West depends, the strategic oil reserves in the Middle East and the strategic minerals in South Africa, and then we will dictate the terms of surrender to the United States and to the West."

The strategic minerals of South Africa are of utmost importance if America wishes to remain an industrial and military power.

A few years ago, the United States Air Force

conducted a study which indicated the Air Force would be grounded within six months of the loss of minerals from South Africa because we would lose our source for chromium, vanadium, magnesium, platinum, and all the other metals which are used in alloys for our jet aircraft. Military leaders in NATO understand this danger as well.

In addition to the strategic minerals, supertankers which are too large to go through the Suez Canal use the Cape of Good Hope shipping lanes. The supertankers carry 90 percent of the oil shipped to Western Europe and some 50 percent of the oil shipped to the United States. If a Russian-backed ANC (African National Congress) regime came to power, and Russia had a major foothold in South Africa as they do today in Mozambique, Zimbabwe, Angola, and many other parts of Africa, in time of war they would be able to shut down the Cape's shipping lanes and bring Western Europe and the United States to their knees, quite literally, overnight. These are only a few reasons why South Africa is very crucial to the United States' interests and why it's targeted by Russia for conquest.

It is important to understand what the racial conflict in South Africa is really all about. Are all South Africans racist, and do Black South Africans hate all the Whites?

Africa has thousands of different tribes with different languages and different cultures. They fight and war amongst themselves. In 20 years, over 5 million Blacks have been killed by other Blacks in tribal warfare across Africa. The Idi Amins kill hundreds of thousands of their fellow countrymen, but they're really not fellow country-men—they're from rival tribes. The continual warring and fighting between rival tribes is one of the realities of Africa. This happened in Nigeria where several million Ibo's were killed a few years ago. The same thing is happening in Communist Zimbabwe where Prime Minister

Robert Mugabe has wiped out 40,000 Metebele tribesmen. Mugabe is a Meshona. The idea of White Western democracy among these Black tribesmen is a joke. They call it, "one man, one vote, one election. Now that I'm elected, I'll declare myself 'President-for-Life,' like Robert Mugabe has done and Idi Amin did, and I'll declare a one-party state. Then we'll take away from you because you're in the rival tribe."

The situation in South Africa is equally complex. South Africa is made up of 12 different tribes with different languages and different cultures. The most numerous and strongest of all the tribes are the Zulus, who are 7 million strong. If there were one man, one vote elections in South Africa like there are in the United States, it would be a hands-down victory for Mangosuthu Buthelezi, the chief minister of the 7 million Zulus, because they are the most numerous tribe. But what would happen next is that the Xhosas, the Vendas, and the Swanas would not want to live under a Zulu government, so they would find guns and spears and probably return to the bush. Instead of forming a loyal opposition, they would oppose that government because they don't want to live under a Zulu. (Intertribal fighting is taking place in South Africa today between the Xhosas and the Zulus, South Africa's two largest tribes, which have long hated one another.)

The racial situation in South Africa is very complex. There are almost 5 million Whites, 2 million mixed-race (Coloreds), and 1 million Indians, along with over 20 million Blacks.

Into this situation came apartheid. Apartheid started out meaning "separate development." There is apartheid even in Black Africa. The daughter of Haile Selassie, the former Black emperor of Ethiopia who was overthrown and murdered by the communists, stated once in Europe to a group of Americans, "You know, apartheid is the best thing that ever happened in Black Africa." What she meant was the separating of the various tribes because they don't mix or intermarry, but they do fight one another in tribal warfare.

Apartheid originally meant that each Black tribe would be able to have their own tribal homeland. They moved into these tribal areas and settled there hundreds of years ago. They would be able to develop their own cultures in those areas, and the Whites would have their own areas.

But out of that came petty apartheid, a lot of discrimination, and racial injustice. But 90 percent of that has been abolished. Apartheid is actually almost gone, but you would never know that because the Western press refuses to report the positive reforms. The real problem in South Africa is not between Blacks and Whites. There is a tremendous amount of good will and affection between Blacks and Whites. The real problem in South Africa is Blacks and Whites versus Reds, or communists. There are Black communists and White communists in South Africa, and they want to control that country. There is a tremendous reservoir of good will between the majority of South African Blacks and the majority of South African Whites.

Looking to the ANC is not a solution. The ANC simply wants to institute a communist government. The ANC is a surrogate of Russia and is controlled by the South African Communist Party. The ANC is the vehicle through which the Russians hope to establish a Soviet South Africa. It will be called the People's Republic of Azania.

The Russians have a three-fold strategy for the revolution in South Africa. The *first element* of the strategy is to put extreme military pressure on South

Africa from the north. There are five communist front-line states to the north and west which surround South Africa. Those communist nations are Tanzania, Zambia, Mozambique, Zimbabwe, and Angola. There are actually six now because the communists recently took over South West Africa, also called Namibia, with the coming of Sam Nujomo to power. In those front-line communist states are 400,000 communist troops, and 80,000 to 90,000 are made up of Russians, Cubans, East Germans, Bulgarians, Czechoslovakians, and other Eastern European bloc troops. The Eastern Europe bloc militaries have not disbanded as many people think. The same people believe that communism is dead and the Cold War is over. As discussed earlier, neither is true.

The Russians have shipped $5 billion of military hardware into Angola over the past few years. They moved in excess of $1 billion of military supplies into Mozambique and about half that amount into Zimbabwe. The military shipments included 400 Soviet MiG war planes and 2,850 Soviet tanks, along with a massive amount of Soviet missiles, armored vehicles, and other military equipment.

The *second element* of the Soviet strategy is to put economic pressure on South Africa via sanctions. They have influenced their "friends" in the U.S. State Department, the U.S. Congress, the U.S. media, and the political left in the West to place these sanctions on South Africa, not to bring down apartheid directly, but indirectly by putting hundreds of thousands of Blacks (they hope eventually millions) out of work, impoverishing them so the revolutionaries can influence and radicalize them, and draw them into the revolution.

The reason America has leveled harsh economic sanctions against South Africa with whom we do an immense amount of business and send aid to the brutal regimes of the People's Republic of China and Russia is because our leaders are hypocrites. They believe in selective morality whereby we can overlook the 80 to 90 million people, according to Alexander Solzhenitsyn, that the Russians have killed, and the millions that still remain in the Russian gulag. We can overlook the 60 million people killed in Red China, the 7,000 students killed in Tiananmen Square last summer in front of television cameras, and the 120,000 people in China who have been purged or killed since last June. George Bush and his friends continue to give billions and billions of dollars of aid and business projects to Russia and Red China. It is the height of hypocrisy to place sanctions against South Africa for alleged human rights violations and concurrently aid and trade with Russia and Red China.

The effect of the sanctions has been to put hundreds of thousands of Blacks out of work and to greatly destabilize the region. The majority of the Blacks are now beginning to turn against America. Between 85 and 90 percent of the Blacks are moderate, anti-communist, and Christian. There is probably a much higher percentage of Black Christians in South Africa than there are Christians in the United States, Europe, and most of the West. They don't understand why America is putting their people out of work. This writer has spoken in many Black townships in South Africa, and Black mayors, town counsellors, and women will come up with tears in their eyes, asking, "Why do you Americans hate us Blacks in South Africa so much? Why do you want to take our jobs away from us? Why do you want to put us out of work? What have we done to hurt you? Why do you want to help the communists come to power?" They know that the African National Congress and the Mandelas are communists.

They can't understand how the United States can impose sanctions on South Africa and at the same time become friends with the Russians and Chinese. They think the United States is insane, immoral, and hypocritical.

We have put hundreds of thousands of South African Blacks out of work, and why? To pacify liberals in Washington so they can return to their constituents and say, "Look what we're doing for the Blacks." The United States has very high Black unemployment in the ghettos of American cities. The Black and White liberal congressmen are not doing anything to help those people, so to pacify them, they throw them a bone and tell them, "We're squashing the White South Africans, and we're helping the Black South Africans." The Black South Africans curse these Black and White American liberals because they are impoverishing their families and helping set the stage for the communist revolutionaries to succeed in South Africa.

The leaders in authority in the Bush Administration, especially in the State Department and Congress, want the African National Congress to come to power. It was the U.S. State Department and the leftists in Congress who enabled the Sandinistas to come to power in Nicaragua in 1979 when they helped overthrow Somoza. They also helped to bring the communists to power in Zimbabwe. A Black moderate government under Bishop Abel Muzorewa had come to power in 1979 in what was then called Zimbabwe-Rhodesia. The U.S. State Department and the leftists in Congress weren't happy until Robert Mugabe, a Marxist/Leninist communist backed by Russia, could be installed in power. The same people pulled support from the Shah of Iran and helped put Ayatollah Khomeini in power. Unfortunately, the political left in Washington has a long-term record of kicking our friends from power and bringing our enemies into power.

These same people are supporting the African National Congress, so who is the ANC? The ANC was founded in 1912 and taken over by the South African Communist Party in 1948. The South African Communist Party was the first external communist party outside Russia after the Bolshevik Revolution in 1917. It is the most virulently pro-Russian communist party in the world. For years, it has been led by a man named Joe Slovo, a White Lithuanian communist and a colonel in the Soviet KGB. He is head of Umkwonto We Sizwe, the military wing of the ANC, and chairman of the South African Communist Party. Of the ANC's 30 board members, 23 belong to the South African Communist Party. The revolutionary movement in South Africa is thoroughly controlled from Moscow through the KGB, through the South African Communist Party, and finally through the African National Congress.

The ANC is very up-front and honest about the fact that they want to establish a Marxist/Leninist government. They state very clearly that when they come to power, they will nationalize all the mines, banks, and property. They will eliminate the moderate Blacks, and all those who have opposed them from the beginning. The ANC is a terrorist organization and has killed and maimed thousands of men, women, and children. Its favorite technique is the "necklace" treatment whereby they terrorize moderate Blacks. (Keep in mind that 85 to 90 percent of the Blacks in South Africa are moderate, anti-communist, and pro-Christian.) The "necklace" treatment is where they take the moderate Blacks, put a tire around their neck, fill it with petrol, and light it with a match. It takes 20 to 30 minutes for these people to die the most excruciating death you can imagine. Several thousand

Blacks have been murdered in this manner. For those readers who would like more information and documentation on this horrible atrocity, a video tape called *The Soviet Strategy for the Conquest of South Africa* is available from the Don McAlvany offices in Colorado, which shows a woman actually "necklaced" and burned to death by the revolutionaries. This is the most incredibly cruel form of death and torture ever conceived by evil men. (To order this two-hour video, call 1-800-525-9556. Cost is $25.)

This is now happening all over South Africa. The ANC is bringing in AK-47s and limpet mines from Mozambique through Swaziland into the Natal. The Zulus, a beautiful, wonderful people, are not armed. The ANC is butchering Zulus by the thousands in their current revolutionary onslaught.

The ANC is a brutal, communist, revolutionary organization, yet it is supported by the leaders in the Bush Administration, the Reagan Administration before that, the Congress, the media, and in particular our State Department. They want to see an ANC government in South Africa and we have put a gun to the head of the South African government, demanding that if they don't negotiate a new government with the ANC, we will impose more sanctions. It's as if our government has suicidal tendencies. We are trying to destroy our most strategic anti-communist friends.

The Western media has painted a picture of Nelson and Winnie Mandela as the "father and mother" of the nation and that they are supported by most of the Blacks in South Africa. The majority of South African Blacks hate Nelson and Winnie Mandela. The Mandelas are communist revolutionaries, and again, the vast majority of South African Blacks do not espouse communism.

There's not a moderate Black you can meet in South
Africa who hasn't had a friend or relative killed by
Mandela's people. They have no great love for him. They
also hate Bishop Desmond Tutu, who is a Marxist/
Leninist leader of Liberation Theology. He runs inter-
ference in South Africa for the communists.

Nelson Mandela joined the ANC in 1944, and over
the next 18 years, he became one of the most important
leaders in the ANC and the South African Communist
Party. In 1963, he was jailed for terrorism when he and his
fellow ANC and South African Communist Party sabo-
teurs were caught with 48,000 Soviet-made anti-personnel
mines, 210,000 grenades, and documents showing proof
of their involvement with Russia, Algeria, Red China,
and Czechoslovakia. This writer flew to Washington in
March of 1987 and interviewed a high-ranking Cuban
official from the Cuban foreign ministry, Juan Benemelas.
He had gone to South Africa in the early 1960s with the
Cuban revolutionary, Che Guevara, where he met with
Nelson Mandela on three separate occasions in Ghana
and other parts of northern Africa. They provided
Mandela with millions of dollars of Soviet weapons.
During Mandela's treason trial, a 62-page document in
his own handwriting on how to be a good communist was
presented as evidence. This is the man our State Department wants to be the next state president of South Africa,
and he very well may be.

The leftists in our media and our entertainment
industry worship this man, and the following is a direct
quote from Nelson Mandela's own handwriting:

*"In our country, the struggles of the oppressed
peoples were guided by the South African
Communist Party and inspired by its policies.*

The aim of the South African Communist Party is to defeat the nationalist government and to free the people of South Africa from the evils of racial discrimination. . . .

"Under a Communist Party government, South Africa will become a land of milk and honey. There will be enough land and houses for all. There will be no unemployment, starvation, and disease. . . .

"We Communist Party members are the most advanced revolutionaries in modern history and are the contemporary fighting and driving force in changing society in the world. To become the most advanced communist revolutionary, it is not enough to understand and just accept the theory of Marxism and Leninism. In addition, a Communist Party member must subordinate his personal interests to those of the Party. . . .

"In South Africa, a Communist Party member must take part in the mass struggle initiated by the South African Communist Party, the African National Congress movement, or the other political bodies within the liberation movement.

"The people of South Africa, led by the South African Communist Party, will destroy capitalist society and build in its place, socialism. The transition from capitalism to socialism and the liberation of the working class cannot be effected by slow changes or by reforms, as reactionaries and liberals often advise, but by revolution. One must therefore be a revolutionary, and not a reformist." (emphasis ours).

On February 11, 1990, Nelson Mandela was released from jail. In a speech the next day broadcast all over South Africa, and raising his communist clenched fist, he talked about how wonderful the Communist Party was. He saluted them and their great efforts over the years, and he looked forward to them joining him in attaining power. Mandela stood in Cape Town in front of a Soviet flag draped over the balcony. He has stated many times before and since his release that he still advocates the nationalization of all gold mines, White properties, banks, and businesses.

Mandela's wife, Winnie, is also a hardcore Marxist/Leninist revolutionary, as well as a vicious murderess who is responsible for the deaths of dozens (if not hundreds) of innocent Blacks. On Radio Moscow a few years ago, she said:

"I have waited for long years personally to send my militant salute to the land of the Soviets, to thank it for its fraternal solidarity. The Soviet Union is a torch bearer for all of our hopes and aspirations. We have learned, and are continuing to learn, resilience and bravery from the Soviet people."

She also calls for the liberation of South Africa via the "necklace" treatment.

Winnie and Nelson Mandela are communist revolutionaries who are surrogates of Russia. If they attain power, South Africa will become a communist dictatorship and be renamed the People's Republic of Azania; America will lose its strategic minerals; and our country will be in deep, deep trouble.

In light of all the documentation and solid intelligence

information on Nelson and Winnie Mandela's leadership in the communist revolution in South Africa, it is incredible how President Bush and our Congress fawned over them when they visited America during the summer of 1990. They were given a ticker tape parade in New York, wined and dined by President Bush at the White House, allowed to speak before a joint session of Congress, and given more acclaim and honor than any world leader, nobility, or hero in U.S. history except for maybe Gorbachev. The spectacle of America literally kneeling at the feet of these communist revolutionaries is just one more indication of how far to the left we have moved and how far we have declined morally and politically. As a country, we now treat evil and evil people as if they were good, and good people as if they were evil.

If events continue to go in the same direction they are headed now, another ally in Africa will fall to a communist-backed revolution. South Africa presently has a very weak and appeasement-oriented government which is operating under the dictates of the U.S. State Department. They have agreed, with the U.S. government gun to their head, to negotiate a new dispensation with the ANC.

The problem is not Black rule in South Africa. If the moderate Blacks take over (and they represent a great majority), or if Chief Minister Buthelezi should come to power, that's fine. A Black, or White, or multiracial Christian, anti-communist government in that part of the world is in the best interests of the United States. But the U.S. government is dictating to them that they must have who our government calls the "legitimate leaders"—the ANC—as their new government. The ANC, of course, agrees. Our government is actually dictating a communist government for South Africa.

If they do reach a negotiated settlement, there will be

a two-stage revolution. First, a coalition government with the ANC will be in control for the next few years. Ultimately, there will be a final communist takeover two or three years hence.

We need to put pressure on our congressmen and pressure on our president to lift the sanctions, or at least treat South Africa as well as we treat "our good friends," the Russians and the Chinese communists, both of whom are bloody butchers. This is a vital country and so important to U.S. interests. If South Africa is lost to the communists, and we are pushing them down the road toward communism just as certainly as we did Nicaragua, and just as certainly as we pushed out the Shah of Iran, the United States will suffer tremendously. The communists view the conquest of South Africa as a major stepping stone to the eventual conquest of the United States of America.

Chapter Nine

Mesmerized by the Bear: The Great Russian Deception

What is happening in Eastern Europe? Is communism really dead? Is the Cold War over? Are Yeltsin, Gorbachev, and Shevardnadze really sincere men of peace, or are they pulling off the greatest deception in modern history? It was Lenin who said: "We advance through retreat." The military strategist Sun Tsu, who lived in 500 B.C., said: "At your pinnacle of strength, feign weakness." J. Edgar Hoover called the Russians "masters of deceit." They are the most brilliant geostrategic strategists in the world. They are also chess champions, understanding deceptive strategy and how to plan many moves or years ahead. We live in a time of deception, confusion, danger, and a blinding acceleration of global events. It's as if we are in a time warp—it's remarkable how rapidly world events are moving.

Shortly after a very clever deception campaign by Russia's Czar Nicholas II in 1889, Rudyard Kipling wrote an allegory entitled *The Bear That Walks Like a Man*. Kipling wrote about a man who was maimed and blinded when a bear he was hunting stood up, as if in supplication. The hunter, "touched with pity and wonder, withheld his fire, only to have his face ripped away by the steel-shod paw." Kipling continued:

"When he stands up as pleading in wavering
man-brute guise,
When he veils the hate and cunning of his little
swinish eyes,
When he shows as seeking quarter with paws
like hands in prayer,
That is the time of peril, the time of the truce of
the bear."

We live in that time of peril, in the time of the truce of the bear.

It is important to watch what people, leaders, or countries do, as well as what they say. What the Russians are saying and what they are doing are almost diametrically opposite. Yeltsin and other leaders of Russia are speaking about peace, but they are preparing for war. They are undergoing the largest military buildup in the history of Russia, or indeed, in the history of the world. In the last seven years under *glasnost* and *perestroika*, the Russian military has been expanded 45 percent. Billions and billions of dollars in weapons are being shipped to various parts of the world from Russia. Surrogates are being supported with those weapons in Central America, South Africa, the Middle East, Libya, and the Philippines. Even though Gorbachev was *Time* magazine's "Man of the Year" in 1988, these things happened under his leadership. By "strange coincidence," 50 years ago, in 1938, Adolf Hitler was also *Time* magazine's "Man of the Year," just a year or so before he launched World War II.

The current period is very similar to the period immediately preceding World War II. There was much talk of peace. Great Britain's prime minister, Neville Chamberlain, went to Munich to meet with Adolf Hitler. After a long meeting, he came out declaring, "There will be peace in our day." Hitler was talking peace, but he was preparing for war. War broke out 11 months later and lasted for over five years, taking 50 million lives. Jeremiah 6:14 and 8:11 say that people will cry, ". . . *saying, Peace, peace; when there is no peace.*" I believe we have entered such an era, and the actions of the Russians over the next three to five years will bear this out.

Meanwhile, the Russians are very clever, and they are seducing America and the West into massively disarming (even as they accelerate their military buildup) and into building them up economically. By introducing and promoting *glasnost* and *perestroika*, the Russians are influencing the West to help them financially and economically. *Glasnost* and *perestroika* are not new policies for the Russians: they have been using them periodically since the 1920s. These terms mean openness and restructuring, with the Russians promising to confess the bad side of Russia and communism, to clean up their act, and to become more moderate.

Six Glasnosts

There have actually been *six glasnosts*. The *first* was from 1921 to 1929 under Lenin. He saw the Revolution was going broke, and he needed Western aid. So Lenin came to the West, "very humbly," and told the West that they had gone too far with communism, that they wanted to liberalize and become more capitalistic and give more freedom to their people. But Russia needed their help in the form of Western financial aid, and that aid from the West came pouring in. It was about this time that Lenin said, "We will sell the Western businessmen the rope with which we will hang them."

The Russians obtained a lot of aid from the West

during the 1920s, but *glasnost number one* ended abruptly in 1929. Tens of millions of Russians were shot or imprisoned shortly thereafter.

The *second glasnost* was under Stalin (in 1936 and 1937) who said essentially the same thing. He spoke about a restructuring of the Soviet economy along capitalist lines, calling it *perestroika*. Stalin said he wanted his country to have a Western-style constitutional government. Western aid again poured into Russia and Western leaders cheered the apparent reforms. *Glasnost number two* came to an abrupt end in 1938, and the brutal purges known as the Great Terror followed shortly thereafter.

Stalin initiated the *third glasnost* in 1941 to 1945. Stalin and Hitler had signed a nonagression pact, but Hitler double-crossed Stalin in 1941 and invaded Russia. In 1941, Stalin again reversed his story, telling the West, "We want to be friends with you in the West. We really want to eliminate communism, we want to be moderate and abolish the revolutionary aspects of our society." Following this announcement, $10 billion in lend-lease aid came, but at the close of World War II, *glasnost number three* ended in 1945 with the annexation of the Baltic States—Latvia, Lithuania, Estonia, and parts of Poland, Romania, Prussia, and Finland. Over 100 million people were enslaved under communism, and tens of millions subsequently died.

The *fourth glasnost* occurred from 1956 to 1959 under Khruschev. He launched more political reforms including "a return to competition and free enterprise." Khruschev told the West, "We have many underground businesses and a flourishing free market, but we need more aid from the West and peaceful coexistence and disarmament." He quoted Lenin almost exactly when he said:

Don McAlvany — 189

"If we cannot give our peoples the same standard of living you give your peoples under the capitalist system, we know that communism cannot succeed."

The West has been hearing almost the same thing from Gorbachev and Yeltsin. Massive U.S. financial aid came flowing in. *Glasnost number four* began to end in 1959 with the Soviet-backed communist takeover in Cuba, the shooting down of an American U-2 plane, massive arrests of Soviet dissidents, and the erection of the Berlin Wall.

The *fifth glasnost* was instigated by Brezhnev from 1970 to 1975, and saw the Soviet leader, along with Nixon and Kissinger, launch "detente" and a "relaxation of tensions." Brezhnev began to publicly air Soviet problems and talked of discarding the Revolution, and moving toward capitalism. Russia not only received massive Western aid during this period of *glasnost*, but also convinced the U.S. to enter into the Anti-Ballistic Missile Treaty of 1973. They later deployed anti-ballistic missiles in total violation of the treaty, while America adhered completely to it. *Glasnost number five* began to lose credibility in 1975 when the Soviet-backed North Vietnamese overran South Vietnam in complete violation of Russian promises to Kissinger. In the years following, widespread arrests of Soviet dissidents began again, covert actions abroad resumed, and in late 1979, the Soviets invaded Afghanistan.

With the *sixth period of glasnost* under Mikhail Gorbachev and Boris Yeltsin, we are falling for the same propaganda and deception which we've fallen for before. *Glasnost number six* started in 1985, and is actually a script written by the KGB. For 15 years, the head of the

KGB was Yuri Andropov, an incredibly evil man who was presented to the West as a very pro-Western individual who drank American scotch, wore American-style suits, and listened to classical music. The media portrayed him as a "good guy," someone just like us. Andropov ascended to the presidency in 1983, but died in 1984. He and his KGB officials wrote the script for *glasnost number six* in 1980-1981. After Andropov, Chernenko came to power but died within a year. Andropov's protege, Mikhail Gorbachev, rose to power in 1985, and was the leader designated to implement the script.

Glasnost Number Six—The KGB Script

The *sixth glasnost* was designed to exact massive concessions from the West; but to be effective, the Russians had to appear to be giving a lot in order to receive those concessions. One of the concessions the Russians appear to be making is the yielding of "nominal" control of Eastern Europe. Why do we say "nominal"? The Russians are not really giving up control of Eastern Europe. There has been a purge of some of the leaders, but that is typical. Purges of communist leaders, in which old ones go and new ones come in, "cleanse and purify" the communist political structure.

For example, Nicolae Ceausescu fell from power on Christmas Day, 1989, and was executed. However, the secret police (the Securitate) are still intact in Romania but with their name changed. The communist military is still intact. The old communist leaders now call themselves "noncommunist" in Romania, where they presently call themselves the New Salvation Front. When Ceausescu was overthrown and executed in a typical communist purge by the communist military, the former number

three man in the Romanian Communist Party, Ion
Illiescu, was brought to power as the leader of the
country. Illiescu was a former college roommate of
Gorbachev's and was handpicked by him. Illiescu is also a
hardcore Marxist/Leninist, but he is presented as a
noncommunist.

Another "concession" under *glasnost number six* is
to superficially encourage democracy movements in
Eastern Europe and Russia. The top leader in Poland is
still a communist, and the communist military is still in
place. Until all the former communists have been removed
from positions of power (including the secret police, who
are still pulling the strings from behind the scenes, and the
communist military) nothing has really changed.

Included in the strategy to superficially encourage
these democracy movements was the plan to talk about
free elections. The communists would drop all reference
to communism, would call themselves Social Democrats,
and would use a lot of high-sounding terms which the
people in the West understand and believe in.

The next thing the Soviet Union planned to do was to
open the Iron Curtain and tear down the Berlin Wall. What
most people in the West don't know is that now tens of
thousands of KGB agents and Spetsnaz troops are pouring
out of Eastern Europe and Russia into Western Europe.

Another part of the strategy was to allow reunification of East and West Germany, something the Germans
have always longed for. What the Germans are now
implementing is a coalition government between communist East Germany and noncommunist West Germany.

Another part of the KGB script is to declare communism dead, the Cold War over, and the communist
parties in Russia and Eastern Europe irrelevant. It's one
thing to declare something dead, but it's another thing to

really be dead. For example, someone declares themselves to be Santa Claus, and from now on they are known by that name. But they are still the person they were before they changed their name. A rose by any other name is still a rose. But the Russians feel that for Western consumption it is critical to declare communism dead.

This plan, scripted by the KGB, is described in a book by a former KGB agent, Anatoly Golitsyn, written in 1984. *New Lies For Old* describes in great detail what the Russians would do, which is everything they are doing right now. The scheme is to deceive the West into disarming, into giving massive amounts of aid to the Soviet bloc, and into dismantling NATO—to mislead us into thinking they are doing one thing, when in fact they are doing the opposite. They are masters at deception and chess-type strategies; they think five or ten moves (or years) ahead.

Glasnost Number Six— Western Concessions To the Soviets

According to the Soviet script, the United States and the West are supposed to assume the financial burden of Eastern Europe for Russia, and indeed we are doing exactly that. Supporting Eastern Europe financially has cost the Russians $40-$50 billion each year, and America, Western Europe, and Japan are now going to pick up that bill, which tremendously relieves the financial burden on the Russians.

The next thing the West was supposed to do was to allow reunification of Germany, which is now a *fait accompli*. The Russians are demanding that Germany become neutral. Even if Germany doesn't leave NATO, the East German secret police and intelligence services will be brought into NATO, completely infiltrating it. It is like bringing the fox into the hen house. Germany is NATO's anchor, and if Germany goes neutral, so will NATO, which will turn into a political organization. Its military role in defending Europe will be eliminated by the mid-1990s.

The Russians also hope to achieve, and indeed are achieving, the withdrawal of American troops from Western Europe. They have already persuaded the U.S. to remove its missiles from Western Europe through the INF Treaty signed by Reagan and Gorbachev. The United States had Pershing and Cruise missiles which were our nuclear umbrella to prevent a vastly superior Russian nuclear or conventional force from attacking Europe. According to several former NATO commanders, that umbrella prevented war for some 25 years. It has now been removed.

Under Ronald Reagan, and after him George Bush, we withdrew all Pershing and Cruise missiles from Europe, while the Russians were allowed to keep 93 percent of their missiles still targeted on Western Europe. They even deceived U.S. leaders during the INF Treaty negotiations when they said they only had 650 SS-20 missiles, while in reality 550 more were hidden. SS-20 missiles began to surface in Cuba in 1991. Since the INF Treaty was signed and ratified, Russia has deployed an even greater number of SS-24 and SS-25 road and rail mobile missiles. While we think peace, they prepare for war. Lenin said, "They disarm, we arm." The Russians have persuaded America to remove their troops and missiles, which is happening at this moment. George Bush is planning that within three to five years all American troops in Europe will have been removed.

The next part of the Soviet plan is to convince

America and the West to massively finance and bail out the basket case Soviet economy, as they have done five times before since 1921. Remember what Sun Tsu said, "When at your pinnacle of strength, feign weakness." Obviously, the Russians are not at their pinnacle of economic strength. The country has been a financial basket case since the communists came to power in 1917. Why have the communists never gone out of business? Why hasn't Russia collapsed over the past 75 years? The reason is because the United States and the West have not allowed them to do so.

In each of the five *glasnosts*, we have sent them immense amounts of aid. The Western powers will be pumping hundreds of billions of dollars into Russia over the next three to five years. It is not as if this was a new idea. Lenin understood the capitalist mind, when he said:

> *"The capitalists of the world and their govern-*
> *ments, in the pursuit of the conquest of the*
> *Soviet market, will close their eyes to the*
> *indicated higher reality, and thus will turn into*
> *deaf, mute, blind men. They will extend credits*
> *in giving us the materials and technology we*
> *lack. They will restore our military industry,*
> *indispensible for our future victorious attacks*
> *on our suppliers. In other words, they will labor*
> *for the preparation for their own suicide."*

In the early 1970s under the leadership of Richard Nixon and Henry Kissinger, the United States helped build the Kama River truck factory in Russia. Over the last 15 years, that same truck factory has produced 300,000 Soviet military trucks and armored vehicles per year. In the past few years, it has started to become obsolete, lacking state-of-the-art computers and equipment. But in 1990 George Bush announced that the U.S. would send the Soviets millions of dollars of technology in order to help them update the Kama River truck factory.

There is also great significance between the political liberalization of Eastern Europe and the European Economic Community's union in 1992. Part of the communist plan is to have Eastern and Western Europe merge economically. Before this can happen, Western Europe must first be neutralized, NATO must be gone, America's influence must be diminished in Europe, and all American troops withdrawn. Then an economic union can occur, and the kingpin country in Western Europe will be reunified Germany. Germany will be a very powerful industrial and economic force which will tilt from neutrality toward Russia. The Eastern and Western blocs will be able to consolidate economically. This should be an accomplished fact by 1994 or 1995.

The great majority of people in Western Europe and America believe that a United States of Western Europe is wonderful, but we must realize who is promoting this economic/political union. It is not those who believe in a free market, or the Christians, or conservatives. The staunchest socialists in Europe are behind the unifying of Western Europe. They believe this is a giant step toward a one-world government. There are also powerful political leaders in the United States who believe a world government will emerge from all these events before the decade of the 1990s is over. Ronald Reagan, George Bush, many of their counsellors, the Kissingers and Rockefellers, and other leaders in the liberal Eastern Establishment talk openly about the New World Order, how this will arrive, and how the differences between our good friends and partners, the Russians, and America are diminishing. We are being pushed rapidly toward a world government, with Establishment leaders believing they can usher in this New World Order during the decade of the 1990s.

Also on the Russian agenda for what the West is supposed to give up is our military strength in the post-communism, post-Cold War era. Since the early 1960s, the United States has signed a series of disarmament treaties with the Russians. Some of those include the Nuclear Test Ban Treaty of 1962, the Anti-Ballistic Missile Treaty of 1973, Salt I, Salt II, and the INF Treaty, and the START Treaty, whereby the United States and Russia agreed to cut their strategic forces by half. The Russians have violated every treaty they have signed, and that's why the Rand Corporation stated recently that the Russians have a five-to-one lead in conventional forces over the United States. The Soviets have 214 combat-ready divisions versus 31 for the United States. The Russian military numbers about 5 million (not including 1.5 million KGB and 250,000 Spetsnaz) versus 2 million for America, of which only about 500,000 are combat-ready troops. Their navy is approximately four times the size of the U.S. Navy. The Soviets have 450 submarines, versus 138 for the U.S. The Soviets have ten times more tanks and armored vehicles than the U.S. In tanks, the Soviets lead America 70,000 to 22,000 while building 3,500 new tanks per year.

Dimitri Manuilski said in the Lenin School for Political Warfare in the 1930s:

"War to the hilt between communism and capitalism is inevitable. Today, of course, we are not strong enough to attack. Our time will come in 30 to 40 years. To win, we shall need the element of surprise. The bourgeoisie . . . will

have to be put to sleep. So we shall begin by launching the most spectacular peace movement on record. There will be electrifying overtures and unheard of concessions. The capitalist countries, stupid and decadent, will rejoice to cooperate in their own destruction. They will leap at another chance to be friends. As soon as their guard is down, we will smash them with our clenched fist."

This is what the Kremlin leaders are doing today—they are seducing the West into disarming (which we are doing rapidly at this very moment), while they arm rapidly. This entire process is accelerating very quickly. Today in the Kremlin, the Soviet military and the KGB are in control, and their men are Yeltsin, Shevardnadze, and Gorbachev. The Russian military and KGB are preparing for war.

Soviet espionage is also increasing. Western intelligence leaders have witnessed a four-fold increase in Russian espionage activities since the beginning of *glasnost number six* in 1985. The Soviets are trying to convince the U.S. to discontinue support for the anti-communist resistance movements around the world, such as the Contras in Nicaragua, UNITA in Angola, and the Mujahideen in Afghanistan. After all, if communism is dead, why should the United States continue to support these resistance movements? The United States is also succumbing to pressure to withdraw its troops from South Korea and the Philippines.

This is a time for Christians to wake up and see what is actually happening in our world today. The Russians are neutralizing their western flank and trying to dispose of NATO and the American missiles and troops—

effectively neutralizing Western Europe. They will soon sign a nonagression pact with China, much like the one Hitler and Stalin signed in 1939, to neutralize their eastern flank. The Soviets are also running out of oil. They are the world's largest oil producer, but they are going to have a major oil crisis in the next three to five years, and anyone in the intelligence or oil business knows this to be true. What will the Russians do? They will have neutralized their eastern and western flanks, and there is oil for 80 cents a barrel straight to their south in the Persian Gulf. The Russian strategy in the latter half of the 1990s is to move into the Persian Gulf area. Meanwhile, Russia will be able to intimidate a disarmed Western Europe and United States with their vast military superiority.

All of these events have enormous biblical significance. Ezekiel 36-39 talks about Russia moving into the Middle East and being aligned with Libya, Ethiopia, Persia (Iran), Togarmah (Turkey), and Gomer (Germany). All of these developments appear to be shaping up on the world scene in the latter half of the 1990s. There could be extraordinary biblical prophetic consequence to what is happening in Eastern Europe today. This is a time for Christians to be very alert. Instead, most Christians are celebrating a new peace. They have forgotten that Jeremiah said to be beware when men cry, *". . . saying, Peace, peace; when there is no peace"* (Jer. 6:14). 1 Thessalonians 5:3 says, *"For when they shall say, Peace and safety; then sudden destruction cometh upon them. . . ."* These are exciting times in which to be alive, especially if you are a Christian, and to see and understand what is happening in the world. It's as if we are in a time warp; everything is moving very quickly—economically, monetarily, and politically. These are exciting times, but these are times in which Christians need to be alert and seeking God's wisdom and guidance on how to live as Christians in the very exciting and challenging 1990s.

Let's examine the evidence of Russian deception and insincerity as they push *glasnost number six* upon us. Watch what people do, not what they say. This holds true for American politicians, as well as Yeltsin and Russia. If you say one thing and do exactly the opposite over and over again, ultimately we must judge you by what you do, not by what you say. The Russians are currently sending massive quantities of arms to their surrogates in Africa, the Middle East, the Philippines, etc. They shipped $5 billion worth of arms into Angola and southern Africa, first to eradicate the anti-communist resistance movement of UNITA and eventually to be used against the pro-Western Republic of South Africa. The Russians have also shipped $6 billion worth of arms to Nicaragua, and they have sent 36 MiG-29 Fulcrums to Cuba. The MiG-29 Fulcrums are nuclear-capable fighter-bombers. They have the range to launch nuclear weapons throughout the southeastern United States. This is happening right now while they are talking peace. Are these actions not inconsistent with all the talk of peace coming from the Russians?

Chapter Ten

The Russians:
Masters Of Deception

"All warfare is based on deception."
          —Sun Tsu, 500 B.C.

*"For the great majority of mankind are satisfied
with **appearances** as though they were **realities**
. . . and are often more influenced by the things
that **seem**, than by those that **are**."*
          —Machiavelli

The Soviet Strategy of Deception

*"The point is that the communist goal is fixed
and changeless—it never varies one iota from
their objective of world domination, but if we
judge them only by the direction in which they
seem to be going, **we shall be deceived**."*
          —Elena Bonner, widow of Sakharov

General Sir Walter Walker, former NATO commander-in-chief and friend of your author, wrote recently:

*"The West is so ignorant of Gorbachev and the
intentions of this evil man. The real story of the
last ten years goes something like this: the rise of*

Gorbachev is the result of a KGB 'coup' which took place in the early 1980s during the dotage of Leonid Brezhnev.

*"This coup was executed by Yuri Andropov —the chairman of the KGB. The helter-skelter of **perestroika** is an attempt by the clever men in the KGB to parlay the country's economic weakness into a winning position, vis'-a-vis' the West. With our attention focused on the Soviet Union's current weaknesses and Third World economic status, we will lower our guard and let the Russian wolf into the European home."*

According to Sir William Stephenson, head of Combined Allied Intelligence Operations during World War II, Mikhail Gorbachev said in a speech to the Soviet Politburo in November 1987:

*"Comrades, do not be concerned about all you hear about **glasnost** and **perestroika** and democracy in the coming years. These are primarily for outward consumption. There will be no significant internal change within Russia other than for cosmetic purposes. Our purpose is to disarm the Americans and let them fall asleep. We want to accomplish three things: One, we want the Americans to withdraw conventional forces from Europe. Two, we want them to withdraw nuclear forces from Europe. Three, we want the Americans to stop proceeding with Strategic Defense Initiative."*

The Strategic Deception Script for *Glasnost/Perestroika* Number Six

In 1981, Anatoly Golitsyn, a major in the Soviet KGB, defected to the West and wrote a book entitled *New Lies for Old*, which was published in 1984. In that book, Golitsyn laid out the KGB script for *glasnost/perestroika number six* which Gorbachev began to implement in 1985. This script would be the most elaborate *glasnost/ perestroika* script of all and was designed to take the Russians to their goal of world domination on or before the turn of the century.

The latest upheavals in the Soviet Union, the coup and countercoup (which this writer believes were phony), the end of the KGB, the death of the Communist Party, the collapse of the Soviet Empire, etc. are all part of that elaborate KGB script for *glasnost/perestroika* number six—*Russian high theater at its best.* Gorbachev, Yeltsin, and Shevardnadze are all part of the cast—actors employed by the Central Committee of the Communist Party of Russia and the KGB.

The Russian Strategy to Dominate Europe

The key element of present Russian global strategy is to dominate Europe (Eastern *and* Western) in what the Soviets openly call "the common European home." The Russians have a Machiavellian strategy for dominating all of Europe (and not necessarily or exclusively by military conquest) even as their empire "appears" to be crumbling. This domination of Europe is a key stepping stone to their long-term strategy of world domination.

An all-European integration (and eventually Russian domination) is only possible if a radical change in both the Western and Eastern European political systems takes place. That change is taking place in Western Europe in 1992 and beyond as the United States of Europe emerges. Though sold to the peoples of Europe and England as a grand free market adventure, the fact is that Western Europeans are about to turn their political sovereignty and independence over to a European superstate dominated by socialist, leftist, globalist, and Euro-communist bureaucrats in Brussels, and heavily infiltrated by the KGB. *Merging the new Commonwealth of Independent States (C.I.S.) with the United States of Western Europe will be far easier than integrating the C.I.S. with 12 separate nation states— all of whom might tend individually to want to protect their sovereignty from the Russians.* There are six major prerequisites for the Russians to dominate an integrated "common European home":

1. A united Western Europe—a *fait accompli* in 1992;
2. The exclusion of America militarily from NATO and from Europe;
3. Russian domination of Eastern Europe;
4. Russian domination of a reorganized, restructured Commonwealth of Independent States;
5. A C.I.S. which is seen to be "democratic" by the Western Europeans; and
6. Russian military dominance (the "big stick") over the entire region—from the Atlantic to the Urals (or as Gorbachev said, from the Atlantic to Vladivostok [the Pacific]).

Let's briefly examine these prerequisites.

First, a European superstate (socialist in orientation) will be far easier to integrate or merge with a Russian superstate (socialist in orientation—but pretending to be democratic) than merging or integrating dozens of truly independent East and West European states.

Second, the Soviets are maneuvering and manipulating to get America out of Europe militarily (and as much as possible, economically). The INF Treaty eliminated America's intermediate-range nuclear missiles (e.g., Cruise and Pershing II's) from Europe. The Conventional Forces in Europe Treaty and Operation Desert Storm have maneuvered America into a major withdrawal of conventional ground forces (men, tanks, planes, materials, etc.). The U.S. is presently pulling out of, or closing, 79 military bases in Western Europe. Because of the "alleged" death of communism, end of the Cold War, and collapse of the Soviet Empire, Bush and the American Establishment plan to pull the American military almost completely out of Europe over the next few years.

In the meantime, the Soviets are trying to undermine America's commitment to NATO by signing a series of treaties with Germany, France, Italy, Greece, and Spain (six treaties in all) which compromise those countries' commitment to NATO in a crisis. France has agreed to represent Russian interests within the European Community, GATT, the IMF, the World Bank, and NATO. The Italian treaty contradicts Italy's commitment to NATO. The German treaty committed Germany to help keep the Baltic states within the Soviet Union. *Tass* reported in late July 1991:

> *"The treaty on friendship and cooperation with Greece . . . serves as yet another element in the architecture of the common European home. The treaty can be placed in the same category as similar international documents concluded between*

the Soviet Union and Italy, Spain, France, and Germany."

The Russians have now obtained a foothold within the European Community and NATO, and are in the process of driving a wedge between America and its European NATO partners. This writer predicts that within two to four years, America will be militarily out of NATO and Europe, and NATO (or at least its military mission of defending Europe) will have collapsed. Europe by that time will be almost totally neutral, it will gradually become dominated by Russian military might, and will become Finlandized (i.e., dominated by the Russians like Finland has been since the end of World War II).

Third, as discussed above, the Russians have never really relinquished full control of Eastern Europe. They still have 500,000 troops stationed there, there are low profile communists (or communist collaborators) in many key positions in Eastern Europe, and the communist secret police and military organization are still largely intact. Furthermore, the Soviets have recently concluded a series of treaties with the Eastern European countries that gives them a growing foothold in those countries.

Fourth and fifth, to seduce Western Europe into integrating into *one (East/West) European home*, it must convince the Europeans that the former U.S.S.R. has become democratic, and that the new C.I.S. (which has been on the drawing board for a decade) is free, independent, and democratic as well. *The present disintegration of the empire is not accidental or spontaneous. It has been well planned and thought out for years by Gorbachev, Yeltsin, and the Kremlin leaders who know that the present form of the Soviet Empire is archaic and counterproductive, and that a deep reorganization of the imperial structure is unavoidable.* The new federation must *appear* to be free, independent, and democratic (but in reality it will be dominated by Russian military might), just as Finland appears to be free but in reality does Russia's bidding because of the Soviet military gun at its head.

Sixth, Soviet military superiority over Eastern and Western Europe *is already a present reality.* Several more years of Western disarmament, Russian arms buildup and Russian military hegemony over *all* of Europe (e.g., the Finlandization of Eastern and Western Europe) will be a *fait accompli.*

Another aspect of the Russians' Machiavellian strategy to *absorb* Western Europe is the *perestroikist* propaganda that has substituted in place of the concept of "defense," the concept of "security." "Security" has been presented as real only if it is "collective." Europe and America have been convinced that "collective security" (e.g., a joint-venture police enforcement action between East and West) is the only way to make the globe safe against terrorism, "Hitlerite dictators" such as Saddam Hussein, the environmental crisis, etc.

Hence, during Operation Desert Storm, for the first time in its history, America felt obliged to ask the U.S.S.R. for its authorization to wage war—to provide for the "collective security" of the Middle East. Out of "collective security" grows the concept of "global security" (e.g., against terrorism, drugs, environmental pollution, dangerous Third World dictators, etc.) and "global security" can only be provided by a *global* police force, a *global* court system, a *global* set of laws, a *global* monetary system, etc.—such as is envisioned by Bush's New World Order. The "global police force" would be a U.N. police force made up of U.S., Russian, European, and Third World troops.

"Collective security" for Europe means (according to the Kremlin propagandists) a joint-venture security arrangement between Western Europe, Eastern Europe, and the new Russian C.I.S. Guess who would dominate that joint security arrangement? The country with a 6.75 million-man army, 30,000 warheads, 75,000 tanks, and the largest military machine in the history of the world—Russia.

As surely as Europe was swallowed up by the Nazi Third Reich in the late 1930s through subtlety, deception, manipulation, disinformation, and finally overwhelming military pressure, so the Europe of the 1990s is laying itself open to being swallowed up by an even more deceptive, Machiavellian, Russian bear.

Gorbachev-Shevardnadze-Yeltsin— Three Peas In the Same Pod

The Russians are masters at creating, controlling, and marketing to the West their opposition. *Opposition to most human endeavors will arise in time, but if you own it, it will never be a real threat to your enterprise— and it may be able to choke out legitimate opposition.* Nothing in Russia really happens by chance, by accident, or by quirk of fate. There is a well-defined plan and purpose behind most significant events in the C.I.S. *Present Russian developments are much more easily understood if Russia is seen as a giant theater, and the present upheaval as scenes or acts in the drama.* Three of the leading actors are discussed below:

Mikhail Gorbachev—did not just happen to emerge on the scene in 1985. He was groomed for his position from the 1970s by his mentor, Yuri Andropov—hardline chief of the KGB. As a KGB operative and protege' of

Andropov, this hardcore Marxist/Leninist was sprung by the Kremlin leadership from relative obscurity in 1983 and 1984 on the world stage, and portrayed as a great democrat, lover of freedom, reformer, and friend of the little man by Soviet propaganda/disinformation specialists. (Andropov was similarly portrayed as a "Western-style closet liberal" by Soviet propagandists just a few years earlier.)

This is the same Mikhail Gorbachev who said in *Pravda* on December 11, 1984:

> *"In the struggle for peace and social progress the Communist Party of the Soviet Union pursues a consistent policy of rallying the forces of the international communist and working-class movement in every possible way. We uphold the historical justness of the great ideas of Marxism-Leninism, and along with all the revolutionary and peace-loving forces of mankind, stand for social progress, and peace and security for all nations. This is what should determine the resolute nature of our propaganda."*

Eduard Shevardnadze—In the mid-1980s, the Kremlin began to elevate another actor to center stage—Eduard Shevardnadze. This life-long hardcore Marxist/Leninist was minister of the interior for the Republic of Georgia from 1968 to 1972—over the secret police, border guards, and all internal security forces (e.g., in charge of the Georgian KGB). In 1972 he was elevated to first secretary of the Central Committee of the Communist Party of Georgia and remained in that position until 1985, when he was elevated to minister of foreign affairs of the Soviet Union—replacing Andre Gromyko.

Shevardnadze (who has become a close friend of George Bush and especially with Secretary of State James Baker) resigned from his position as foreign minister in December 1990, protesting the U.S.S.R.'s move toward "a dictatorship by the 'hardliners.' " He is protrayed by the Russian and U.S. media as a reformer, a liberal, a staunch democrat, and lover of freedom—and a close friend of Gorbachev's. He was sent to America on a Soviet fund-raising drive in the first half of 1991 and was shuttled around the U.S. by America's liberal Eastern Establishment—requesting $90 billion (for starters) in Western financial aid for the U.S.S.R.

Handsome, suave, and sophisticated in appearance, Shevardnadze has been suggested by such Establishment publications as the *New York Times* and *London Economist* as the next head of the United Nations. Since the August 1991 coup/countercoup drama, Kremlin leaders have begun to move Shevardnadze back to center stage—where, if they decided to write Gorbachev out of the script (as in a TV soap opera), they could move Shevardnadze into the top position. In November 1991, Shevardnadze was reappointed Soviet foreign minister by Gorbachev and in early 1992 he was appointed president of the Republic of Georgia.

Shevardnadze has been well-packaged for Western leaders and the public as a democrat and lover of freedom by his Kremlin PR (disinformation) handlers. We are told his favorite book is *The Federalist Papers*, that he quotes from it often. He would bring great credibility to the "reform/democracy/end of communism" coup if the communist leadership should decide to place him at the top. *But, he is still a hardcore, lifelong Marxist-Leninist revolutionary dedicated to Soviet world domination.*

Boris Yeltsin—is the Kremlin's latest major entry

onto the stage of Soviet theater. Also a lifelong, hardcore Marxist/Leninist (like Gorbachev and Shevardnadze), Yeltsin has been portrayed as a staunch anti-communist, democrat, lover of freedom—the Russian "David" willing to risk his life and career by standing up to the "hideous, hardline communist monster—Goliath." Americans love a courageous underdog, and Yeltsin's character has been tailored by the Kremlin scriptwriters to elicit great admiration and respect from middle America, Europe, etc. The "man on the street" in the West can identify with this two-fisted, hard-charging, hard-drinking, outspoken "champion of democracy"—a Russian "John Wayne-type."

The *reality* of Boris Yeltsin is somewhat different. In 1961, at the age of 30, Yeltsin joined the Communist Party. In 1968, he became a full-time Party worker in the Sverdlovsk Communist Party in Siberia. He went on to become Party secretary, and in 1976 became first secretary of the Regional Committee. At this post, the hard-driving Yeltsin was noticed by the communist leaders in Moscow. In April of 1985 he was elevated to head the Communist Central Committee Construction Department, and in December 1985 was appointed head of the 1.2 million-member Moscow City Party Committee (the largest communist organization in the entire Soviet Union).

As with Gorbachev and Shevardnadze, powerful figures in the CPSU Central Committee and KGB put Yelstin on the *fast track to the top—something which does not happen in Russia unless one's Marxist/Leninist credentials are impeccable.* Yeltsin's position as the powerful head of the Moscow Communist Party opened the door for him to be placed on the Politburo (though he was removed in 1987 in a "quarrel" with Gorbachev).

In June 1991, Yeltsin (promising "swift moves to establish greater democracy and market economics") was elected (in the first-ever such election) president of the Russian Republic—which has 150 million of Russia's 285 million people. Following that election, the Western press enthusiastically described Yelstin as "Bigger Than Life—The Russian People Love Him."

His image, credibility, and standing in the West went into orbit as he *appeared* to "stand in the gap" against the hardline "gang of eight" coup perpetrators during the August 1991 coup/countercoup drama.

As he "appeared" to stand off the entire Soviet army and KGB almost singlehandedly, the Western media and public opinion went ballistic. Americans were barraged with articles with typical headlines such as: "The Right Stuff: Yeltin Joins the Ranks of Robin Hood, Moses, and Churchill." For almost a week in August, Yeltsin would have been accepted as president of the world—had such a position existed.

Yeltsin's "thinking" is reflected in speeches he has made at the 26th and 27th Party Congresses of the CPSU where he highly praised the tremendous strivings of the CPSU as well as the monumental advancements and great successs of Russia. As he said at the first of those Party congresses:

*"Today we find the mighty productive forces which possess our society, the wealth supplied to the Soviet people by unfettered socialism. **And all of this is the result of a wise collective brain, titanic work, unbreakable will, and the unsurpassable organizational talent of the Communist Party and its Central Committee and Politburo. . . .***

"Under the leadership of the Central Committee, our Party and the state have actually

continued to lead in the hard rebuttal of the aggressive machinations of imperialism [e.g., America]. *The communists and all the workers of the Sverdlovsk Central Committee* [headed by Yeltsin until April 1985] *assure the congress delegates and Lenin's Central Committee that they will fight with their entire revolutionary fervor and give **unswerving dedication to the cause of the Communist Party**."*

In July 1990, the Kremlin script called for Yeltsin to resign from the Communist Party (as Shevardnadze and Gorbachev have now done) and *Yeltsin is now referred to as a "non-communist reformer." Yes, but he is still a hardcore Marsixt/Leninist revolutionary—an important distinction.* In early 1992, Yeltsin replaced Mikhail Gorbachev as the supreme dictator of the old Soviet Union (now the Commonwealth of Independent States).

Yeltsin, like Gorbachev, Shevardnadze, and the reform (liberal) wing of the Communist Party, is totally dedicated to *perestroika* (a restructuring and reorganization of the Communist Party and Russia from top to bottom). Yeltsin is for purging hundreds of thousands (or millions) of bureaucrats, aparatchiks, and the Nomenclatura (the privileged ones)—*not to terminate communism, but to accelerate its thrust toward world domination.* He would go even further and faster than Gorbachev—hence the "alleged" rivalry between the two.

Yeltsin is not against Gorbachev, nor against communism. He is against the entrenched bureaucracy (and the stagnation it has begotten) which he and Gorbachev believe is self-serving, bloated, and slowing down the communists' timetable for world revolution.

When Yeltsin and Gorbachev talk about a multi-party system in Russia, they are talking about *multiple communist parties all functioning within the communist system.* Hence, Yeltsin's pronouncement to found a new party "to the left" of the communists. It will be anti-free enterprise, anti-capitalist, and hardcore Marxist/Leninist, but will use all the terminology of free markets, democracy, etc.

In Russian politics and theater, there is the concept of the "liar" and the "liar's helper." Gorbachev was the liar—Yeltsin was the liar's helper. Now Yeltsin is the liar.

Conclusion

Gorbachev, Shevardnadze, and Yeltsin are all actors in a dramatic stage play (like *Hamlet* or *King Lear*). The Russians organize their politics according to a well-developed scenario which sometimes includes the death or permanent exit of the main hero. It helps to understand the plot, to understand the position and relationship among the actors, as well as the intended influence or impact upon the audience—the world. Nothing in Russia is accidental: the words, the stage, the violins, or the plot.

The three actors described above are all hardcore Marxist/Leninists (on the same side) with their directors in the Central Committee of the CPSU, the KGB, and the Russian military orchestrating the plot, its pace, and each new twist in the plot (e.g., the August 1991 coup/countercoup, the termination—*actually the renaming*—of the Communist Party of the Soviet Union, the KGB, and the U.S.S.R. itself). Just as Western audiences are fascinated by the next episode of TV's *Dallas*, so the Kremlin leaders plan to mesmerize and manipulate the West with the next act of Soviet political theater.

And the ultimate goal: to convince the West that

communism has collapsed in the U.S.S.R., that democracy has arrived, that massive U.S. (and Western) aid and disarmament should follow, and the integration of East and West (starting with Europe) should occur—*by the mid to late-1990s.*

The big three actors described above will be joined by others. Watch another rising star—Alexander Yakovlev —a close confidante of Gorbachev and Shevardnadze.

Soviet Disinformation

"Telling the truth is a bourgeois prejudice. Deception, on the other hand, is often justified by the goal."
—Vladimir Lenin, 1921

"When we are weak, boast of strength . . . when we are strong, feign weakness."
—Vladimir Lenin

The present Soviet leadership has developed history's most comprehensive and Machiavellian plan to destabilize the West and defeat it through systematic deception. *The Russians have learned that the American people have a very short attention span; are easily seduced by media-generated illusion; find it easier to believe words (when pronounced with "sincerity") than deeds—even when the deeds contradict the words; and find it difficult to detect camouflage and deception.* The Soviet leaders are presently creating the *illusion* of peace, the death of communism, the breakup of the empire, the demilitarization of the Soviet Union, democracy in the C.I.S., friendship with the West (and perhaps even economic collapse)—while planning and perpetrating exactly the opposite.

To facilitate this strategy of deception, the Russian leaders (primarily via the KGB) utilize *disinformation— the deliberate false portrayal of the true conditions and practices of the communist world to elicit desired reactions from the non-communist world.* In periods of true weakness and crisis within the communist world, the carefully crafted image is one of aggressive strength and expansion, and all communist practice is geared to create that image. In periods of actual strength and solidarity within the communist leadership, the system is portrayed as weak, struggling, transitional, and open to cooperation with the Western family of nations.

To wage ideological war against the West, Russian disinformation/propaganda specialists concentrate on two kinds of studies. One is the study of Western people and their psychology. The other consists of developing a working method of using unnoticeable, subliminal propaganda for achieving victory in ideological, political, and economic areas. *The Russians have mastered the art of telling Americans what they want to hear and making it believable.*

1. *The Disinformation Network* — The Russians have tens of thousands of KGB agents worldwide devoted specifically to disinformation and propaganda in the world media. Of tens of thousands of KGB agents in America, James Tyson in *Target America* estimates that 2,000 function within the U.S. media. TASS, the Soviet official news (disinformation) agency, has bureaus in 126 countries— staffed almost exclusively by the KGB.

   The Novosti Press Agency has 3,000 employees around the world (mostly KGB) who feed information and reports into 4,000 information services worldwide. Novosti publishes thousands of books and 24 illustrated magazines (in 45 languages) in foreign countries around the world (12 in India alone). Novosti publishes magazines and newspapers (printed in Libya) in 32 different African countries and distributes millions of copies of books, newspapers, and magazines in Europe and North America.

The Russians know that the best dissemination of propaganda lies in supplying properly edited TV news reels and newspaper galley proofs to Western media outlets. Westerners in turn are impressed that *glasnost* "allows" this and eagerly transmits or publishes everything with no thought or question as to the validity of the material—most of which is prepared by the KGB.

The TASS News Agency is the outlet on which all the world relies for its information about Russia. TASS produces tens of thousands of communiques, magazine and news articles, programs and commentaries each year, which appear to be unbiased and objective, but which are in fact clever, sophisticated disinformation or propaganda pushing the present Russian thinking, strategy, or manipulations. These are, in turn, fed into tens of thousands of Western and Third World media outlets and reach an audience of billions of unsuspecting people worldwide.

This disinformation is virtually always what the Western (especially the American) audience wants to hear. Presently it dwells on the collapse of the Russian economy, the dissolution of communist parties, chaos in Eastern Europe, the end of communist regimes, the dissolution of the Soviet

Empire, etc. *It is noteworthy that there is almost a total absence of any information on the Russian military. This is not by accident!*

2. *Are the Russians Understating Their Economy as Part of Their "Feign Weakness/Get Western Aid" Disinformation Campaign?* This writer recently saw statistics from a 1988 Soviet publication of world statistics comparing Russian and U.S. production in a number of areas. These statistics show amazing Soviet economic *strength* in a number of areas—strength that runs completely counter to all appearances that Russia is a total economic basket case.

A few examples of Russian versus American production numbers are worthy of reflection: Overall production is 80 percent of America's; crude oil production—140 percent of America's; natural gas production—139 percent; cast iron—286 percent; steel—214 percent; iron ore—504 percent; mineral fertilizers—162 percent; tractors 463 percent; cement—168 percent; cotton fabrics—293 percent; woolen fabrics—515 percent; sugar—149 percent; railway freight—273 percent; students in universities and colleges—83 percent; number of physicians—218 percent; beds in hospitals—369 percent.

This writer has seen Soviet grain production statistics for 1990 that make him wonder if they have not vastly *understated* their true production. *We have been led to believe that the Russians are technical/industrial/financial buffoons.* But more than half of the engineers in the world live in the former Soviet Union. The average Russian university graduate is *far better educated* than the average U.S. university graduate today, something most Americans would not like to admit. The Russians produce two and a half to three times more world patents per year than Americans. They already have a powerhouse based on "plasma" (not blood)—a self-generating powerhouse like the sun.

The Russians built the first nuclear power plant. The Russians built the world's first nuclear-powered icebreaker in the 1950s. They are presently deploying a Star Wars-type space-based defense system that America has chosen not to build. They have an operational space station in outer space—for military purposes. America cannot afford to put one up.

They have an operational rocket that lifts a 100-ton payload into outer space, verses a 32-ton maximum rocket payload America can lift (a three-to-one edge in lifting capacity). They have built the largest military air transport in the world, far larger than America's C5A Galaxy. *They even developed America's favorite video game—Nintendo.* They build a nuclear submarine worth $3 billion per copy every six weeks that is as good as any America can turn out. *Their weapons industry is five to ten times the size of our own, turns out weapons that, in many instances, are as sophisticated as ours, and in five to six times the quantity of our own.* In areas where they are technologically behind America, they beg, borrow, steal, or are given what they need by the West.

Financially, they may not be the incompetents we perceive them to be in that they always best us price-wise on large commodities deals—they are actually very sophisticated market operators (or manipulators). When they sell gold (as the world's third largest producer), they sell into strength to maximize their profits. *The Soviet economy is actually less vulnerable to the coming depression in the West than our own* because they do not have a huge internal debt pyramid to collapse as we do (America's is $16 trillion and rising). Most Russian debt is international—*owed to the West!*

Furthermore, a major deflationary economic (or price) collapse in the former Soviet Union is unlikely because the government owns everything and controls all prices. People will not be dumping assets or investments to get liquid—they don't own any! The Russians are not major exporters—they consume most of their production. But they are major importers, and import prices will drop sharply in a depression. *The Soviet economy will be relatively insulated from a Western global depression.*

What's the point? Sun Tsu, the Chinese military strategist (whom the Russian leaders idolize) said, "When at your pinnacle of strength, feign weakness." The Russians *may not be* at their pinnacle of economic strength (they never have been) but neither are they the economic basket case or technical/industrial/financial incompetents which Russian disinformation portrays them to be. As a few of the above facts would seem to indicate, they may be far stronger economically, industrially, technologically, and scientifically than we have been led to believe.

One highly respected Soviet-born Sovietologist even believes that the primary motive behind the Russians seeking massive Western financial aid is *not* need, as much as the desire to destroy the fragile U.S. and Western economies by overstretching our resources. One hundred billion dollars or more in international loans to the C.I.S. suddenly defaulted upon could also help to precipitate a financial collapse in the West.

The Russians *are*, however, at their pinnacle of military strength (their current "seeming" political upheaval notwithstanding), and that strength versus the West's is growing every day. General Douglas MacArthur once said, "It is most dangerous to underestimate your enemy." Is it possible that the Russian disinformation and Western gullibility about true conditions in the C.I.S. is causing America and the West to dangerously underestimate Russian military, industrial, and technical strength and to overestimate our own? Are the Soviets carefully crafting the "buffoon" image? Are they really "dumb like foxes?"

One good rule for Russian watchers when considering Russian disinformation is to *assume that almost everything is the opposite of what it appears to be.* Another rule to remember is that *if you own the guns, you still own the country.*

The Soviet Pseudo-Coup— Soviet Theater At Its Best

On Monday, August 19, 1991 Mikhail Gorbachev was ostensibly overthrown in a coup by military, KGB, and Communist Party hardliners not satisfied with the results of his *glasnost/perestroika* reform program. Within three days, the coup fell apart, the eight coup leaders were arrested, and Gorbachev was restored to power. While the communist and world press, as well as Bush and other Western leaders trumpeted the genuineness of the coup and countercoup, *there were some very strange aspects to the entire affair that cause this writer to conclude that the coup was staged:*

1. The U.S. and world press were warned about the

coming coup for several days leading up to August 19. *Seldom is the world press given advance notice of such events.* Western intelligence sources knew of the coup several months in advance. Also curious was the fact that *in spite of the advance publicity of the coup, Gorbachev made no moves to head it off or avert it.*

2. All of the eight coup leaders were Gorbachev appointees and confidants.

3. Coup leader Gennady Yanayev referred to himself only as "acting president" and spoke of Gorbachev returning to power after recovering from "his illness."

4. The coup leaders did not cut the internal or international communication lines—something which is always done in a coup or revolutionary upheaval.

5. The coup leaders made no attempt to control the press—neither the Soviet nor the foreign press stationed in Russia—which had complete access to international phone lines throughout the coup.

6. Anti-coup leaders such as Yeltsin had access to international phone lines *and operators* throughout the coup.

7. Only minimal troops were used throughout the coup, and troops *loyal to Yeltsin were sent to surround Yeltsin in the parliament building.*

8. The airports were all left open.

9. Utilities in the parliament building were never cut.

10. *In a legitimate coup, the KGB would have killed Yeltsin, Gorbachev, and other reform leaders.* No attempt was even made to arrest Yeltsin, but the coup plotters did arrest Godiyan, a well-known enemy of Gorbachev's.

The president of Soviet Georgia came out shortly after the coup and accused Gorbachev of having masterminded the coup, and 62 percent of the Soviet people (according to private polls) believe the coup was a fake. Even Eduard Shevardnadze (Gorbachev's former foreign minister) said that Gorby may have been behind the coup. *Certainly Gorbachev and the Soviet leadership had much to gain from a pseudo or staged coup:*

1. If Gorbachev could be seen as wresting control of the nation from reactionaries and restoring constitutional authority, his popularity and legitimacy among the people might rise.
2. It was hoped that the coup and coutercoup would quiet the restive Soviet people—holding out hope for improvement of their living conditions.
3. The coup and countercoup would *raise the credibility of the Soviet reform/democracy/glasnost/ perestroika movement in Western eyes—opening up the floodgates for even more financial and high-tech aid.* The Bush's of the world could say: "See, our good friend Gorbachev and the Soviet forces of democracy just 'dodged the hardliner's bullet'—now we *really* have to help them if we want to see democracy and reform succeed and survive."
4. The coup was to remind the West how wonderful Gorby really is. He was losing credibility due to his huge military buildup, his killing of people in the Baltics, etc. After the coup, he could blame all these indiscretions on the "hardliners."
5. The "restoration of democracy" to Russia and the "demise of the hardliners" is now *an excuse for the West to accelerate its disarmament* and for the

globalists in America, Europe, and Russia to
accelerate their merger into the New World Order.

6. The coup and countercoup are *an excuse to launch
a long overdue purge of hundreds of thousands of
inefficient Communist Party, KGB, or government
bureaucrats—tens of thousands of whom will be
shot or imprisoned.* This purging (or cleansing) of
the Party has been done periodically since 1917. It
is like pruning a grape vine or rose bush to make it
stronger. *A huge Communist Party purge is now
underway in Russia.*

7. The coup and countercoup would be *the excuse
for reorganizing and renaming the Communist
Party of Russia, the KGB, and the U.S.S.R. itself.*
This strategy of reorganizing, restructuring, and
streamlining the former Soviet Union from top to
bottom has been on the drawing boards for several
years. Under the impetus (or smokescreen) of the
coup and countercoup, this restructuring is now
being done in one huge quantum jump.

8. Another goal of the coup/countercoup was to
raise Boris Yeltsin to superstar status so that he
could be thrust into leadership if the people did
not rally around Gorbachev. *Soviet theater always
has an understudy for the star ready to be brought
on stage at a moment's notice.*

It appears that the eight leaders of the coup
(Kryuchkov, Yazov, Pavlov, Pugo, Yanayav, Baklanov,
Starodubtsev, and Tizyakov) were enticed into setting up
the coup (which they may have believed was genuine).
They were set up, entrapped, and then double-crossed.
Pugo is said to have committed suicide, but was more
likely murdered by the KGB since he was shot in the head

three times. The remaining seven will be tried, imprisoned, or shot. *This is the communist way—to double-cross and liquidate their own top leadership.* They overthrew and killed Trotsky (in Mexico); they purged and executed Bukharin (Lenin's closest associate and a "hero of the Revolution") in 1936 because he would not support Stalin's *perestroika* in 1936 and 1937; and they executed Beria (head of the NKVD) in 1956. Kryuchkov and friends may well suffer a similar fate—sacrificed for the long-term good of the Party. And *the sacrifices of Kryuchkov, Yazov, Pugo, Pavlov, etc. (who apparently walked into a trap) lends immense credibility to the whole coup/countercoup scheme.*

Historical Precedent

There are numerous precedents for purges, duplicity, double-crosses, and brutal executions in Soviet history since 1917. But there is also a precedent for a pseudo-coup in Russian history in 1564 when Ivan the Terrible was czar. Ivan became distraught over his inability to remake Russia in his image. The ruling class (the old guard) tried to thwart him at every turn. Ivan also believed that the ruling class had murdered (poisoned) his wife Anastasia. So, he packed up as if to go on his vacation, and once he reached his destination, he sent word to the ruling class elite that he was abdicating the throne.

This sent a shockwave of fear through the ruling class. The peasants would revolt and they would not get any help from Ivan's merchant class followers. So they sent word to Ivan—"come back, please!" He replied, "I will, but on *my* conditions." They thought about it and then decided it was the lesser of evils. Ivan returned to the throne and he renewed his reform efforts with much less resistance from the ruling class.

One thing seems to have gone wrong with the phony coup/countercoup. The Soviet people were supposed to rally around Gorbachev. They did not! Many saw through the charade, and most would simply not forgive his six years of despotism. So, it could become advantageous to move Yeltsin and/or Shevardnadze to center stage. But remember, both are hardcore Marxist/Leninists cut out of the same cloth as Gorbachev. As the French proverb says, "the more it changes, the more it remains the same."

Chapter Eleven

Reorganizing and Restructuring the Old Soviet Union

"We are not going to change Soviet power, of course, or abandon its fundamental principles, but we acknowledge the need for changes that will strengthen socialism."
— Mikhail Gorbachev, *Perestroika*

The Western media has been filled with headlines over the past year that the Soviet Empire is disintegrating, that communism and socialism are abandoned and dead at last, and that the Communist Party of Russia and the KGB are being dismantled, disbanded, and relegated to the "dust bin of history." Certainly the demise of the "gang of eight," the rise of Yeltsin to power, the official condemnation of the CPSU and KGB, and the independence of many of the Soviet republics would all seem to signal the end of the "evil empire." But looks can be deceptive and so can the Marxist/Leninist dialectic.

The Soviet Empire is not disintegrating as the Western press and leaders keep telling us. It is restructuring, rearranging, reorganizing, streamlining, purging the deadwood, and rearming preparatory to its final thrust for world domination over the next five to ten years. As Gorbachev said in 1989:

*"Through restructuring [perestroika] we want to give socialism a **second wind**. To achieve this, the Communist Party of the Soviet Union returns to the origins and principles of the Bolshevik Revolution, to the Leninist ideas about the construction of a new society."*

And in 1987 Gorbachev said:

"In October 1917, we parted with the old world, rejecting it once and for all. We are moving toward a new world, the world of communism. We shall never turn off that road."

Does this sound like a man who is presiding over the death of communism? The Lenin whom Gorbachev worships, quoting Sun Tsu, said:

"We advance through retreat . . . when we are weak, we boast of strength, and when we are strong, we feign weakness."

The old dialectic Leninist doctrine of taking two steps forward and then one back to confuse your enemies is certainly being applied by his disciples, Gorbachev and Yeltsin, today. It is called "scientific socialism" by the faithful, and of course Gorbachev and Yeltsin have said that they do not want to discard socialism, but renew, restructure, and strengthen it. *It should be remembered that all present changes in the Soviet Union are within the framework of socialism.*

Abolishing the Communist Party of the Soviet Union and the KGB

The Russians are *not* abolishing the CPSU or the

KGB, they are renaming them, reorganizing them, purging them of inefficient deadwood, and *expanding* their mission.

1. *The KGB* has had six name changes since 1917:
   a. CHEKA
   b. OGPU
   c. GPU
   d. NKVD
   e. MVD
   f. KGB

   All of those name changes were accompanied by purges (where thousands of heads at the top rolled), by restructuring or reorganization, by an expansion of the role of the secret police, and by public pronouncements that the secret police had been abolished. In the 1950s, Beria, the brutal and infamous head of the NKVD, was purged and executed. Vladimir Kryuchkov (head of the KGB until the recent phony coup and countercoup) has similarly been removed to make the coup/counter-coup seem more genuine.

   The KGB has about 1.5 million members worldwide, with about 50,000 sequestered in the U.S. KGB *military* units will now be moved under the Soviet army command (the new KGB will fall under the Soviet military command), and tens of thousands of inefficient KGB bureacrats will be sacked (or worse). *This is not being done to destroy the KGB, but to make it stronger, more efficient, lean and mean, etc.* It was seen to be becoming, fat, dumb, lazy, and bloated. Just as the Romanian secret police, the Securitate (which was 50,000 strong under Ceausescu) continues to operate in a Romania which is allegedly non-communist—but still is dominated by the communists—so the KGB will continue to function in Russia, which will be allegedly non-communist—but will still be dominated by the communists.

In 1991, the KGB was divided into three departments:

a. *Inter-Republican Counter-Espionage Service*—in charge of domestic political repression;
b. *Central Intelligence Service*—in charge of external espionage;
c. *State Committee for the Defense of C.I.S. Frontiers*—in charge of the uniformed military contingents of the KGB.

In early 1992, these three departments were reorganized or consolidated into one giant Russian ministry of security and interior affairs and restructured along the lines of the old KGB under Stalin and Beria in the 1950s. Today, the KGB is larger and stronger than it has ever been, and its agents (along with GRU agents—Russian military intelligence) are pouring into the U.S. and Western Europe.

2. *Restructuring and Renaming the Communist Party of the Soviet Union*—the CPSU has 20 million members and another 45 million members in its Lenin youth organization, Komsomol. (Komsomol is a young adult organization with members from the Red army, the KGB, the Red navy, the air force, and a majority of the young factory workers.) The CPSU has grown top-heavy and inefficient with bureaucratic deadweight. It is about to be reorganized, restructured, trimmed in size (or purged) to increase its efficiency, *and renamed. It*

*is not going to be abolished as Gorbachev, Yeltsin,
Bush, and the press keep telling us.*

It should be remembered that the Communist
Party of the Soviet Union has undergone a
number of metamorphoses in name: At its inception, it was called the Russian Social Democratic
Worker's Party. In 1912, following an internal
feud, it split into the Bolsheviks and Mensheviks
(the "big ones" and the "little ones"). The big ones
ate the little ones. The name then became the
Russian Social Democratic Worker's Party of
Bolsheviks. In 1918, it became the Russian Communist Party (Bolshevik). In 1925, the name was
changed again to the All-Soviet Communist Party
(Bolshevik). *In 1952, it became the Communist
Party of the Soviet Union, which it has remained
until the present. It is now operating with no
name, but may eventually be renamed the Social
Democratic Party or some other innocuous name.*

Each of these name changes was accompanied
by major fanfare, "absolute proof that the communists had completely changed," and the declaration that all the political, economic, and repressive
evils had been perpetrated by the *previous* party—
but that the *new* party would be benign, democratic,
freedom-loving, etc. In reality, all of the old evils
continued under the new, revamped party—nothing
changed! *The present charade will not alter any of
the principles or the goals of the CPSU.*

Each of the major Communist Party name
changes under Lenin and Stalin were accompanied
by massive purges (called "party rejuvenation") to
streamline the organization and bring it under
formidable discipline. Millions of Russian com-

munists went to the wall or the gulag in those purges. Today's CPSU has become fat, dumb, lazy, careless, apathetic, and passive, and is *ten times larger than during World War II*. It has lost sight of its goal, it has become diluted, and will probably be trimmed by several million members. This is not abolition of the Party—it is reorganization, restructuring, and *strengthening* of the Party.

The communists believe that Americans and most Westerners are shallow, superficial, gullible, and easily seduced by media-generated illusions. *Hence, if they change the name of one of their fronts or parties, and declare the old organization to be dead, most Westerners will believe it.* For decades they have routinely changed the names of their communist-front organizations in this manner. In 1990 they renamed the Communist Party of *Italy*, now calling it the Democratic Party. In *Poland*, they renamed the Communist Party (which was called the Polish United Worker's Party) to the Social Democratic Party. In *Romania*, they renamed the old Romanian Communist Party, calling the new party the New Salvation Front. In none of those cases (or many others), did they really abolish those communist parties. They simply renamed, reorganized, and restructured the parties, while gullible naive Westerners believed the charade. It has been said, "a rose by any other name is still a rose." *Calling the CPSU the Social Democratic Party (or some such name) will not alter the fact that it is the same old CPSU with a new label and some new faces. The present strategy of having no name for the CPSU is brilliant. Westerners cannot believe that an organization with no name can really exist.*

Today, the Communist Party of Russia operates through elected representatives, the Politburo, and the Central Committee. The Central Committee of the CPSU (made up of 300 to 450 members) wields the real power in Russia, and an inner circle of about 100 members really calls the shots. These Central Committee members dominate the military and the KGB, as well as the "visible" politicians such as Gorbachev, Yeltsin, Shevardnadze, and the various cabinet ministers. Yeltsin and Gorbachev are simply actors, employees who are implementing the policy laid down by the Central Committee since the early 1980s when they (and the KGB) drafted the script for *glasnost/perestroika number six.*

The new refurbished Communist Party was discussed at length at the CPSU's 27th and 28th Congresses in 1986 and 1990. Gorbachev described the "new Party" as:·

> *"A Party of **socialist choice** and **communist perspective.** . . . A Party adhering to **humanistic ideals** common to all mankind . . . intolerant of chauvinism, nationalism, racism, and **any manifestation of reactionary ideology** and obscurantism. . . . A Party open for contacts, **co-actions with the communists, social democrats, and socialists of various countries.**"*

Reading the "new Party" profile as conceived by the CPSU leadership, it is clear that the only difference between the "old Party" and the "new Party" is in the new one's wide acceptance of all revolutionary movements throughout the world.

'Socialism' to be Substituted for 'Communism'

"The concept, the main idea, lies in the fact that

*we want to give a new lease on life to socialism
through perestroika and to reveal the potential
of the socialist system."*
    —Mikhail Gorbachev, October 1989

*"Today we have perestroika, **the salvation of
socialism**, giving it a second breath, revealing
everything good which is in the system."*
    —Mikhail Gorbachev, December 1989

The word "socialism" will be substituted for "communism" and the latter will be almost completely stricken from the communists' vocabulary. From Lenin to Yeltsin, the communists have used the two words interchangeably. Socialism, as defined by Karl Marx in the *Communist Manifesto*, is what has been imposed on the peoples of the U.S.S.R., China, Cuba, etc. Socialism, as the stepping stone to the final Utopian goal of communism, involves abolition of private property, Draconian political and financial regulations and controls on the people, huge bureaucracy, a progressive income tax, an end to inheritance, a monopolistic central bank, central control of education, and state control of the family, children, religion, etc. (This sounds ominously like the socialist America which is emerging in the 1990s.)

  What do George Bush, Helmut Kohl, John Major, most Western leaders, Mikhail Gorbachev, Boris Yeltsin, and Eduard Shevardnadze all have in common? They are all socialists, secular humanists, and globalists—working for a common socialist global government—called by Bush and Gorbachev the "New World Order."

  A few years ago the "convergence theory" of history emerged. It held that America and the West would move to the political left, the Russians would move to the political right, and we would all meet and merge in the middle as socialists or social democrats. The "convergence theory" of history seems to be right on track. Socialist Russia, socialist Eastern Europe, and socialist Western Europe are all moving toward merging into one giant unitary state or federation over the next five years or so. A massive Soviet subversion and absorption of Western Europe will follow.

Reorganizing the U.S.S.R. from Top to Bottom

Soviet leaders in the Central Committee, the Politburo, the KGB, and the Soviet Academy of Sciences *began to conclude over a decade ago that in spite of Russia's vast natural and human resources, that the country was utilizing those resources in a most "barbaric manner."* They have concluded over the past decade that Russian industry is lagging badly behind the West, especially in controlling wastefulness of materials and energy, as well as human resources. Russian industry uses between two and two and a half times more material resources and between one and one and a half times more energy per unit of production than Western countries do.

Gorbachev, Yeltsin, and the Soviet leaders have therefore called for the reorganization of Russian society from top to bottom—*but within the framework of socialism.* The "new economic policy" is called "free market" and borrows much terminology from the West, but *to Yeltsin and the Russian leadership, "free market" means state- and collectively-owned property, businesses are still state-run and state-controlled, and business or investment profits are still illegal, etc. To the Russians, "free market" means only that they will trade with us, while to Westerners, when the Russians use the term, they think Russia is in a transition to capitalism.*

Another example of word/concept manipulation is "liberation theology." The Russians hatched "liberation theology" about 15 years ago, which is a diabolical and seductive use of Marxist/Leninist doctrine wrapped up in Christian/biblical terminology, doctrines, etc. Liberation theology has been a smashing success for the communists in Central and Latin America, South Africa, and the Philippines. *Now they are taking Marxist and socialist concepts and wrapping them up in free market terminology, concepts, etc.—to seduce gullible Western political and business leaders.*

When Yeltsin or Gorbachev talk about stagnation, electronization of industry, opening the country to market economy, democratization of society, etc., they are really talking about getting rid of the corrupt, overpaid, inefficient bureaucrats who are now running Russia instead of the workers. The bloated bureaucracy is about to be cut away "because it has lost its revolutionary fervor."

As Gorbachev said at the 28th CPSU Congress:

"What we see today is not the working class running the Soviet Union, but the bureaucracy— which is satisfied to occupy soft and lucrative positions, but is hardly interested in revolutionary movements, political underminings of the rest of the world, or military expansion of communism. This is clearly stagnation."

The New Soviet Approach: The Velvet Glove Versus the Ironclad Fist

Since 1917, the communists have hated nationalism

and nationalists—who stand for strong national entities as opposed to the international order sought by the communists. According to the socialist/communist ideology, nationalism hinders the development of socialism and eventually communism, and is counter-internationalist. From the 1960s to the 1980s, nationalists in the Baltic states, Byelorussia, and Ukraine have been under incessant attack by the communists.

However, with *glasnost/perestroika*, the situation seemingly changed. National symbols such as flags and other objects were suddenly allowed. Literally overnight, people turned to the old national emblems, parading them in front of the communists as if they had won the battle for national survival. The nationalists in the Baltics and other republics exposed themselves and left no doubt as to who they were. *This bringing to the surface of potential enemies was probably the main goal of the CPSU. Over the past few years, the Russians have allowed nationalistic opposition to emerge, and have then turned around and infiltrated it, financed it, and co-opt (or taken over) much of it.*

The Russians are masters at either creating or taking over their own opposition. They did this with Solidarity in Poland, the New Salvation Front in Romania, and with Shevardnadze and Yeltsin in Russia. Much more advantageous than destroying their opposition is to create or co-opt it so they can use it for their own purposes.

We hear a great deal about the "hardliners" versus the "reformers," or the "conservatives" versus the "liberals." Western leaders and media describe the "hardliners" (or "conservatives") as unrepentant communist hawks, (i.e., such as the "gang of eight"); and the "reformers" (or "liberals") as lovers of freedom, democracy, and free markets (such as Gorbachev, Shevardnadze, and Yeltsin).

In reality, both groups are hardcore Marxist/ Leninist communists, hell-bent on Soviet world domination or conquest. They simply disagree on the most advantageous method for our destruction. The "hardliners" would bludgeon us to death with an ironclad fist; the "reformers" would strangle us with a velvet glove. The result is the same—our destruction. The quarrel between the so-called "conservatives" and "liberals" is over *methodology*—not results or the final outcome. The reformers believe you can catch more flies with honey than vinegar.

Yeltsin and Gorbachev are widely viewed and described as reformers, liberals, and lovers of democracy. And yet, in December 1989, Gorbachev said:

"I am a communist, a convinced communist. For some that may be a fantasy. But for me, it is my main goal."

In November 1987, Gorbachev said:

"In our work and worries, we are motivated by those Leninist ideals and noble endeavors and goals which mobilized the workers of Russia seven decades ago to fight for the new and happy world of socialism. Perestroika is a continuation of the October Revolution."

That same Gorbachev, described to the West as a lover of democracy and freedom, said in November 1987:

"We are moving toward a new world, the world of communism. We shall never turn off that road."

And in June 1990, Gorbachev "the reformer" said:

"I am now, just as I've always been, a convinced communist. It's useless to deny the enormous and unique contribution of Marx, Engels, and Lenin to the history of social thought and to modern civilization as a whole."

Gorbachev, Shevardnadze, Yeltsin, and the reform wing of the CPSU are dedicated communists, they hate the American and other Western "imperialists," and they still believe in the inevitability of the communist conquest of the world, but they believe a different strategy is presently needed for success. *They want to discard the old "hardline" strategy of confrontation, divide and conquer, making enemies, etc., and instead adopt a strategy of cooperation, of embracing the West, making the West friendly to the socialist world; and eventually they intend (through subtlety, deception, infiltration, subversion, and manipulation) to "absorb" the West. (Western Europe will be the first to be so absorbed.)*

The "reformers" want to incorporate their "new thinking" into the world thinking process in order to ultimately control world politics. They want the economy of the world to be integrated with the economy of the old Soviet Union. They plan to take over the world the way the AIDS virus takes over the body—slowly, subtly, surreptitiously.

It is important for the West to understand that Gorbachev, Shevardnadze, and Yeltsin (the "reformers") are enemies—just as dangerous to our survival as the "gang of eight" (the "hardliners"). In fact, these reformers are more dangerous because they have caused the West to lower its threat perception—to lower its guard. (Better the enemy you can see and defend against than the enemy who comes to you as a friend—as Brutus did to Julius

Caesar before he stabbed him.) *The "reformers" will tell us what we want to hear—they will talk about democracy, free elections, free markets, multi-party systems, freedom, independence, etc., while giving these words their own Marxist/Leninist twist or meaning.* If you are strangled by the hand in the velvet glove (instead of being bludgeoned by the mailed fist) you are still dead!

The New Soviet Federation

We have been told that the Union of Soviet Socialist Republics (U.S.S.R.) has collapsed. That is not really true. It is being *voluntarily* disbanded by the Soviet leadership in favor of a new federation (or union), presently called the Commonwealth of Independent States. *This restructuring (not disintegration as it is portrayed by Soviet disinformation and the Western media) of the U.S.S.R. has been on the drawing boards since before Gorbachev came to power (actually dating back to the late 1970s).*

The leaders of Russia at that time began to realize that the present form of the Soviet Empire was archaic, inefficient, and counterproductive to further global expansion, except in remote areas of the world (e.g., Africa and Nicaragua) not contiguous to the U.S.S.R. In a certain sense, the Western policy of "containment" and the advent of NATO in the 1950s had been reasonably successful in restricting the U.S.S.R.'s European growth beyond Eastern Europe and the Soviet republics. Just as slavery in the old American South had become unprofitable, unproductive, and uneconomical before the U.S. Civil War, so the Soviet Empire was seen over a decade ago to need deep reform in its imperial structure.

Remember Lenin's admonition: "We advance through retreat." *The "apparent" demise of the Soviet Empire will speed the dismantling of NATO; Western Europe's and America's military structures will be dismembered in the new "era of peace, death of communism, end of the Cold War, and collapse of the evil empire"; and the U.S.S.R.'s long-term goal of the neutralization of their western flank—preparatory to the absorption of Western Europe (politically, economically, and militarily)—will have been accomplished.*

It is essential that as the new commonwealth replaces the old union, that the new be seen to be made up of sovereign, independent states, democratically oriented, with multi-party political systems and free market economies. That will be the *perception* (as it is today in Poland, Romania, Nicaragua, etc.) but it will *not* be the *reality.* The *rhetoric* will be "free market" and "democratic." But the *reality* is that the Russian military and the KGB (regardless of its new name), through a series of treaties *with*, infiltration and subversion *of*, and economic pressure *on* the so-called "sovereign independent republics" *will continue to maintain control of those republics.*

As Dr. Francoise Thom, respected Sovietologist and professor at the University of Sorbonne at Paris said recently:

> *"We fail to see the great design underlying Moscow's* **new imperial policy**. *This failing leads to the misunderstanding of the Soviet European policy, because since the launching of perestroika, Moscow's European policy has become* **a continuation of Moscow's great imperial design.**
>
> *"It is essential for us to understand this*

strategy: for Moscow, the preservation of the empire depends more and more on the domination of the international community. When the Kremlin's influence, or even hegemony, on Europe is fully established, the Baltic's quest for independence will seem irrelevant."

Professor Thom points out that the political elite in the U.S.S.R. saw the need for restructuring and reorganizing the imperial empire over a decade ago, but that "inertia of the Soviet power apparatus" delayed the process until now. This explains *the real* conflict between the reformers and the hardliners. The former are more enlightened regarding the need for change. *They are not only trying to purge, reorganize, and restructure the Communist Party and the Soviet system in order to save and strengthen it, but the entire empire as well. This is also essential to seduce Western Europe into integration and merger with the new "democratic" Russian federation.*

To better understand Russia's present incredibly devious strategy of deception, this writer recommends that the reader go to a video store and rent the film *The Sting*. Sophisticated, complicated scams or cons are run all the time. Most honest people simply don't understand them and cannot believe that people are deceptive or clever enough to put them together. But remember, *the Russians are the world's chess champions and they always lie* (when it is to their advantage to do so). The latter is part of their Marxist/Leninist doctrine. As Professor Thom continued:

"The current upheaval in the Soviet Empire led the present Soviet leadership to seek an accelerated all-European integration, i.e., the 'com-

*mon European home' Gorbachev has talked about in CPSU congresses since coming to power in 1985. **This is possible only with a radical change of both West European and East European political systems. All European integration is conceivable only if an homogenization of the political structures of East and West takes place.***"

What we are seeing is the "convergence or merger theory" in a European context first, then globally—including the U.S. The "radical change in the West European political system" Professor Thom refers to is the U.S. of Western Europe—the political merger of Europe in late 1992 under Euro-socialists in Brussels whereby the European countries will yield their sovereignty to the European superstate. The "radical change in the East European political system" is the restructuring/reorganizing of the CPSU, KGB, the U.S.S.R. from top to bottom, and the empire itself. Thom went on:

*"In order to achieve hegemony over the political processes in Europe, a new, apparently **'democratic legitimation'** of the Soviet Empire (the ratification of a new union treaty by **elected** parliaments) had to be accomplished. Without this 'democratic legitimation of the Soviet Empire, the building of a 'European home' is unthinkable."*

The Form and Substance of the New Soviet Federation

If one studies the proceedings and speeches of Gorbachev, Yeltsin, and other Kremlin leaders of the

26th, 27th, and 28th Congresses of the Communist Party of the Soviet Union (in 1981, 1986, and 1990), one will see that they have been talking about and planning for the new federation or commonwealth since 1981.

Elements of the New Commonwealth— For the Existing Republics

The new commonwealth or union will include the following elements in regard to the current 15 Soviet republics:

1. The old Soviet Union as we know it will be dissolved and a *new* union or federation established —to be called the Commonwealth of Independent States (for the moment).
2. Under the new union, each republic will have more independence at the *cultural and economic level*, will "appear" to be an independent multi-party democracy at the *political level*, and will still be under the military influence or domination of the Russian republic at the *military level*. *(The "sovereign" republics will "appear" to be freer and more independent than they really are.)*
3. The huge Russian republic will have more power in the new set-up and will look more like Germany during World War II. It will dominate the C.I.S. (In the early stages of the C.I.S. the Russian republic will be portrayed as equal to the other republics. This will be part of the charade to fool the West and the republics.)
4. Each of the 15 republics will have a vote in the U.N. (whereas only the U.S.S.R., the Ukraine, and Byelorussia have had votes since its inception).

As these republics retain their loyalties to the old U.S.S.R., that is potentially 12 more votes against America in the U.N.

5. The republics will be made to look independent and sovereign, will talk about and actually move to more free market economies, multi-party systems, and economic freedom, but will continue to be controlled by covert communists and in reality by the Communist Party of Russia, the KGB, and the Soviet military, no matter what their new names turn out to be. (At this writing, every republic is run by communists who are either KGB agents or controlled by the KGB.) The *Washington Post* wrote on February 1, 1992, *"It is now known that **the KGB infiltrated the independence movements and democracy parties that sprang up around the Soviet Union as a result of liberalizing policies of former Soviet leader Mikhail Gorbachev. Since many of these parties have now come to power, it means that KGB agents and informers are represented in the highest levels of government.** . . . At parliamentary meetings last week, Russian security chiefs acknowledged that the pro-Yeltsin democratic Russia faction includes numerous KGB agents."*

6. Treaties between the C.I.S., the Russian republic, and these republics (tying them back to the Russians) have been signed. Lenin said, "A treaty is a means for gaining strength," (e.g., the Ukranian communist leadership declared independence in 1991 and then turned around and signed a treaty of military and economic cooperation with Russia. They came right back into the C.I.S.) *Question*: When is "sovereignty" not really "sovereignty"?

Answer: When it's fake!

The *A*nti *B*olshevik *N*etwork, a German publication, was recently quoted by Pat Buchanan as attacking the Ukranian parliament "reformers" as being a group of phonies who actually support the communists. This situation will be found in the other republics as well.

7. Most of the "independent republics" are economic basket cases. They will get sympathy and free market rhetoric from the West, but very little in the way of economic aid or trade. (Unfortunately they are not credit worthy, can't pay their bills, and don't really understand free enterprise.) So, they will remain defacto dependent on the Russian republic and the C.I.S. economically. They will continue to get the raw materials for their industries from the Russian republic and sell their finished products back to Russia.

This situation has a recent historic parallel in South Africa, where four tribal homelands became independent a decade or so ago, but remained economically dependent on South Africa (their former Mother Country and an economic colossus compared to the homelands). Those new countries were allowed to have armies (albeit small, weak, poorly armed defense forces) but those are dwarfed and can be easily dominated by the relatively huge South African Defense Force. Those countries will probably be reintegrated back into the New South Africa in the foreseeable future—which seems likely to come under the rule of the communist ANC over the next year or two.

8. The "sovereign, independent" republics will be allowed to have armies, but these will be *miniscule*

compared to the gargantuan Russian military force—functioning more like local militias or the National Guard in the various states of America.

9. There will be much talk about "multi-party democracy" in the sovereign republics, but most of these parties will be Marxist/Leninist (either overtly or covertly) and/or controlled and manipulated by the KGB (as is the case in much of Eastern Europe today).

10. The sovereign republics will be more free, but still within the walls of the Russian prison. For the Russians, the word "sovereignty" is really a matter of semantics. It doesn't mean to them what it means to us. To them it doesn't mean total independence—only partial.

Elements of an Expanded Russian/C.I.S. Federation— Beyond the Old Borders

Of even greater importance are the Kremlin leaders' plans for expansion of the new Russian-dominated federation beyond the existing borders of the old U.S.S.R.:

1. The new Soviet federation is designed to suck Eastern Europe into the union via a series of economic and military treaties. Soviet influence in the former East European satellite countries is still very strong. For example, consider Romania—a country of 24 million people: roughly 4 million are Communist Party members; 8 million are Komsomol members; 8 million are children (and don't count politically). That leaves 4 million non-communist adults out of a total population of 24

million. The president (Illiescu) is communist. The ruling party (New Salvation Front) is communist. The secret police (49,000 members) is communist. Who controls Romania today?

2. The new Soviet federation is designed to eventually encompass Eastern Europe, the U.S.S.R., Afghanistan, Cambodia (Kampuchea), Vietnam, Laos, Mongolia, a *United* Korea, and the People's Republic of China. In other words, the grand design of the Soviet strategists is by giving up the present, antiquated, stagnant empire, and the outdated, ineffective Warsaw Pact, to put together a far larger, *voluntary* Marxist/Leninist-dominated federation encompassing 1.5 billion people. (Remember, Lenin said: "We advance through retreat.")

3. Another group of countries (in the region of the Indian Ocean Rim) will be brought into the new Soviet federation sometime later. Those will include: Iraq, Iran, Syria, Lebanon, India, Sri Lanka, the Philippines, and Indonesia (the latter three have yet to fall to communist insurgencies but are targeted by same).

4. The most important part of the new federation is to get the other socialist countries to join it. The goal is "voluntary" under communism (or Marxism/Leninism or social democracy if the word "communism" is abolished). The mortar which will ultimately hold together the bricks of the new federation is economics and socialist ideology. But Russian military power will also play a major role as well, as the "defender of unity."

The Russians never set timetables, but with the speed at which world events are now transpiring, much of the new federation's *internal* restructuring should be a *fait accompli* within one to three years. The *external expansion* of the new federation should be well advanced within five years.

Conclusion

By Russian definition, peace, democracy, and social progress does not exactly stand for capitalism. World communism (or should we call it social democracy), on the other hand, includes in its basic ideals the premises of peace, democracy, and social progress. Therefore, current Russian developments are strictly in line with the reorganization of the country *in order for it to achieve a better opportunity for expansion.* In the future, all political parties in the world with communist or socialist leanings, including the social and national democrats, will become partners with the CPSU for a common world movement.

As the 28th Congress (1990) stated, "The U.S.S.R. is in a transition from a unitary state to a *friendship of nations.*" This friendship of nations will comprise hundreds of millions of people not now in Russia and a greater number of nations also not now in the U.S.S.R. *We are witnessing today the birth of a new socialist-communist conglomerate which will be much more potent economically, politically, and militarily than the old Soviet Union. In countries ruled by monarchies, when the king dies, the cry goes up: "The king is dead—long live the king" (meaning the new king). In the present case it can be said,* "The empire is dead—long live the empire."

The Russians are chess geniuses (the best in the world). They see the continuing contest between the East and the West as a giant chess match. *The ultimate goal of the match is to take or checkmate the king—which is*

America. But the intermediate goal is to take the queen— which is Western Europe. Once the queen, and perhaps some of her bishops, rooks, or knights (e.g., South Africa, the Philippines, perhaps South Korea, etc.) have fallen, the king (e.g., America) becomes vulnerable. It will only be a matter of time until he falls. In the meantime, if the Soviet chess masters have to sacrifice some of their pawns, rooks, or knights (e.g., such as the Baltics, a few Eastern European countries, and some of the Soviet republics) for the greater gain of taking her opponent's queen (e.g., Western Europe), the present sacrifice is worth it. In this chess match, however, the Soviet chess masters hope to get all, or most, of their pawns, rooks, bishops, and knights back.

Chapter Twelve

The Russian Military Buildup Versus U.S. Disarmament

"Even with the START Treaty, you [the Russians] *will have the ability to destroy the U.S. in 30 minutes."*
—Gen. Colin Powell

"The effectiveness of our foreign policy is secured by the might of our country, the component part of which is our armed forces."
—Mikhail Gorbachev

In spite of the incredible political shake-up which is taking place in the old Soviet Union, the gargantuan Russian military machine remains intact and virtually unchanged. The KGB will ultimately be moved under the Russian military command, which hardly means a diminishing of the role of either organization. The Russian army still has 5 million men, 250,000 Spetznaz commandoes, and 1.5 million KGB soldiers and/ or operatives. They still have a five-to-one conventional military lead over America and a five or six-to-one strategic nuclear lead over America. At this writing, they still have 30,000 nuclear warheads targeted on America contained on some 12,000 missiles (ICBMs) and another 19,00 tactical nuclear weapons. *If the "hardline" coup had been for real, the Russian military could have launched those nuclear missiles against America, and we have zero defense against them.* We cannot stop even one of them, regardless of who is in charge—"hardliners" or "reformers."

Russian Military Education and Indoctrination

Since the Russian Revolution, the Soviet Union has considered military power as the most important force to protect the gains of socialism. Russian military forces are educated to conform with the latest theories of "scientific communism," and their armaments are updated according to the most recent developments of the sciences. *Unlike the soldier in Western countries, the Russian soldier does not serve his country first, but swears and owes his first allegiance to the Communist Party of the Soviet Union.* This is true as well for the Communist Sandinistas in the Sandinista army of Nicaragua.

To teach and to control the ideology of communism, commissars and political leaders are attached to each military unit. All Russian men undergo training and serve in the army. The training, aside from martial arts, strategy, and operation of the different types of armaments, involves a heavy dose of political and patriotic education.

During the Great Patriotic War (World War II) all education and propaganda was directed against the Nazis. But with the death of Naziism, the Russians retrained their sights from German Naziism and Japanese militarism to American imperialism. *Unfortunately, in spite of the current flagrant disinformation, we Americans remain enemy number one, and the basic education of the Russian soldier is directed at proving his superiority over the American soldier.*

Over the past 46 years since World War II, the Russians have developed an incredibly sophisticated, comprehensive, and exhaustive system of political indoctrination. It begins with children five years old up through young adults (both in and outside of the schools). The two primary organizations for this indoctrination are Komsomal (the Young Communist League) and DOSAAF (Voluntary Society for Cooperation with the Army, Air Force, and Navy).

While Komsomal is instrumental in political indoctrination, DOSAAF is the most important organization in preparing the Russian youth for war. DOSAAF operates under the military division of the Central Committee of the CPSU and the ministry of defense of the U.S.S.R. It does the compulsory pre-military training of all young men and women between the ages of 16 and 18. Most of the young population of Russia retain their membership in DOSAAF. In 1988, DOSAAF's membership exceeded 107 million people.

In the C.I.S. (the new Soviet Union), the political education of the entire population, especially of the army and pre-draft age youth, is of paramount importance. It is strongly believed that only a soldier who has been politically indoctrinated is ready to fight and perform heroically in the defense of the socialist state. Typical of the kind of anti-American political indoctrination the entire youth of the U.S.S.R. receive from age 5 to 20 is the following passage from the book *Youth Become Men In the Ranks* by General M.I. Druzhinin (a leader in DOSAAF education):

"U.S. imperialism has unleashed a previously unheard of arms race. It insolently rattles with

*the most barbaric arms of mass destruction. It
aspires to squash, with its power, liberation
movements and peoples fighting for peace. It
threatens to drag humanity into a destructive
conflagration of nuclear war. It is capable of
burning to ashes the entire civilization on our
planet. . . .*

*"It is not in vain that the Soviet armed
forces are not only the proven sentinel of our
Motherland, they are also the guarantors of
peace on earth. Were our army and navy not as
mighty as they are, were they not in possession
of such a fighting potential representing in
themselves a perfect mixture of high technology,
military mastership, and invincible moral spirit,
the reactionary imperialist circles, especially the
United States of America, would have long ago
attempted to perform aggression against the
Soviet Union and other socialist countries in
order to realize their black reverie—the destruction of socialism as a political system.*

***"Now it is common knowledge that in the
immediate past American presidents have
approved plans for nuclear attacks on our
Motherland, and not just once or twice. These
plans have had code names, "Trojan," "Drop-
shot," etc. Only the Soviet soldiers' mighty
power of retaliation and the readiness to answer
the aggressor's blow with a destructive blow,
have torn apart their fanatic plans."***

This is a small sample of the kind of anti-American
propaganda that Russian youth are being indoctrinated
with even as the Russian leadership *pretends* to be

America's friend and partner.

Recently, the trend to inject more political ideology into the armed forces has become even stronger. The reason given is the crystallization of "extremely complicated conditions of acute antagonism between the two social systems—imperialism and socialism." As Oleg A. Belkov wrote in his book, *Ready To Defend the Motherland*:

> *"Future historians will be amazed to find that to guarantee the chance of victory, the responsible individuals were counting the number of present communists in the army with more diligence than the number of machine guns and pieces of artillery."*

In other words, political indoctrination is more important than weapons.

The Russian military leadership believes war with the American imperialists is inevitable. In their writings they constantly refer to the "inevitable upcoming war." They believe that only Russia, with its armed forces, can save the world. As General Druzhinin explains the Russian view:

> *"As long as imperialism exists with its anti-humane, reactionary, and militarist essence, the danger of military attack on our Motherland remains a fact. **In recent years the danger of such aggression has especially grown**. We must be fully armed to be able to ward off probable aggression and trustfully guarantee the security of the State. Experience shows that preparation must be started beforehand to solve this problem. **We cannot wait for thunder to strike. We must***

initiate, leaning on youth of all ages. We cannot waste time. Such loss is irreplaceable and during war costs a great amount of blood. Take heed, my friends, and make your own conclusions."

Another ominous development in Russian military education and indoctrination is the resurrection of the writings, strategies, and tactics of Field Marshall Alexander Suvorov, a prominent 18th century Russian general, military genius, and strategist. Suvorov's writings on warfare strategies and tactics (first published by Suvorov in his life work, *Science To Conquer*) have recently been republished and rewritten; hundreds of thousands of copies are being widely distributed throughout the Russian military and political hierarchy. Suvorov's successful tactics of speed, maneuverability, audacious attack, etc. are now being widely studied in Russia, much as Sun Tsu's *Art of War* has been a Bible for the Russian military and KGB for decades. The resurrection of Suvorov in Russia could signal a new and far more aggressive Soviet military strategy.

Soviet Arms Acquisitions

In spite of all of the Russian's financial and political problems at home, the following areas of military expansion and war preparation continue apace:

1. Between the years of 1988 and 1990, the Russians out-produced us in eight major weapons categories.
2. In the first six years Gorbachev was in power, the Russians outproduced America in nine separate weapons categories.
3. In 1991, Gorbachev just increased the budgets of

the KGB and the Soviet military 20 percent and 37 percent for the next 12 months. Russia (according to *Time* magazine) spends 50 percent of its GNP on its military/industrial complex. America spends 6 percent (about to drop to 4.5 percent, and then 3.5 percent).

4. Gorbachev and Yeltsin have promised a mass conversion of Russia's 600 military weapons factories over to consumer goods factories. *Only six have been converted.*

5. The Russians have placed and still maintain tactical nuclear and chemical weapons in Eastern Germany, where they also still have 380,000 troops stationed. They still have a half million troops in Eastern Europe in spite of the supposed independence of that region.

6. The Russians still maintain 60 to 70 active divisions and 30 mobilization divisions in the Atlantic-to-the-Urals zone.

7. The Russians have now completed 75 deep underground civil defense structures around Moscow—each the size of the Pentagon. *Why?* They know we won't launch a first strike, but we would retaliate from submarines with SLBMs.

8. The Kremlin has just deployed 18 new rail-mobile first strike SS-24 missiles and housed them in 1,100-yard-long sheds mounted on trains. They are presently moving SS-20 missiles with a 3,000-mile range into Cuba.

9. The *Armed Forces Journal* (August 1991) lists a myriad of new conventional and strategic nuclear developments and deployments which the Russians are now implementing, including a large number of road and rail mobile, submarine, land, and air

launched nuclear missiles.

10. The Russian government recently repealed the military draft exemption for 5 million military age students. Many or all of those could now be inducted into the Russian military—which could double it from 5 million to 10 million.

11. Since the August 1991 coup, the Russian military has deployed 320 SS-25 nuclear missiles throughout the C.I.S. (a "peace gesture" no doubt). The Russian nuclear arsenal still has 12,000 long-range nuclear missiles, 30,000 warheads, and 19,000 tactical nuclear arms—all for use against the West. By way of contrast, Bush and the NATO leaders are removing all of our nuclear weapons from Europe as a "good faith" gesture. It makes sense, or does it?

12. *Five new Russian strategic weapons systems are being rapidly developed and/or deployed*, General Colin Powell, chairman of the Joint Chiefs of Staff, told the Senate Armed Forces Committee on October 1, 1991. This in spite of the Russians' present "peace and poverty posture."

13. Powell, saying that "the Soviets remain the only nation on earth capable of destroying us," described the new weapons system as:

   a. a rocket-powered, maneuverable warhead called MARV on their giant SS-18 missile;

   b. a new advanced version of the road mobile SS-25 ICBM (known as "Courier") equipped with three warheads;

   c. a new SS-25 deployment complex in Byelorrusia;

   d. a new class of nuclear submarine being produced near the White Sea port of Severodvinsk; and

   e. two new air-launched nuclear cruise missiles.

Russia, (according to the *New York Times* on February 23, 1992) continues to build sophisticated new nuclear submarines including Oscar and Akula attack submarines, and new Typhoon and Delta class submarines (launching platforms for nuclear ballistic missiles are being built at the shipyards at Severodvinsk).

U.S. Intelligence has identified 16 sites in the former Soviet Union where offensive biological weapons are being stored. The U.S.S.R. signed and violated a 1975 treaty "agreeing not to produce or stockpile" these weapons. The Russian (or C.I.S.) biological weapons arsenal includes deadly anthrax spores, additional genetically-engineered micro-organisms that cause deadly diseases; and synthetically-produced mycotoxins including the extremely deadly T-2. The Russians are making no moves to destroy millions of tons of such weapons they currently possess.

14. General George Keegan, former head of the U.S. Air Force Intelligence, says, **"The Soviets are currently implementing the most aggressive and expensive peace time civil defense program in history.** . . . Every major Soviet factory is equipped with a giant underground shelter hardened to 145 pounds per square inch; the entire Soviet worker population is protected from all but a direct nuclear hit. Every worker's apartment house built since 1980 is equipped with a similar basement shelter—so it is no longer necessary to evacuate cities."

Since the Russians know that America will *never* launch a first strike, what are they preparing for? *Answer:*

Our retaliation after *their* first strike. *While the Russian "reformers" are talking peace, cooperation, and partnership, their military is continuing a crash expansion program and is preparing for war. They are talking peace and as a country moving onto a war footing.*

The Russian Nuclear War Plan Against America

The overall Russian nuclear war plan for the U.S. (called by the Pentagon RISOP, for Red Integrated Strategic Operations Plan) is believed to cover 2,500 targets. Chief among them in approximate priority order:

1. 1,000 Minuteman and MX ICBM silos, 100 ICBM launch control centers for those silos, and another 50 command and control facilities and nuclear weapons storage depots. That makes a total of at least 1,150 "hardened"—that is fortified—weapons facilities targets. These would be hit by at least two and probably three Russian warheads each.
2. Another 54 nuclear bomber and bomber dispersal bases and at least three naval bases that service missile-firing submarines. Although these are relatively "soft" targets, they would also be targeted for multiple hits to ensure that runways and missiles would be disabled.
3. About 475 other naval bases, airfields, ports, terminals, military camps, depots, and other military installations associated with nuclear as well as conventional forces.
4. About 150 industrial facilities that have Defense Department contracts for $1 million a year or more in military hardware.

5. About 325 electric power plants that generate 70 percent of the nation's electricity.
6. About 150 oil refineries that turn out 70 percent of the nation's petroleum products.
7. About 200 "soft" economic communications, transport, chemical, and civilian leadership targets.

In these last four categories, many targets are located sufficiently close together so that only one nuclear weapon would be needed to destroy them.

Only the Strong Survive

The following article (written in late 1991) is a warning to the people of the free world from this writer's good friend, General Sir Walter Walker, former NATO commander-in-chief. General Walker, a British military hero and one of the world's greatest geo-strategic experts, has written several excellent books on Russian strategy and tactics. He accurately warned in advance about the Indonesian invasion of Borneo and the Russian invasion of Afghanistan. Like this writer, General Walker sees the Russian bear preparing for war.

"I consider it my duty, as a former NATO commander-in-chief, to tell you of the extremely dangerous threats that lie ahead. It is because I know for certain that we are now in a period of the greatest strategic deception, perhaps in all history, that I feel I should not allow this occasion to pass without warning you of the future that lies ahead in the next decade.
"I say most emphatically that the Cold War is not yet over, but only in a state of remission.

To give you examples: in spite of the number of Soviet citizens still queuing for food, the Soviet Union is continuing to provide arms not only to Iraq, but to the communist regime in Afghanistan and to its satellites, such as Cuba and Libya. Meanwhile, more and more money is being poured into the size of the cake they have cut for their own armed forces.

"In dealing with Moscow the risks will be more disturbing and much greater. The man in the street has not been told that the Soviet Union is still devoting a vast proportion of its resources to sustain a military machine capable of threatening the West.

*"As an example, their navy is engaged at present in a major rebuilding program. It has launched the 65,000-ton Tiblisi—its first major carrier. **The Western public is unaware that Gorbachev is launching one new nuclear submarine every six weeks.** The aim of this naval buildup is to sever the strategic link between America and Europe and to control the waters of the Persian Gulf and the sea lanes around the Horn of Africa. NATO without control of the seas is a nonsense.*

*"**Amid all his difficulties, Gorbachev has now increased the Soviet military budget by 37 percent at the insistence of generals and KGB masters. This represents 40 percent of the country's GNP.** On the same day that he made this increase, our defense secretary announced that 40,000 British troops, a quarter of the entire British army, would be axed. A suicidal decision. Furthermore, Western disarmament and tech-*

nology transfer is what Gorbachev and his hardline military leaders have in their sights. It is this
that would make any Grand Bargain with him
not mere folly, but a Grand Swindle.

**"The Soviet military threat has NOT
evaporated. The neutralization of NATO has
long been one of the Soviet's prime glasnost
deception goals.** Production of tanks continues
unabated, replacing old tanks, and they have
also introduced several new helicopters, a huge
transporter, a fighter designed to kill other
helicopters, and a sophisticated anti-tank
helicopter.

"Despite the collapse of the Soviet economy
—the Kremlin—under pressure from the military
—is actually increasing the military budget by
$42 billion to more than $162 billion. In contrast,
only $7.5 billion is being earmarked for educa-
tion, and a mere $4.5 billion for health. But even
consuming over **40 percent** of their GNP, this
amount may not be enough to satisfy the
military elite. If there is the risk of economic
catastrophe in the Soviet Union, then surely the
West should insist that butter must come before
guns. Any help from the West must lay down
strict conditions, the foremost being **true** freedom
and independence within the Soviet Union and
the Balkans.

**"In spite of the signing of the Conventional
Forces in Europe (CFE) Treaty on the 19th of
November, 1990, the Soviets have already moved
about 17,000 thousand tanks plus much more
equipment (e.g., 70,000 units in toto)** to the
other side of the Ural mountains—beyond the

geographical area of the treaty. And some Soviet aircraft from Hungary were repainted in Soviet naval colours, also outside the treaty.

"There has been a lot of talk recently about NATO's new look. One keeps on reading the words—I quote: 'NOW THAT THE COLD WAR IS OVER.' In light of what I am telling you, I say most emphatically that the Cold War is NOT yet over, but only in a state of remission. The hard truth is that the dreaded KGB is being strengthened and expanded. Last year the American FBI apprehended 30 foreign spies, 28 of whom were KGB, a new record. Today the KGB employs 1.5 million people and 6 million informers. And despite the Soviet economic crisis, the KGB has received a 20 percent increase in its latest budget.

"I leave you with the stark fact that unless we stand fast and stop the rot, the demonstrable truth is that, contrary to the Kremlin's self-serving pose of humility, the Soviet Union is not 'on the verge of collapse.' Western defense, on the other hand, is."

The American Stampede to Disarm

"They disarm, we build."   —Vladimir Lenin

"The Soviets intend to conceal vast 'reserves' of missiles and warheads, hiding them in places throughout the expansive Soviet Union where the 'imperialists' could not spot them. Later, they could be launched in a nuclear war."
    —Nikita Krushchev, January 14, 1960

*"Perestroika is expressly designed to enhance
Soviet military capability and combat readiness."*
—An official in the Soviet
Council of Ministers, 1987

*The "apparent" disintegration of the Soviet Empire,
death of communism, end of the Cold War, and resurgence
of the "liberal reformers" (e.g., "the forces of democracy" in
the U.S.S.R.) is causing U.S. and European political and
military leaders to accelerate their disarmament plans.*
Bush has pulled the U.S. nuclear missiles out of Europe; is
withdrawing U.S. tanks, planes, and troops from Europe;
is shutting down our tank, submarine, and F-16 production
lines; is closing hundreds of U.S. domestic military bases,
79 of America's Europan bases, and 535 of America's non-
European military facilities; has closed our huge air base in
the Philippines (Clark Field); is planning to withdraw U.S.
troops from South Korea and the Philippines; is cutting
U.S. Army troop strength by 500,000 men and the U.S.
Marines by 50 percent; is cutting the overall size of the U.S.
military by 25 percent over the next five years; and is
planning to cut America's strategic stockpiles of 91 critical
war materials by over 40 percent.

The U.S. military spending trend is such that the
U.S. will be spending only 3.6 percent of GNP on defense
by 1996 (the lowest level since *before* World War II—
when America was highly disarmed and undefended and
we were attacked at Pearl Harbor). *Meanwhile, the
Russians are spending 40 to 50 percent of their GNP on
their military.*

Bush and Gorbachev signed the START treaty in
1991 which is supposed to cut the U.S. and Russian
nuclear arsenals by 30 percent. But the Russians massively
cheated on the Nuclear Test Ban treaty of 1962; on the

ABM treaty of 1972; on SALT I; on SALT II; on the INF treaty of 1989; on the Conventional Forces in Europe treaty in 1991; and they will cheat on the new START treaty as well. It is tantamount to unilateral disarmament for the U.S. since we will adhere to the treaty, and *we know* that the Russians won't.

Meanwhile, *according to U.S. disarmament negotiator Richard Burt, the Russians are presently developing and deploying five new strategic nuclear systems.* Under START, the Russians will "seemingly" have their heavy missiles cut in half—but arms experts report that what is left will be more lethal because the SS-18s have been modernized with greater accuracy and power, and can be equipped with 14 rather than 10 warheads apiece. We have no such heavy first-strike missiles.

We also have no mobile missiles; *they get to double their number under START.* While we *talked about* MXs and Minutemen, the Kremlin deployed rail-mobile SS-24s and road-mobile SS-25s, *and will be allowed under START to develop the next generation.* Verification will be virtually impossible. During Operation Desert Storm, we couldn't find many of Saddam's Scuds, so why should we think we can find strategic missiles in an area of Russia 20 to 30 times larger than Iraq.

On June 7, 1991, the U.S. House of Representatives voted to terminate U.S. bomber production after completion of just 14 B-2 Stealth bombers now on order, in spite of the fact that the Russians outproduced us in long-range bombers 140-to-1 in 1989 and 1990. The House also voted to restrict maximum production and deployment of Peacekeeper ICBMs to 50 missiles, and to restrict missiles for "reliability testing" to just 12. These cuts were made in spite of the fact that the Russians outproduced us in ICBMs 265-to-1 in 1989 and 1990.

The House also voted (*at the recommendation of the Bush Administration*) to cut U.S. submarine production to one per year in spite of the fact that the Russians outbuilt us in submarines 29-to-14 in 1989 and 1990 and are currently building one new nuclear submarine (worth $3 billion per copy) every six weeks—that's nine per year. The House also voted (*at the recommendation of the Bush Administration*) to reduce U.S. SLBM (submarine-launched ballistic missile) production dramatically to match our downsized fleet of submarines. This in spite of the fact that the Russians outproduced us in SLBMs 375-to-107 from 1985 to 1988 and 165-to-103 in 1989 and 1990.

The House voted (*at the recommendation of the Bush Administration*) to produce *zero* short-range ballistic missiles (SRBMs) in spite of the fact that the Russians built 1,300 SRBMs in 1989 and 1990. And, in spite of continued very high levels of Russian ICBM, SLBM, SRBM, submarine and bomber production, the House voted to slash the Strategic Defense Initiative (SDI) budget—for protection against such strategic weapons— by 40 percent. The Bush Administration had requested $4.6 billion—the House voted for $2.7 billion.

In both the House Armed Services and House Appropriations Committees (which sent these "build-down/shutdown" bills to the House floor, the prevailing rationale for ending or reducing production of these strategic weapons systems was: "Not to worry. The Cold War is over. We won. Peace is at hand. We trust Gorbachev. We need the peace dividend for social programs (e.g., to buy votes)." Unfortunately, this same attitude of wishful thinking extends to the Senate, the White House, the State Department, the Establishment media, and much of the general public.

As attorney and defense consultant Jim Gerard, Jr. wrote recently:

> *"So desperate are many people for the Cold War to be over and for the so-called 'peace dividend' to be real, that they fail to notice that* **at least half of the arms race—the Soviet half— is still raging out of control.** *"*

Those who refuse to recognize the dangers inherent in these numbers are living examples of what George Orwell called "the will to disbelieve the horrible." *The "horrible" thing in this case is, of course, the notion that the Soviet leaders might be intentionally and deliberately pursuing a gigantic buildup in strategic weaponry with some evil purpose in mind.*

Be that as it may, the hard numbers show that during a period when the poverty-stricken people of Russia have not been able to afford toothpicks and toilet paper, *the Kremlin has somehow still found ways to restructure (perestroika) its scarce resources so as to continue outproducing the United States by enormous margins in all segments of the so-called "strategic triad"—missiles, bombers, and submarines.*

In the face of such an unrelenting strategic arms buildup by the Russian leaders, we and our NATO and Japanese allies should reject as wildly preposterous any "Grand Bargain" proposal for massive economic assistance to the C.I.S. (e.g., $35-$50 billion per year has been requested by Yeltsin and is being seriously considered in high U.S. circles at this writing).

The Bush Disarmament of America

On September 27, 1991, citing our move toward a "new world" and a "new age" of peace and cooperation between the superpowers, George Bush announced the most sweeping U.S. unilateral disarmament in American history, described by the *New York Times* as "the most *one-sided* cut in nuclear armaments ever announced by a great power." Aspects of the Bush disarmament include:

1. Elimination of the Strategic Air Command.
2. Grounding and shutting down of America's airborne command and control aircraft and early warning system.
3. *All* strategic bombers (e.g., 280) have been grounded and pulled off of around-the-clock alert status and their bombs placed in storage. These nuclear-armed bombers have flown 24 hours a day for 34 years. It will take 24 hours to rearm them and put them back in the air. *A Russian first strike against America will take less than 30 minutes.*
4. 450 Minuteman II ICBMs were pulled off of alert status and will be scrapped. The grounding of the B-1Bs and B-52s and non-alert status of our missiles was put into effect just hours after Bush's speech. What is the big rush?
5. Two rail-mobile missile basing programs for the MX and Midgetman were cancelled.
6. *All* sea-launched nuclear cruise missiles (including 800 that would have been permitted under START) and *all* tactical nuclear weapons will be removed from *all* U.S. submarines and warships, including *all* aircraft carriers, and from *all* land-based naval aircraft. Intelligence sources say that *all* nuclear weapons will be withdrawn from *all* U.S. warships in the near future.
7. *All* ground-based U.S. tactical nuclear weapons will be removed from Western Europe and Asia,

including South Korea, and destroyed. NATO is now talking about removing *all* nuclear weapons from Western Europe.

8. *All* short-range missile warheads will be removed from U.S. bases all over the world and, along with *all* nuclear artillery shells, will be destroyed.

9. A quarter of the U.S. Air Force personnel will be cut; tactical Air Force Wings will be cut by almost a third from 36 to 26; the number of Air Force Commands will be cut from 13 to 10; and up to a third of the Air Force's 45 bases will be closed.

10. The U.S. Army will be cut by 500,000 troops and the U.S. Marines will be cut by 50 percent to just over 50,000 troops. The Pentagon says that U.S. active duty forces (even before Bush's new cuts) are at their lowest level in over 40 years (since before the Korean War) and are about to drop to their lowest level since 1937 (pre-World War II).

11. U.S. ground-based ballistic missiles with multiple warheads will be dramatically reduced and eventually totally eliminated. Bush has offered to open discussions with the Russians on the same *immediately*.

12. U.S. forces in Europe will be cut from 260,000 to 150,000 and eliminated within five years. Of the U.S. bases in Europe, 79 will be reduced in size or closed and some 500 U.S. military installations worldwide will either be reduced or closed.

The *New York Times* (September 29, 1991) said:

"In a single speech, President Bush had transformed the security apparatus that has shielded Americans for 40 years and has granted much of

the disarmament of the U.S. the Soviet Union has long sought, including elimination of all tactical nuclear weapons abroad and on Navy ships at sea."

America is in grave danger! Communism is *not* dead, the Cold War is *not* over, peace has *not* arrived, and throughout the recent political upheaval in the U.S.S.R., the gargantuan Russian military has *not* been touched or diminished in any way. It still numbers 6.75 million men, including the army, air force, navy, internal police, KGB, and Spetznaz. Ninety percent of the officers of the Red army and navy are members of the Communist Party of the Soviet Union, or the Komsomal Communist Youth League; 80 percent of all pilots in the air force, over 90 percent of all officers of rocket submarines, 95 percent of all officers in anti-aircraft and ABM defense, and 100 percent of the rocket and nuclear forces are CPSU members.

All of these have had an incredibly comprehensive and exhaustive system of indoctrination from age five to adulthood. *Contrary to popular belief in the West, the Russian military is highly disciplined, extremely well-trained, very patriotic, heavily indoctrinated with Marxist/Leninist revolutionary doctrine*, and is not staffed by the stereotype blockheads, buffoons, or dullards which most Westerners have been led to believe.

The Russian military spent a decade training its people and testing weapons, battlefield techniques, etc. in Afghanistan. It is by far the best armed military in the world (five or six times better armed than America). Its weapons are excellent, sophisticated, battlefield functional, and in many instances based on U.S. technology—stolen, sold, or given free gratis.

America is today at a tremendous psychological

disadvantage. *One should never underestimate one's enemy* and yet most Americans have been led to believe that the Russians, their leaders, their KGB, and their military are incompetent, bumbling buffoons. *This stereotype has been exacerbated by Russian disinformation.* Conversely, Americans believe in the wake of Operation Desert Storm that we are invincible, in spite of the fact that we faced third- or fourth-rate Russian weapons, a country the size of the state of Kentucky, and except for Russian air defenses and Scud attacks, Saddam's forces *never* engaged our troops.

The Bible says, *"Pride cometh before the fall."* A very proud, overconfident America now believes that nothing can touch us—certainly not the "bumpkin" Russians. Hence, our stampede to disarm.

If the Central Committee of the Communist Party or the Soviet military high command should decide that the time to take out the U.S. was appropriate, they could do so immediately and totally—and with very little pain from U.S. second-strike or retaliation. America could not stop even one of the incoming missiles. We have *no* missile defense and *no* civil defense. And it should be remembered that the Russian military commanders are not "reformers"—they are *all* "hardliners." And they didn't hestitate to kill 1.5 million innocent men, women, and children in Afghanistan over the past decade.

America, in the early 1990s, is most certainly asleep to its danger, as it was on December 6, 1941; or as Europe was in 1938-39; or as Troy was the day before it brought the giant wooden horse into its gates. Troy had had a long and bloody war with the Greeks. Then suddenly, the Greeks gave up, admitted their inferiority, their inadequacy, and weaknesses, declared defeat and surrender, and sailed their ships off into the sunset.

But first, they left a token of their esteem on the beach—a gift, a good luck omen, a war reparation for their "noble conquerors"—a giant wooden horse. With the gift was left instructions to bring the great horse into their city gates for good luck and as a token of the Greeks' admiration, friendship, and esteem for "their conquerors."

The proud and overconfident Trojans brought the wooden horse into their gates. That night, the Greek ships turned around and sailed back to Troy and their troops inside the belly of the great horse opened the gates of Troy. *That night Troy fell—never to rise again—a victim of strategic deception.* As Sun Tsu and the Greeks understood, "all warfare is based on deception." Could America and Western Europe be the Troy of the 20th century?

Conclusion

This writer concludes that communism is *not* dead; the Cold War is *not* over; the Communist Party of Russia and the KGB have *not* been dismantled; and peace on earth has *not* arrived. *We live in the age of deception. Our leaders are deceiving us* as they push us into a world government, into the New World Order. They see the merger of the common interests of America and the C.I.S., a partnership between the two superpowers, as the cornerstone of their global government under the United Nations.

The Russians are deceiving us as they feign peace, brotherhood, the end of the Cold War, and the death of communism—even as they prepare for war.

The Russians are currently purging the inefficiencies and deadwood from their system; *they are reorganizing and restructuring and renaming the Russian system from top to bottom in order to expand it.* They are inundating the West with disinformation regarding their true intentions. They are "lulling the people of America and the West to sleep with the greatest overtures of peace and disarmament known throughout history," and we are stampeding to disarm.

Today we hear our leaders telling us that "there will be peace in our day," but the Bible warns to beware when men cry, *"Peace, peace, and there is no peace."* And in 1 Thessalonians 5:3 we read, *"For when they say peace and safety; then sudden destruction cometh upon them, as travail upon a woman with child, and they shall not escape."*

What We Should Do

Howard Phillips (chairman of the Conservative Caucus) has published a 10-point plan for victory over communism which this writer believes that U.S. and Western leaders should adhere to instead of their insane policy of propping up and aiding the communist regimes around the world.

1. *Stop Paying Moscow's Bills*—No more foreign aid to still-communist governments, such as Poland, Romania, or the C.I.S. (the new Soviet Union). Let them first dismantle their military, their KGB, and their massive gulag.
2. *Stop Feeding the Soviet Army*—No more multi-billion-dollar U.S. taxpayer-subsidized grain sales to the U.S.S.R. No more write-offs from the Commodity Credit Corporation.
3. *Stop Giving Moscow Advanced U.S. Technology*—Restore the technology transfer limits which President Bush has liberalized or lifted.
4. *Stop Tax-Subsidized Business Ventures In the U.S.S.R.*—No more U.S. Export-Import Bank

credit and loan guarantees. No communist business insurance from OPIC—the government-subsidized Overseas Private Investment Corporation.

5. *Stop Signing Arms Control Treaties With Moscow* —SALT, START, INF, and CFE disarm U.S. strength, while Moscow continues to lie, cheat, and build.

6. *Stop the Unilateral Disarmament of U.S. Military Strength*—Yeltsin (and before him, Gorbachev) is working on a 45 percent buildup of the Russian war machine. In 1991, they outproduced us 3-to-1 in nuclear submarines, and 11-to-1 in ICBMs. But Bush and Congress have agreed to substantial U.S. military cutbacks.

7. *Stop U.S.-Backed Bank Loans to Moscow*—With Bush's help, Moscow now participates in GATT and has now been granted membership in the U.S.-subsidized IMF and World Bank—to which we're being asked to give another $12 billion. This must be stopped.

8. *Stop Delaying Vital U.S. Defense Programs*— SDI must be deployed now. Bush should immediately give six months notice of withdrawal from the ABM treaty which prohibits SDI deployment.

9. *Stop Selling Out Anti-Communist Freedom Fighters*—From Angola to Afghanistan, from Mozambique to Cambodia, the Bush Administration has, and continues to sacrifice brave anticommunists by either aiding the communists or cutting back support for our friends.

10. *Stop Deceiving the American People*—It does not help America to rescue the Communist Party of Russia or its Leninist leadership. Our leaders should be encouraged to tell the truth.

Chapter Thirteen

Racing Toward the New World Order, Part I

"We at the executive level here were active in either the OSS, the State Department, or the European Economic Administration. During those times, and without exception, we operated under directives issued by the White House. We are continuing to be guided by just such directives, the substance of which were to the effect that **we should make every effort to so alter life in the United States as to make possible a comfortable merger with the Soviet Union.**"
> —H. Rowan Gaither, President of the Ford Foundation, 1953

"In politics, nothing happens by accident. If it happens, you can bet it was planned that way."
> —Franklin D. Roosevelt

"U.S. President Bush and Soviet President Gorbachev arrived yesterday on this Mediterranean Island for a summit conference beginning today during which both hope to start the search for a **New World Order.**"
> —New York Times (Dec. 1, 1989)

America is run today by people from what this writer calls the liberal Eastern Establishment. Made up of some of America's wealthiest finance capitalists (e.g., the Rockefellers, Andreas', Hammers, and hundreds more) and certain liberal leaders in the media, the military, academia, and politics, this group dominates both U.S. political parties, the largest U.S. banks, and multinational corporations. It has as two of its prime U.S. political organizations the Council on Foreign Relations and the Trilateral Commission. This Establishment group has controlled U.S. foreign policy since the 1920s, and liaises closely with the British Fabian Socialists, the Bilderburgers, the Socialist International, the Club of Rome and other internationalist groups who are working for a one-world government. Their catch phrases for world government are: "new world," "new world order," "one world," etc.

This group totally dominated the Carter Administration, had heavy influence in the Reagan Administration, and totally dominates the Bush Administration. Building up communist governments such as in Russia and the People's Republic of China, as a stepping stone toward world government and for mega-profits for their banking/corporate allies, is standard operating procedure for this group.

This group believes indeed that the "common interests of America and Russia can be merged" (like any corporate merger or leveraged buyout), much as one of their minions, Rowan Gaither said in 1953. That is why successive U.S. administrations keep pumping billions of dollars in aid and high-tech transfers into communist countries. Actually this group, and its now-deceased associates, have been financially supporting the Bolsheviks since before 1917. Alexander Solzhenitsyn has said of this group:

*"There also exists another alliance—at first
glance a strange one, a surprising one—but if
you think about it, one which is well grounded
and easy to understand. This is the alliance
between our communist leaders and your
capitalists."*

Woodrow Wilson said of them:

*"There is a power so organized, so subtle, so
watchful, so interlocked, so complete, so persuasive that prudent men had better not speak
above their breath when they speak of it."*

These groups are comprised of socialists who not
only look on freedom for the masses with disdain, but
who would feel comfortable running Big Brother's
Orwellian system described in *1984*. They are pushing for
massive socialist legislation in America, for an end to
financial privacy and ultimately a cashless society, and for
a series of regional governments around the world
(probably three) leading toward the New World Order by
the turn of the century. The United States of Western
Europe is emerging in 1992 as one of those; the North
American Common Market including Canada, the U.S.,
and Mexico is another. A Japanese/Pacific Rim Community will be the third. This corresponds to Zbigniew
Brzezinski's trilateral group of North America, Europe,
and Japan. By odd coincidence, George Orwell's *1984*
also had three regional governments: Oceania, Eurasia,
and Eastasia.

The United States of Western Europe

Conceptualized by French socialist Jean Monnet in
the post-war years, the European Economic Community

was born, evolved into the European Community, and in 1992 will become the United States of Western Europe. This economic union is about to become a political union, pushed through and headed by Europe's most fanatical socialists and one-worlders. This united Europe will be run *by* socialists, *for* socialists, and is seen as a quantum jump toward world government before the end of the decade.

George Bush and his Establishment associates want America to join in the union. U.S. Secretary of State James Baker, speaking in Berlin on December 12, 1989, said, "We are Europeans—we will create a new Europe on the basis of Atlanticism."

America's liberal Eastern Establishment wants America to join, as a giant step toward the New World Order which Bush and his associates speak of so longingly. As America enters, the name will probably be changed to Atlantic Community.

Yeltsin and the Politburo want to join for all the economic, financial, and high-tech advantages the Russians would gain, and for the leverage Russia would achieve over Western Europe. Gorbachev has spoken longingly of a united Europe from Vladivostok to the Atlantic—"a common European home for all of us." The Soviet leadership intends to become the controlling partner in this new axis. A reunited Germany would join and economically dominate the newly created Europe. Then a restructured Russia could join and dominate them both. By 1995 all of Eastern Europe and Russia are likely to be part of this European union.

Note: Uniting all of Europe has been tried before. Imperial Rome tried to unite Europe by force, and failed. Napoleon tried twice to unite Europe by force, and failed. But now Europe is to be united voluntarily from the Atlantic to the Pacific. A growing number of students of

Bible prophecy believe that a united Europe is a forerunner to the Armageddon scenario.

The countries in the united Europe will give up a great deal of their national sovereignty. In France, for example, the surrender of sovereignty to Europe has created a situation where 40 percent of France's laws now stem from Common Market directives rather than from the French National Assembly. The same loss of sovereignty would apply for other European members and the U.S. as well *when* we join. And that is *before* Europe is even fully functioning. Only Margaret Thatcher, of all major Western leaders, saw the danger and was trying to keep Great Britain out. The socialists in her own party sacked her because of her opposition to Britain's entry into the European branch of the New World Order.

As Larry Abraham said in his *Insider Report* (March 1990) regarding the emerging New World Order:

> *"All of Europe—not just Russia or the Eastern bloc—is in the process of perestroika, or 'restructuring.' The first step is already finalized with the 1992 common currency for the EEC. This will be followed by the gradual surrender of national sovereignty to the European Parliament.*
>
> *"The so-called Warsaw Pact nations will remain intact but will ultimately join this 'Urals to the Atlantic' federation. Mr. Gorbachev calls it 'our common home.' These steps are being initiated with meetings and agreements with the Conference on Security and Cooperation in Europe (CSCE). Watch for this organization to take on increased importance.*
>
> *"The U.S. and Soviet Union will join together in a 'superpower' alliance to act as world*

cops for preserving and enhancing the New World Order. I have called the process 'The Greening of the Reds.' It will include their participation in such things as environmental protection, the war on drugs, and terrorism. The broad scope of this cooperation was keyed by Mr. Gorbachev in his U.N. speech last December and will start to take shape with new agreements strenghtening the role of the World Court.

"The New World Order agenda has been pursued relentlessly since the end of World War II with no interruptions in strategy and only occasional shifts in tactics. The final question we need to answer is, 'Is it really so bad?' My unequivocal answer is yes. Yes, because in the process we will lose more of our freedoms and most of our wealth. As the insiders' age-old dream of a New World Order comes closer and closer to realization, our personal options will be narrowed. We will, as Carroll Quigley said in Tragedy and Hope, *'be numbered from birth' and 'be followed through life.' It is George Orwell's nightmarish vision of the future come true."*

The New Age World Government

The New Age movement, a loose network of millions of people and thousands of organizations around the globe from environmentalists to occultists to satanists, believe their christ (not the Jesus Christ of the Bible) is alive and well on planet earth today and will soon reveal himself. The New Agers talk of a global government by the year 2000 and their government sounds like the socialist global government of the New World Order crowd, replete with computers and other high-tech devices to control the over-populated masses.

Some New Agers believe that about one-third of the world's population, who cannot adjust to their new program (e.g., about 2 billion people) will have to be terminated (e.g., killed). Before one totally dismisses the New Agers as irrelevant kooks, it should be remembered that their belief system sprang from an Indian-Hindu sect, and is almost identical to the occultic beliefs which permeated and energized Adolf Hitler and the Nazi's Third Reich.

Many New Agers are also part of the New World Order movement, high up in the liberal Eastern Establishment, and bring with them an occultic dimension to their socialist/globalist views. For example, Zbigniew Brezezinski, one of the three founders of the Trilateral Commission and an Establishment leader in the New World Order movement, is said to be a prominent New Ager.

Conclusion

The Club of Rome is one of the most powerful and influential of the elitist one-world groups. The Club states: "Only a revolution, the substitution of a new world economic order can save us." The COR intends to control international trade, world food, world minerals, and ocean management (*H. Du B. Reports*, Apr. 1985).

The COR is pushing for a cashless society. The book *Microelectronics and Society: A Report To the Club of Rome*, edited by Friedrichs and Schaff, states:

"The move to a cashless society seems inevitable, given the technological push provided by micro-

*electronics and significant cost advantages assoc-
iated with the transfer of funds electronically."*

On April 18, 1980, the *Calgary Albertan* carried an
article entitled "Club of Rome Says: 'Messiah Needed.' "
In the article, Aurelio Peccei (now deceased), founder and
president of the COR stated:

*"A charismatic leader—scientific, political, or
religious—would be the world's only salvation
from the social and economic upheavals that
threaten to destroy civilization. Such a leader
would have to override national and international
interests as well as political and economic
structures in order to lead humanity away from
the maladies that afflict it."*

Could that charismatic leader be a Gorbachev, a
Yeltsin, a Bush, or a Perot? Today, Gorbachev is still the
most popular man in Europe and in the world. Whatever
the answer, the 1990s promise *not* to be dull!

Could we soon see the rise of Antichrist? Is the stage
being set for a one-world government, for Armageddon?

Chapter Fourteen

Racing Toward the New World Order, Part II

*"This is an historic moment. We have in the past year made great progress in ending the long era of the Cold War. We have before us the opportunity to forge for ourselves and for future generations a New World Order, a world where the rule of law, not the law of the jungle, governs the conduct of the nations. When we are successful, **and we will be**, we have a real chance at the **New World Order**, an order in which a credible United Nations can use its peacekeeping role to fulfill the promise and vision of the U.N. founders."*

—George Bush addressing the
nation as America began bombing
Iraq on January 16, 1991

"[The Gulf Crisis] **has to do with a New World Order**. *And that world order is only going to be enhanced if this newly activated peacekeeping function of the United Nations proves to be effective. That is the only way the New World Order will be enhanced."*

—George Bush, January 9, 1991

George Bush and his government officials now refer to the *New World Order* one or more times in every speech he makes and has done so since the summer of 1990. Bush invoked the New World Order twice in his Helsinki summit address on September 9, 1990; four times in his address to Congress on September 11, 1990; twice the night he addressed the nation as America attacked Iraq on January 16, 1991; once at the National Religious Broadcasters convention in Washington, D.C. (on January 28, 1991—this writer was present as 3,500 religious broadcasters gave the president a standing ovation); twice in his State of the Union address (January 29, 1991), and dozens of other times. Mikhail Gorbachev and Boris Yeltsin also refer to this New World Order in most of their public speeches. What is this New World Order which the two superpower leaders repeatedly refer to?

Bush's, Yeltsin's, and Gorbachev's vision of a New World Order *is a global government under the United Nations wherein the "common interests" of all the countries in the world are merged into one government and one political system.* In such a world government, all the nations of the world would surrender their sovereignty to the United Nations or to the powerful group which runs that government. It is to be the new Tower of Babel.

Henry Kissinger said in 1965:

> *"The ultimate goal of a supra-nationalist world community will not come quickly . . . but it is not too early to prepare ourselves for this step beyond nation-state."*

Senator Barry Goldwater said in his 1979 book, *With No Apologies*:

> *"In my view the Trilateral Commission represents*

*a skillful, coordinated effort to seize control and consolidate the four centers of power—political, monetary, intellectual, and ecclesiastical. All this is to be done in the interest of creating a more peaceful, more productive world community. What the Trilaterals truly intend is the **creation of a worldwide economic power superior to the political governments of the nation-states involved.** They believe the abundant materialism they propose to create will overwhelm existing differences. **As managers and creators of the system, they will rule the future.** "*

What Is the New World Order?

The New World Order is being pushed by the world's most powerful socialists, communists, internationalists, and New Agers. Willy Brandt, former chancellor of West Germany, chairman of the Fifth-Socialist International, and long-time Soviet collaborator, recently chaired the Brandt Commission which gave a rather accurate definition of the New World Order. (Former World Bank president Robert McNamara, former Secretary of Commerce Peter Peterson, and *Newsweek's* Katherine Graham were all members of that commission.)

The New World Order, as defined by the Brandt Commission, is a world that has a supernational authority to regulate world commerce and industry; an international organization that would control the production and consumption of oil; an international currency that would replace the dollar; a World Development Fund that would make funds available to free and communist nations alike; and an international police force (probably the U.N.) to enforce the edicts of the New World Order.

Note: The first major enforcement effort of the New World Order was the Persian Gulf War.

What is George Bush's definition of the New World Order? When asked in a news conference on February 6, 1991 for his definition of the New World Order, Mr. Bush replied:

> *"It was the farsighted vision of Mr. Gorbachev that enabled us to work together in the United Nations. . . . **My vision of a New World Order foresees a United Nations with a revitalized peacekeeping function.** . . . The peacekeeping function for the most part has not been effective. And one of the reasons it hasn't is because of the veto in the hands of the five permanent members of the Security Council—one of them being the Soviet Union.*
>
> *"When I was ambassador 20 years ago in the U.N., we hardly ever voted with the Soviet Union. Now we're with them on many, many things. **So, the New World Order, I think, foresees a revitalized peacekeeping function of the United Nations.** . . .*
>
> *"And so **it would envision, though, much more cooperation between the United States and the Soviet Union.** . . .*
>
> *"We should have and should strive to have Soviet cooperation all along the way. And that's why I'm not going to back off on my efforts to try to improve relations with the Soviet Union.*
>
> *". . . We've left China out of the equation, and we ought not to do that. They've been through a difficult time. I took on some shots for trying to keep relations with China. . . . It is*

vital to this New World Order."

Note: Liberals and Bush apologists, concerned about the president's overuse of the term *New World Order*, and the furor it has caused among conservatives, have begun downplaying the concept by saying, "It is just meaningless rhetoric inserted in Bush's speeches by an enthusiastic speechwriter." This is called "operation coverup."

A world government, by its highly centralized nature, would be socialistic; would be accompanied by redistribution of wealth; strict regimentation; and would incorporate severe limitations on freedom of movement, freedom of worship, private property rights, free speech, the right to publish, and other basic freedoms.

Some of the elements of a New World Order would be: a world tax system (David Rockefeller says, "The answer is a supra-national political being with the power to tax." Zbigniew Brezezinski said in his 1970 book, *Between Two Ages*, that *the world government would need a global taxation system*); a world court; a world army; a world central bank; a world welfare state; compulsory worldwide economic planning; abolition of private firearms; mandatory population and environmental control; and centralized control of education. A world government will need a world police force, and the U.S. (and eventually the Russian) military are slated to become the core of such a U.N. police force.

Groups such as the Council on Foreign Relations (with 350 of its 2,500 members in the Bush Administration), the Trilateral Commission, the Bilderbergers, Britain's Fabian Socialists, Socialist International, Club of Rome, the Illuminati, the New Age movement, etc., have pushed for world government for decades (in the case of the Illuminati for over 200 years). In the 1930s, globalists quietly placed the inscription *"Novus Ordo Seclorum"* (the New World Order) on the back of the U.S. one dollar bill below the pyramid and the all-seeing eye— which is the symbol of the Illuminati. *These groups have always operated in secret. Now they feel so bold, they feel their (conservative, anti-communist, Christian) opposition is so weak, that the masses are so psychologically conditioned or prepared, that the reality of world government is so near, that they have decided to go public and tell the world their plans. They see their victory, their establishment of the world government as a fait accompli. They believe they can install their New World Order over the next few years (by the mid-1990s).*

What Part Does the United Nations Play In the New World Order?

"I challenge the illusion that the U.N. is an instrument of peace. It could not be less of a cruel hoax if it had been organized in Hell for the sole purpose of aiding and abetting the destruction of the United States."
— J.B. Matthews, former chief investigator for the House Committee on Un-American Activities

After World War I, the League of Nations was established with the hope of its founders that it would become a world government. After World War II, the United Nations was founded with the hope that it would become the new world government. When George Bush recently referred to the "ability of the United Nations finally to become a peacekeeping organization its founders

envisioned," he was referring to world government under
the U.N. As *Time* magazine said in late 1990:

> *"If Bush has led the U.S. to the brink of a
> wrenching war, he has also raised the vision of a
> New World Order. In it, the U.S. and the Soviet
> Union, the superpowers that kept the world in
> dread of nuclear annihilation for 40 years,
> would cooperate to maintain peace and order,
> and the U.N. would deter aggression as its
> founders intended 45 years ago."*

Note: Quite to the contrary, the U.N. has been a
catalyst for war for 46 years, having induced 157 wars
since 1945.

Should freedom-loving people have any concern
about a New World Order under the U.N.? Yes! The U.N.
has been dominated by Russia since their agents (Alger
Hiss—U.S. undersecretary of state, and Harry Dexter
White—U.S. undersecretary of treasury) and 14 other
communists helped write the U.N. charter in 1944-45. Hiss
(a Soviet spy) set up 66 U.N. agencies and staffed them with
500 of his own people. Since 1945, the U.N. has functioned
as a giant pro-Soviet Trojan horse in our midst.

When Hiss and his comrades set up the U.N., they set
up the Department of Political and Security Council
Affairs, which would have jurisdiction over all future
U.N. military operations. Written into the fine print of the
rules and regulations which govern the U.N. is the rule
that the head of this U.N. department will always be a
Soviet citizen, military officer, or person designated by
the Soviets. This has been the case for the past 47 years,
with the following 14 communists having chaired that
vital U.N. post since 1946:

1946-49—Arkady Sobolev (U.S.S.R.)
1949-53—Konstantin Zinchenko (U.S.S.R.)
1953-54—Ilya Tchernychev (U.S.S.R.)
1954-57—Dragoslav Protitch (U.S.S.R.)
1958-60—Anatoly Dobrynin (U.S.S.R.)
1960-62—Georgy Arkadev (U.S.S.R.)
1962-63—E.D. Kiselyv (U.S.S.R.)
1963-65—V.P. Suslov (U.S.S.R.)
1965-68—Alexei E. Nesterenko (U.S.S.R.)
1968-73—Leonid N. Kutakov (U.S.S.R.)
1973-78—Arkady N. Shevchenko (U.S.S.R.)
1978-81—Mikhail D. Sytenko (U.S.S.R.)
1981-86—Viacheslav A. Ustinov (U.S.S.R.)
1987-90—Vasilly S. Safronchuk (U.S.S.R.)

In September 1961, the State Department published Freedom From War—The U.S. Program for General and Complete Disarmament in a Peaceful World. This publication called for disbanding "all national armed forces and the prohibition of their re-establishment in any form whatsoever other than those required to preserve internal order and for contributions to a United Nations peace force." The sharp contraction in the U.S. military over the past 25 years has accelerated in the wake of the Persian Gulf War; and Bush and the New World Order crowd in the U.S., Europe, and Russia will push hard for a New World Order/ U.N. army to replace all national armies as per the Freedom From War blueprint. (The State Department, Freedom From War—publication No. 7277, is available for $1. Write to the John Birch Society, 770 Westhill Blvd., Appleton, WI 54915; or call 414-749-3780.)

Note: George Bush's action in taking the U.S. to war under U.N. authority, rather than U.S. congressional (constitutional) authority, is a strong message that he believes the United Nations treaty, charter, and organization supersedes the authority of the U.S. Constitution. The U.N. police force of a future New World Order world government would be headed by a Soviet military officer, citizen, or designee. This is one reason Yeltsin and Gorbachev are pushing so hard for the New World Order under the United Nations.

The *New York Times* wrote on March 6, 1992, in an article entitled "The New World Army":

> *"The bill for 11 U.N. peacekeeping missions involving 77,000 blue helmeted U.N. troops could approach $3.7 billion this year. Never before have so many U.N. troops been committed to so many costly and diverse missions. . . . U.N. forces were asked to disarm guerrillas, conduct elections, and enforce human rights, first in Namibia, then in Cambodia (e.g., 22,000), in Yugoslavia (e.g., 14,000), and El Salvador. The Security Council recently expanded the concept of threats to peace to include economic, social, and ecological instability."*

The permanent U.N. rapid deployment force is about to be formed. The *New York Times* welcomed the growing power of the U.N.:

> *"One promising possibility is to make fuller use of the U.N. Charter. Article 43 already calls on members to make available 'armed forces assistance and facilities' necessary to maintain international peace."*

The *New York Times* then suggested that part of the

U.S. defense budget *go directly* to the U.N.

In March 1992, the U.N. imposed sanctions on Libya. It still maintains sanctions against Iraq and South Africa. One recent newspaper headline said, "Saddam Can't Be Allowed to Disobey the U.N." Large numbers of U.S. and Russian troops will soon be serving under the U.N. flag instead of their own flags in what is rapidly becoming the New World Order army. Operation Desert Storm was the first major enforcement action of that army.

Note: It should be remembered that the U.S. Constitution says that treaties the U.S. signs supersede the U.S. Constitution—*and that includes the U.N. treaty and charter! This writer predicts that within three to five years, U.N. troops will be stationed on U.S. soil—to maintain the peace, the environment, civil obedience, and human rights, and to help fight the "drug war" and against American "dissidents" (e.g., conservatives, patriots, and upholders of the U.S. Constitution).*

George Bush:
The New World Order President

"George Bush looks upon himself as the chairman of the board of Skull and Bones International. He gets together with all the leaders of the world, and they decide this, that, and the other."
— Patrick Buchanan, *New York Times*, February 1, 1992

*"Some of these fellows have to wake up and realize it's not 1939 anymore. **Most of these folks (the Bush crowd) are globalists. They***

believe in subordinating American sovereignty to some globalist New World Order. When I see European countries giving up their currencies, giving up their control of trade . . . when I see George Bush engaged in the unilateral economic disarmament of his own country, I say watch out."

—Patrick Buchanan in New
Hampshire, February 1992

George Bush has talked about the New World Order over 200 times in public speeches since 1990. It is not just the figment of one of his speech writer's imaginations. *It is the world government under the United Nations (not the U.S. Constitution) talked and written about and planned for decades by globalists, Marxist/Leninists (e.g., Fidel Castro first talked of a New World Order in 1979 and Gorby began to preach the New World Order in 1987), and New Agers. The sovereignty of the U.S. Constitution would be replaced by the sovereignty of the U.N. charter or some international constitution.*

The U.S. military would be under the U.N. flag (as it technically was in Korea and Operation Desert Storm); a global currency, banking system, Environmental Protection Agency, educational system, population control authority, gun control mechanism, and police force under the U.N. are all talked about openly by Bush and his establishment comrades as integral parts of the New World Order. *The welfare of the "citizens of the world" is far more important to Bush and his New World Order associates than the welfare (or jobs) of Americans.*

Bush's Operation Desert Storm, which stopped the U.S. military just short of victory, was fought, in the words of the president, "as a stepping stone to the New

World Order." It was the first military enforcement action of the New World Order.

The New Financial World Order

The following is excerpted from the excellent *Ron Paul Investment Letter*:

"*When Bush goes around the globe implementing the New World Order, he is doing more than signing trade pacts, giving away money, and instituting cooperative military arrangements. He is also making your bank accounts subject to globalist prying. Yet this is part of the New World Order that is never mentioned in the media: the effort to unite the IRSes of the world in a global data base, with an enforcement network to make all financial transactions subject to bureaucratic scrutiny.*

"*The goal is to eliminate private financial transactions wherever they occur. The means include U.N. treaties, pacts among the various members of the Organization for Economic Cooperation and Development, and Treasury Department bullying.*

"*The United States has always taken the lead, as they say in Washington, on tax evasion, money laundering, and financial privacy. This country has some of the worst laws in the world. Today, American banks are an arm of the (usually unjust) law. Even check-cashing companies and wire-transfer businesses have become government handmaidens.*

"*Major retail outlets have been terrified by*

sting operations, and now fear anyone using cash. **Customs, IRS, BATF, and Secret Service all conduct their own investigations to make retailers file 8300 forms on cash users.** *Texas has been swept (agents found $5.5 million in unreported cash); Buffalo, New York ($3.5 million); and so has Arkansas ($2.5 million). Before the Christmas holidays, tax agents visited more than 5,000 businesses. [Note: the form 8300 has a box to check if the customer exhibits 'suspicious behavior.' In the New World Order, we are all to spy on each other, just as in Russia.]*

"The IRS isn't shy about its goals in mandating 8300 filings. 'The information is also much more than a weapon in the war on drugs,' says one news release, continuing, 'the cash transaction reports can also reveal tax evaders who hope to remain hidden by dealing in cash.'

*"***The United States is the only nation in the world to have a full-scale, high-tech, computerized agency devoted to collecting financial information on American citizens, the better to intimidate and prosecute them.*** That agency is the Financial Crimes Enforcement Network. Americans know nothing about it, but **it has become the model for other industrialized nations trying to gain control of their underground economies.***

"Thus, it makes sense that the United States lead in imposing a New Financial World Order. What the U.S. has been able to accomplish toward this end globally may pale with what the government has done to us domestically. But nonetheless, the steps undertaken are unprecedented.

"The primary means is the Mutual Legal Assistance Treaty, or MLAT, the most severe of all international financial pacts. **The MLAT is a written agreement between the United States and other nations to cooperate in collecting information on anything each government deems a financial crime and tracking money flows between countries and within each respective banking system. The MLAT also guarantees mutual assistance in finding people, confiscating property, and taking cases of financial crimes to court.**

"Once all significant countries have MLATs with the U.S., world planners will turn their efforts toward **a world headquarters for tax investigation and prosecution, assisted and implemented by the International Criminal Police Organization, known as Interpol.**

"The first MLAT was signed with Switzerland. It has bred 20 others. The plan is to ensure that the U.S. has an MLAT with every country in the world, especially the 'troubling' countries that have banking systems with relative privacy. And pressure of all sorts is applied. The Canadian and Mexican agreement occurred in the midst of negotiations to create trade preferences for them in the North American trade bloc, and the Panamanian agreement came after our military invasion.

"The financial records of banks, retailers, and individuals are being made available to foreign authorities, without public announcement or the permission of the people harmed. And foreign governments are cooperating in

prosecuting Americans for the crime of doing business away from D.C. scrutiny.

"Thus we see the Financial New World Order. It is the creation of an elite system of interconnected governments and bureaucrats, which conspires to tax, regulate, and inflate away the wealth held by the middle class peoples of countries around the world, in the name of global democracy."

The U.N. International Covenant on Civil and Political Rights

On February 1, 1992, the chiefs of state of 20 countries, headed by George Bush, met at the United Nations and declared:

"The world community can no longer allow advancement of fundamental rights to stop at national borders. . . . That the U.N. abandon its tradition of non-interference in internal affairs of member countries. . . . The U.N. should play a more active role in combating abuses even if that means involving itself in issues that would once have been regarded as off limits to the world body, because they involved a country's internal affairs. Nations are too interdependent, national frontiers are too porous, and transnational realities . . . too dangerous to permit egocentric isolationism."

George Bush, addressing world leaders at the U.N., said:

"It is the sacred principles enshrined in the U.N.

charter to which we will henceforth pledge our allegiance."

Those "sacred principles" Bush refers to were crafted by Soviet spy Alger Hiss and given force by the signatures of Josef Stalin and Franklin D. Roosevelt.

At the same U.N. meetings, plans were discussed to transfer national armies to the control of the United Nations. As the *Los Angeles Times* said on February 1, 1992:

"Creating a standing army under the control of the United Nations Security Council would give the world organization a military punch it has never had before and could convert it into a full-time international police force. The proposal for such a force, advanced by French president Francois Mitterand and immediately endorsed by Russian president Boris Yeltsin and the Hungarian government, would permit the Security Council to act on short notice. . . ."

Even in the first quarter of 1992, the U.N. blue helmets assumed eight new peacekeeping operations, compared to 13 in the prior 40 years. *If this U.N. standing army is created, blue helmeted U.N. troops from Russia, China, Europe, Africa, etc., could be on U.S. soil within three to five years.* Harvard professor Joseph S. Nye (a former State Department official and a member of the Council on Foreign Relations and Trilateral Commission) in a *New York Times* editorial on January 27, 1992, was blunt in coming out for a "fire brigade, or U.N. rapid deployment force—led by the U.S.—for the coming New World Order."

This writer believes that the liberal Eastern Establishment will try to slam dunk the New World Order on America during the next four years with a state of national economic emergency declared in 1993 or 1994 and used as a smokescreen for implementation of the New World Order. It is very possible that the November 1992 presidential election in America could be the last of its kind—for a long, long time. The Establishment knows that Americans are waking up, and hence is dramatically accelerating all of its plans.

Another important point on the New World Order— the New World Order will be no friend of conservatives, fundamental, evangelical Christians, or Orthodox Jews (not the liberal establishment types like Kissinger). *As the New World Order is installed, it will progressively take more and more steps against these groups (e.g., social and legal pressure leading eventually to persecution and/or imprisonment). A study of how the pressure built against these groups in Nazi Germany during the 1930s and of how the underground church has functioned in Eastern Europe, Russia, and China over the past 40 years might prove very informative to the reader.*

On February 15, 1992, the Bush Administration proposed to make churches, synagogues, and temples report to the IRS the names of *all donors who give them more than $500 per year. Soon all tithing members will be tracked and monitored by the government.* If implemented, this will mean the computerized monitoring of tens of millions of American church-goers who attend 350,000 churches, synagogues, and temples. The IRS says it "wants churches to help catch fraudulent church-goers who claim false church-related deductions."

As the *Rocky Mountain News* pointed out in an article entitled "Another Bush Regulation" on February 28, 1992:

"Even as some Orthodox priests in the old Soviet Union are being unmasked as KGB informants, the U.S. government would jettison more than two centuries of separatist tradition and deputize the entire American clergy as tax snitches. To try and cover a supposed $25 million annually lost to offering plate cheating, the Bush IRS rule would put a new accounting burden on every house of worship from St. Patrick's Cathedral to the smallest chapel in the wildwood."

Note: This computerized monitoring of church givers (both Christian and Jew) will also enable the government to compile computerized lists of all U.S. church-goers and Christians (by church, amount of contribution, etc.) for future use in the coming New World Order/New Age dispensation—which will be highly anti-Christian. Imagine how the Soviets or Red Chinese could have used such a list in 1917 and 1949 (and following) in their persecution of Christians.

The New World Order/New Age Connection

The New World Order is actually converging with the occultic New Age movement, both of which believe that they can help deliver us to world government during the 1990s.

When George Bush talked about a "thousand points of light" during his 1988 campaign, or "serving a shining purpose, the illumination of a thousand points of light" in his State of the Union address on January 29, 1991, he was actually drawing from H.G. Wells' (a one-world internationalist) writings on the open conspiracy *and from the New Age prayer for world government.* Wells wrote in his book, *Experiment in Autobiography*, in 1934:

> *"I believe this idea of a **planned World-State** is one to which all our thought and knowledge is tending. . . . It is appearing partially and experimentally **at a thousand points**. . . . When accident finally precipitates it, its coming is likely to happen very quickly. . . . Plans for political synthesis seems to grow bolder and more extensive. . . . The New Plan in America and the New Plan in Russia are both related to the ultimate World-State."*

The New Age movement has a prayer called the "Great Invocation," a 13-line mantra/prayer which invokes the presence of the "Christ" on earth. The "Christ" this prayer is calling for is Lord Maitreya—not the Jesus Christ of the Bible. Some would call him the "anti-Christ." The "Great Invocation" says:

> *From the **point of light** within the mind of God*
> *Let the stream forth into the minds of men.*
> *Let light descend on earth.*

> *From the point of love within the Heart of God*
> *Let love stream forth into the hearts of men.*
> *May Christ return to earth.*

> *From the center where the Will of God is known*
> *Let the purpose guide the little wills of men—*
> ***The purpose which the Masters know and serve.***

> *From the center which we call the race of man*

Let the Plan of love and light work out.
And may it seal the door where evil dwells.

Let Light *and Love and Power* **restore the Plan**
on Earth.

Note the H.G. Wells reference to the "planned world-state appearing at a thousand points," and the New Age "Great Invocation" (first line) reference to the "point of light." Hence, the synthesis of George Bush's "thousand points of light," and the merger of the New World Order and the New Age movement. As the last light of the prayer says, "Let the Light . . . restore the Plan on Earth." Occultist Alice Bailey also used the term "a thousand points of light" as a catch phrase.

Apparently, this is Bush's way of letting the one-world government advocates and the New Agers know that he is one of them, and that his New World Order and the New Age world government are one and the same, and are on track for installation in the near future.

Note: Pastor David Smith, editor of *Newswatch* magazine, recently communicated the following to this writer:

"On January 3, 1989, the Arizona Daily Star *and the* Los Angeles Times *carried an article describing how President-elect Bush had accepted an invitation from the Millennium Society (a New Age group) to be their guest of honor on December 31, 1999 at the Pyramid of Cheops at Giza, Egypt to help them welcome in the New Age millennium (the year 2000)."*

The article described Bush's acceptance (for he and

Barbara) of the invitation. New Agers have long held occultic, Luciferian initiations and ceremonies at that pyramid.

The Earth Summit

The largest New World Order/New Age/environmental summit in history was held in Rio de Janciro in June 1992 under the auspices of the United Nations Conference on Environment and Development. With 160 heads of state including George Bush in attendance, the Earth Summit is believed by knowledgeable insiders and outsiders to be the launching pad for a quantum leap into the New World Order and the New Age.

The Earth Summit was spearheaded by Maurice Strong, a powerful Canadian billionaire and one of the top global leaders in the New Age movement, and sponsored by dozens of leftist, communist, peace, environmental, and New Age groups. George Bush was an enthusiastic backer and an important participant in the Earth Summit. The New World Order/ Establishment crowd, the New Age movement, and the communists have found a vehicle whereby they can slam dunk their U.N.-backed world government on all of us—it is called "environmentalism." The old "reds" have now turned "green."

The plunge toward the New World Order, the New Age, and a U.N.-policed world government is going ballistic in the wake of the Earth Summit and will accelerate dramatically in 1993 or 1994. (See Chapter Fifteen for more information on the Earth Summit and the Green movement—and how they are being used as a vehicle for the New World Order.)

304—Toward a New World Order

Conclusion

The New World Order under the United Nations envisions a convergence of the goals and interests of the U.S. and C.I.S. (the new Soviet Union) in a world government that will control the nations of the world; bring about world peace; and a synthesis of West and East, of capitalism and communism into a hybrid of democratic socialism like that allegedly breaking out in Eastern Europe.

If the New World Order comes into being, the U.S. Constitution and Declaration of Independence will be scrapped, and an all-powerful world government will force the redistribution of America's wealth to other nations (dragging down our living standard); it will control and restrict Americans' freedom of movement, freedom of worship, and private property rights; and turn America into the socialist nightmare described in George Orwell's *1984*.

An international police force (under the U.N.) will be used to enforce the New World Order, much as it is being used against Iraq at this writing. Computerizing everyone from the cradle to the grave, computerizing their finances, their movements, and all aspects of their lives will be part of the Orwellian enforcement of the New World Order. The government computerization of all Americans (in process for the past seven years) is now completed. Christians and conservatives will come under persecution in the coming New World Order/New Age dispensation.

Chapter Fifteen

Saving Mother Earth: The Environmental Juggernaut

"Ostensibly to save the environment, misinformed and uninformed Americans are being mobilized to create the appearance of popular support for a radical agenda intended to altar our lifestyles and subvert the independence of our country. If this agenda is implemented, it will not improve the environment but will fulfill a long-sought-after goal of the Establishment. For this very reason, the Establishment has supported the radical environmental cause."
—Gary Benoit, *The New American* magazine

"Humanity needs a world order. The fully sovereign nation is incapable of dealing with the poisoning of the environment. . . . The management of the planet, therefore—whether we are talking about the need to prevent war or the need to prevent ultimate damage to the conditions of life—requires a world government."
—Norman Cousins—Earth Day 1970

Introduction

The world political left have found a brilliant

Machiavellian way to slam dunk socialism and world government onto the unsuspecting people of America and the entire world. It is not war; it is not communism; it is not even revolution—it is environmentalism, the "save Mother Earth/save the planet" movement. Over the past 22 years (since 1970) the Establishment globalists have pushed down our throats more socialism, more people control, more restrictions on free enterprise and private property in America and throughout the industrial West, all in the name of environmentalism, than the communists have been able to achieve in 75 years.

Just some of the environmental legislation which has passed since the EPA (Environmental Protection Agency was set up in 1970 includes the Clean Air Amendments Act; Clean Water Act; Endangered Species Act; Insecticide, Fungicide, and Rodenticide Act; Forest and Rangelands Renewable Resources Planning Act; Marine Protection, Research, and Sanctuaries Act; and Federal Land Policy and Management Act. Tens of thousands of regulations, many with criminal penalties, emanate from these acts, and most are enforced by the EPA.

Red is out, green is in! Under the guise of protecting the environment, we are about to lose many (if not most) of our remaining God-given, Constitutionally-guaranteed freedoms, and be submerged into a global government run by and for the elite—under the United Nations.

The Establishment/New World Order crowd know that they must have crises, either real or manufactured (i.e., war, the Cold War, the drug war, the environmental crisis, etc.), in order to implement socialistic, people-controlling "crisis management." Hence, the *drug war* has been used as justification for a host of anti-privacy, money-laundering, people-watching laws and regulations designed to move Americans toward a cashless, computerized society. The present U.S. *crime wave, escalating riots, and social upheaval will be used as an excuse for gun registration, and eventually confiscation.*

And the pseudo-ecology (or environmental) crisis is becoming the justification for thousands of laws and regulations that are emasculating our free enterprise system in America, neutralizing our private property rights, and moving us into a world government under the United Nations.

The Establishment/one-world planners are using the Hegelian Dialectic, via their manufactured environmental crisis, to move us into the New World Order and their socialist dream for America. As Don Bell recently wrote in his *Don Bell Reports* (P.O. Box 2223, Palm Beach, FL 33480):

1. A crisis is discovered *or created.* In this case industrial pollution, global warming, ozone depletion, overpopulation, food shortages, deforestation, acid rain, nuclear fallout, clean air and clean water needs; these are all packaged together to create a global crisis.
2. The masses are made aware of the crisis through the media, public meetings and speeches, sermons, conferences, etc. and are agitated into demanding a solution which will save and protect "our common home, Mother Earth."
3. The pre-planned solution is presented to and accepted by world leaders at special summits or conferences (such as the recent Earth Summit), and the people cheer as their leaders sign into world law (via U.N. treaties) the applicable measures for controlling the crisis—measures designed to move us all into a world government.

Don Bell, quoting from *The New American*, said:

"Here in America, the dialectic developed as follows: It seems that the Club of Rome was assigned the leadership in the environmental management by crisis project, with the large tax-exempt foundations (i.e., Ford, Carnegie, etc.), the Council on Foreign Relations, the Trilateral Commission, Bilderbergers, other international clubs, and the New Age network all joining in to complete the job in the 1990s.

"Accordingly, the Club of Rome had its first conference in America in 1969. In order to hasten the scheme, the 'Scissors Strategy' was decided upon; that is **pressure to be applied from above and below simultaneously.** *At the top of the pressure pyramid in July 1970, President Nixon submitted to Congress his plan to create an 'Environmental Protection Agency,' Congress concurred, and the EPA began operating in December 1970. Today, some 22 years later, thousands of EPA regulations will cost over $130 billion in 1992 alone (or over $1,000 per family per year).*

"While the EPA began its pressure at the top of the pyramid, below, at the grass roots level, there was organized the **1970 Earth Day** *observance. Also, at about this time, Lawrence Rockefeller, David's brother, using Rockefeller brother's funds, organized the* **Environmental Task Force,** *whose task was primarily propaganda, publicity, and promotion of the environmental crisis scam. In 1972, the program 'went global' with the U.S. Stockholm Conference on*

the Environment. Concurrently, CFR member Lester Brown, president of Worldwatch Institute, wrote World Without Borders, *in which he stated:* **'Arresting the deterioration of the environment does not seem possible within the present framework of independent nation-states. ... The list of national problems which can only be solved at the global level is lenghtening.'**

"In 1974, CFR/Trilateral Commission member Richard Gardner (a former U.S. ambassador to Italy) wrote in Foreign Affairs *(the journal of the CFR) as part of his plan for a New World Order, that* **'we must make an end run around national sovereignty, eroding it piece by piece.** ... *The next few years should see a continual strenghtening of the new global and regional agencies charged with protecting the world's environment.' Then to strengthen the pressure below, Lawrence Rockefeller wrote an article that appeared in the 1976* Reader's Digest *in which he stated: 'Either through voluntary discipline* **or state compulsion,** *human society would have to be reconstructed.' He predicted that* **'authoritarian control would be necessary to save the earth.' "**

The following year, 1977, the Rockefeller Task Force published *The Unfinished Agenda*, a

". . . consensus document intended as a blueprint for global environmental policy. It proposed an almost identical agenda to that which was just discussed at the Earth Summit in Rio: population control (using abortion and sterilization), the

redistribution of the world's food supplies through a transnational food cartel, the adoption of water distributional policies, severe taxes on gasoline and other disincentives for automobile ownership, recycling surcharges on consumer items, etc. The report also recommended the appointment of a three-person Economic Planning Board that would preside over America's economy; the board would be appointed, not elected."

The Establishment must have global crises (war, Cold War, drugs, AIDS, etc.) in order to stir the people of the world into requesting (or demanding) world government, in order to save the world. (Remember, many people in the recent Los Angeles riots begged for martial law in order to stop the pain.)

In 1963, 15 Establishment (CFR) leaders in the Kennedy Administration met at Iron Mountain, New York to formulate a substitute for war and promote the goals of world government and the New World Order. This special study group worked for two years to produce a supersecret report called "The Report From Iron Mountain." On page 66 of that report, they wrote:

"It may be, for instance, that gross pollution of the environment can eventually replace the possibility of mass destruction by nuclear weapons as the apparent threat to the survival of the species. . . . *It constitutes a threat that could be dealt with only through social organization and political power. But . . . it will be a generation, to a generation and a half before environmental pollution, however severe, will* *be sufficiently menacing on a global scale, to offer a possible basis for solutions."*

In 1990, UNCED (the United Nations Conference on Environment and Development, which just sponsored the Rio Earth Summit) wrote in a booklet, *In Our Hands, Earth Summit '92:*

"The world community now faces together greater risks to our common security through our impacts on the environment than from traditional military conflicts with one another. . . . We must now force a new 'Earth Ethic' which will inspire all peoples and nations to join in a new global partnership of North, South, East, and West."

Since 1990, UNCED has formed working groups to write treaties, agreements, and programs dealing with sustainable development, biodiversity, oceans, fresh water, air, land use laws, sewage, hazardous waste, population growth, forests, deserts, transportation, energy, health care, housing, taxation, etc. As William Jasper recently wrote in *The New American*, "There is virtually no area of human activity or environmental concern that they have not arrogated as their own, to plan, supervise, regulate, and control." As Richard Gardner said, *"An end run around national sovereignty, eroding it piece by piece."*

This chapter will analyze the manufactured (or pseudo) environmental crisis; the makeup of the environmental movement; and the real agenda of the environmental movement: socialism, people control, and the New World Order.

Creating a Manufactured (Pseudo) Crisis

The environmental crisis is a giant scam, a sham, a staged pseudo-crisis (like the pseudo-coup in the Soviet Union in August 1991) designed to give national and international government bureacrats and globalists the excuse to impose socialistic, communist bloc-type controls on people, business, private property, and virtually all aspects of our lives—"in order to save Planet Earth for future generations." Elements of this pseudo-crisis include: global warming; ozone depletion; the greenhouse effect; endangered species ranging from spotted owls to snail darters, from giant pandas to humpback whales; receding rain forests to advancing deserts; polluted water, land, and air; the disposal of toxic wastes; the population explosion; saving the trees; chemical poisoning of food; etc.

Note: It should be understood that there *are* legitimate pollution and environmental problems. No one hates Los Angeles smog or polluted lakes or rivers more than this writer. There are 150 million acres of eastern hardwoods which have been assaulted in recent years by a variety of imported diseases and pests. For example, 90 percent of the nation's fir trees in the Southern Appalachians are dead or dying because of the woolly adelgid. The spruce budworm has eaten millions of acres of red spruce in Maine, and many more millions of acres in Canada. The environmentalists ignore these *real* environmental problems.

The environmental movement concentrates instead on a few real or fabricated environmental problems, and exaggerates and multiplies them into a planet threatening, global crisis which can only be solved by control of people, by curtailing our freedoms, and by world government.

This writer has debated hard-core environmentalists on a number of radio talk shows, and is amazed at the incredible religious fervor which the environment issues generate. There are environmentalists who would actually kill people in defense of Mother Earth. *This movement should not be simply dismissed as a bunch of "hug-a-tree" freaks. It is one of the most powerful, occultic, and potentially evil forces in the world today.*

A growing number of highly degreed scientists are beginning to step forward and debunk global warming, the ozone crisis, the greenhouse scenario, the endangered species crisis, and most of the extreme positions of the environmentalists. *The earth is not warming*—if anything, it's cooling slightly. Ozone depletion is *not* a problem—ozone levels in the stratosphere have remained more or less constant for centuries. *Hence, the stampede to outlaw chlorofluorocarbons (CFCs) from refrigerators, aerosol sprays, foam packaging, and cleaning agents is a total pseudo-crisis.*

To put the "endangered species crisis" in perspective, in spite of a few hundred species of birds, fish, mammals, or insects which the environmentalists say (but can't prove) are endangered species, according to David Raup (a paleontologist at the University of Chicago and author of the book *Extinction: Bad Genes or Bad Luck?*), "there are 40 million species alive today and somewhere between 40 and 50 billion species may have lived during earth's history." And to put the "population explosion crisis" in perspective, you could put all of the planet's 5.4 billion people inside the state of Arkansas with 10 square feet each and have the balance of the earth left over for growing food.

Acid rain is another hoax. The National Acid Precipitation Assessment Program (NAPAP) spent hundreds of millions of taxpayer dollars over several years proving conclusively that "acid rain" is *not* a problem. *Only 240 out of 7,000 northeastern lakes are acidic and most of those were acidic before the Industrial Era.* The number of acidic lakes is *not* growing, and the 240 acidic lakes in the northeast could be de-acidified with *500,000 pounds of lime per year (for all of them)* versus billions of dollars for an elabaorate government acid rain program.

The so-called "greenhouse effect," caused by man-made carbon dioxide emanating from burning fossil fuels, is also a hoax. Recent scientific data show that 96 percent of all carbon dioxide in our atmosphere is naturally occurring. At an April 1992 conference on "Climate, Volcanism, and Global Change" in Hilo, Hawaii, Dr. Robert E. Stevenson, the secretary general of the International Association for the Physical Sciences of the Ocean, reported:

> *"Mean sea level has not changed in the past century (which puts the lie to the ecologists' argument that global warming is melting the polar ice caps); atmosphere temperatures, though having up and down cycles, have not established a trend in either direction; ozone holes are natural reactions to ultraviolet light variations and volcanic matter in the stratosphere; and the gases in the stratosphere caused by human's activities are insignificant."*

A group of 44 eminent, highly degreed scientists, part of the Science and Environmental Project, wrote recently:

> *"Environmentalist policy initiatives derive from*

highly uncertain scientific theories. They are based on the unsupported assumption that catastrophic global warming follows from the burning of fossil fuels and requires immediate action. **We do not agree.**

"The majority of scientific participants in a survey (summer 1991) agreed that the theoretical climate models used to predict a future warming cannot be relied upon and are not validated by the existing climate record. Yet all predictions are based on such theoretical models.

"We are disturbed that activists, anxious to stop energy and economic growth, are pushing ahead with drastic policies without taking notice of recent changes in the underlying science. We fear that the rush to impose global regulations will have catastrophic impacts on the world economy, on jobs, standards of living, and health care, with the most severe consequences falling upon developing nations and the poor."

The Makeup Of the Environmental Movement: Who Are the Players?

Four major groups comprise the environmental movement. Berit Kjos, in her recent book *Under the Spell Of Mother Earth*, describes three distinct sectors of the environmental movement which comprise *the marriage of the political left and the occult.* On the book cover, Kjos points out:

"Concern for the environment has joined with mysticism to spark a return to ancient forms of nature worship. How can Christians responsibly

care for the earth, but still resist the pervasive pagan beliefs that are entering our lives through the media, schools, and churches?"

The sectors of the environmental movement which are rapidly merging into one are:

1. *The Conservation Movement*—While generally left-wing politically, the groups in this sector have concentrated more on education and land preservation. They include organizations such as the National Wildlife Federation, the Audubon Society, and the Sierra Club. (In recent years, these groups have been taken over, however, by Green extremists.)

2. *The "Radical Green" Sector*—is composed of groups that advocate socialist policies and carry out vandalism in an effort to protect natural resources. Many of the Greens would force society "back to nature" regardless of the cost. One such "radical Green" educator Steven Van Matre, says, "Let's cage ourselves and let the animals run free. . . . Let's tear down our egocentric structures." *Their agenda goes far beyond ecology, to gay rights and the abolition of nations and private property.* The "Radical Greens" have become a powerful political force in Western Europe, and are becoming one in America as well.

3. *The "Deep Ecology" Sector*—is heavily based in New Age and pagan religion. These are the worshippers of the "Gaia" (pronounced guy-a) spirit of the earth. They include New Age educators in great numbers in our public schools, modern witches and pagans, and occultic oriented scientists.

Their goal has been the New Age transformation of individuals and nations, as the means to solving environmental problems and achieving "oneness" with the universe.

4. *The Liberal Eastern Establishment In America, Europe, and Elsewhere*—(not emphasized in Kjos' book) is epitomized by the Council on Foreign Relations, Trilateral Commission, Yale's Skull and Bones, Club of Rome, the Bilderbergers, Socialist International, the Fabian Socialists, and such globalists as David Rockefeller, Henry Kissinger, Baron Edmond de Rothschild, George Bush, James Baker, etc. If one person can be cited as head of the world environmental movement, it is Baron Edmond de Rothschild.

The Anatomy Of America's Green Lobby

Who or what groups make up the environmental or Green movement in America at present? Today, there are more than 400 Green groups at the national level, with additional thousands at the state and local levels. *These groups have one common denominator upon which they can all agree: they hate private property and the free enterprise system, and have dedicated their energy to stamping out both. Their efforts are concentrated on frustrating all private development of resources by promoting a growing government role in protecting, managing, and ultimately owning the environment.* They are continually cultivating the image of all businessmen and entrepreneurs as evil, greedy villains.

There are six major American "non-governmental organizations" (NGOs) which are helping to orchestrate America's descent into a planetary eco-dictatorship. Bill

Grigg describes these NGOs in a June 1, 1992 article in *The New American* entitled "Pressure From Above and Below" as *the National Resources Defense Council, the Sierra Club, the Environmental Defense Fund, the National Audubon Society, the National Wildlife Federation, and Friends of the Earth.*

These six have formed the Consortium for Action to Protect the Earth '92 (CAPE '92) which, according to Bill Grigg in *The New American,*

".... could be considered the lineal descendants of the Environmental Task Force, which was assembled in the mid-1970s with the aid of the Rockefeller Brothers Fund. Most of the CAPE '92 organizations had previously belonged to the Rockefeller Task Force. ...."

Hilary French of the Worldwatch Institute describes NGOs as "far-flung organizations responsive to *global* constituencies rather than to parochial national interests." The National Resources Defense Council is the most influential of the six organizations under the CAPE '92 umbrella.

All of the CAPE '92 organizations are well funded and well connected, with huge financing coming from the large tax-exempt foundations, from government grants, and from large multi-national corporations such as Dupont, Dow Chemical, Mobil, Monsanto, Weyerhauser, and other major corporations. The corporate philosphy seems to be "if you can't beat 'em, join 'em." Large U.S. corporations are trying to buy favors (it's called "blackmail," or "buying protection") from their environmental enemies, and to project an "environmentally correct" image.

The entertainment industry and the news media (both comprised mainly of pro-Green liberal secular humanists) works closely with the Green movement. (They even have an Environmental Media Assocation— EMA.) Over two years ago, these groups got together and designated White House Chief of Staff John Sununu as the "nation's chief environmental foe." An orchestrated media campaign of attacks against Sununu finally culminated in his forced resignation.

The CAPE '92 Green groups and others liaise closely with governmental agencies such as the U.S. Council on Environmental Quality, the Agency for International Development, the EPA, the National Oceanic and Atmospheric Administration, and 27 other federal agencies, according to Bill Grigg. The U.S. government involvement in UNCED is supervised by the UNCED Working Group of the Policy Coordinating Committee *of the National Security Council* (i.e., the highest levels of the U.S. government).

As Grigg concluded, "Accordingly, *the work of binding America to the decisions made at the Earth Summit will proceed with or without the explicit approval of President Bush.*" So, Bush can maintain for public/conservative pre-election consumption, an aloof, even confrontational stance with the Earth Summit and the Greens, *while his Administration continues to quietly implement their program for a socialist America.*

In addition to the CAPE '92 groups, the Green movement in America is comprised, according to Bill Jasper (also writing in the same issue of *The New American*) of

". . . hordes of U.N. bureaucrats, an army of ecology 'experts' from Greenpeace, Nature

Conservancy, Planned Parenthood, Zero Population Growth, United World Federalists, Worldwatch Institute, National Organization of Women, World Council of Churches, Socialist International Women, and literally hundreds more of what the U.N. calls NGOs."

These groups, in turn, liaise with international leftist/global groups such as Club of Rome, Bilderbergers, Socialist International, and thousands of international Green groups.

Note: The old anti-war, anti-nuclear, anti-Vietnam War, leftist/socialist/communist crowd now comprise the U.S. and global Green movement, but with a hundred times more muscle, clout, respectability, influence, financing, and momentum than they had before Red became Green! They now plan to set up a planetary dictatorship under the guise of environmental stewardship. As Bill Grigg wrote:

"By creating a sense of environmental panic, the Green movement is preparing the public to accept draconian measures that will limit economic growth, curtail personal liberties, and destroy American sovereignty."

The Power and Money Of the Environmental Movement

In an article in the September 1, 1990 issue of the Washington weekly, *Human Events*, Congressman William Dannemeyer (R-CA) discussed what he referred to as the Environmental Party, and said:

"I describe them as a political party because of the massive monetary and grassroots resources they have managed to tap across this country."

Data from the Federal Election Committee reveals that Republican organizations took in contributions of $71.1 million in calendar year 1989. Democratic organizations took in $18.6 million in the same year. The donor base for Republicans is 1,881,260, while the donor base for Democrats, which is not available, is estimated to be around 489,000. All told, the two parties took in around $89.7 million and have an approximate donor base of 2,370,300.

Now consider the Environmental Party. Twelve organizations comprise the base of support for the Environmental Party: Center for Marine Conservation, Clean Water Action Project, Environmental Defense Fund, Greenpeace USA, National Audubon Society, National Wildlife Federation, Natural Resources Defense Council, Nature Conservancy, Public Interest Research Group, Sierra Club, Wilderness Society, and World Wildlife Fund.

According to Congressman Dannemeyer:

"All told, the Environmental Party has an operating budget of $336.3 million (1988) and has a donor base of 12,959,000. That's nearly $250 million more than the Republican and Democratic parties combined and a donor base of some 10 million persons more! The Environmental Party is an awesome new dimension in American politics."

Incredible! They have four times more funding than the Republican and Democratic parties combined.

The Environmental/New Age Connection

Marlon Maddoux, in his April 1992 *Freedom Club Report*, described the New Age connection with the environmentalists:

> *"It's April—the month of Earth Day (on the 22nd). The goals of one-world government and religious unity are being accomplished with the help of an explosive new factor—the emerging ecological 'crisis' and* **the conversion of the powerful environmental movement to New Age religion.**
>
> *"While 'the confused sects of Bible-thumping Christianity celebrate the myth of Easter,' the world is being prepared to find true rebirth in the thrilling effort of protecting the planet. And in the process,* **millions are discovering 'the divine life' that infuses all rocks, plants, dust, trees, and themselves.** *Out of self-preservation, the planet is awakening to its own divinity. At last, the New World Order is coming into view."*

The New Age movement is the supernatural (or occultic) dynamic behind environmentalism. *Time* magazine (June 22, 1992) referred to the recent Earth Summit in Rio as "*a New Age carnival.*" The New Agers are providing the spiritual dimension as well as the globalist agenda to the environmental movement. Berit Kjos points out that in 1990:

> *"Suddenly books about Goddess worship burst into public view. Formerly secular minded feminists and ecologists began to see the Goddess'*

spirit—or Gaia—as a useful symbol for their goals. But many also saw it as a real spiritual force which manifested itself as a higly evolved 'nature spirits' once worshipped by pagans in ancient civilizations and forests."

Mother Gaia—The Earth Goddess who allegedly pervades us all

As Kjos points out:

*"The Sierra Club, for example, once a basically secular organization, now has published a book called **Well Body, Well Earth,** that promotes New Age visualization rituals to 'contact the voice of the living Earth . . . and trust what it provides.' "*

The National Audubon Society, the National Science Teachers Association, and even the Boy Scouts and Girl

Scouts of America have endorsed an econoly manual for children written by Joseph Cornell, who believes that global unity will come when people "realize that at the center of the universe swells the Great Spirit (Gaia), and that this center is really everywhere."

Marlon Maddoux went on to describe the New Age/Environmentalist plan for global victory:

> *"This new, stronger environmental movement has both a distinct philosophy and action plan. The philosophy includes these chilling aspects:*
>
> *"1. Christianty has caused an environmental crisis. Because Christians believe God is above creation, not part of it, they allegedly have a low view of nature.*
>
> *"2. The only way to save the earth is a revival of pantheism (God is everything) and paganism (God is expressed in spirit-beings and nature).*
>
> *"With the right religious perspective, one world government and planetary salvation will be achieved through affirming the unity with our divine Mother, Gaia, the goddess who pervades us all.*
>
> *"What about their action plan? New Age ecology is even now flexing its muscle in the following crucial centers of power in our world:*
>
> *"**Religion**. Many Christian churches are being subverted by modified forms of pantheism through environmentalist propaganda. At one 'Christian' conference on the environment, attended by many evangelicals, Kjos encountered workshops directly promoting the concept that 'everthing is God.'*

"Madeleine L'Engle, a 'Christian' fiction writer favored by many evangelicals, has endorsed a book for children in which the hero, a boy named Jimmy, is given telepathic powers and told by nature spirits to 'bring humans back to tree entities so that we may share our wisdom. . . .'

*"**Culture.** Outside the church, 'Goddess' and 'eco-feminist' doctrines preached by the late pagan university professor Joseph Campbell have spawned a whole line of books, videos, and TV series. And films such as* Dances With Wolves *are promoting pagan imagery while their stars travel to Washington to speak out for global action to preempt environmental 'crises' and preserve idol-worshipping cultures.*

*"**Education.** Environmental curricula now mandated in many states is fusing with the globalist education already firmly in place. The ecological angle in public school education gives an urgency to the New Age spiritual and political agenda that it didn't have before."*

Note: The excellent book *Under the Spell Of Mother Earth* by Berit Kjos is highly recommended for further reading on the environmental/New Age connection.

Who Is Maurice Strong?

Maurice Strong is a man to watch! The billionaire Canadian businessman is an employee of the United Nations; an employee of the Rockefeller and Rothschilds trusts and projects; a director of the Aspen Institute for Humanistic Studies; the organizer of the first World

Conference on the Environment in 1972; the founder and first head of the U.N. Environment Program; the secretary general (and chief organizer) of the UNCED Earth Summit in Rio in June 1992, and a leading socialist, environmentalist, New World Order manipulator, occultist, and New Ager. In the mid-1980s, Strong joined the World Commission on the Environment where he helped produce the 1987 Brundtland Report widely believed to be the "incendiary" which ignited the present "Green movement."

Strong, who spearheaded the Earth Summit, has complained that "the United States is clearly the greatest risk to the world's ecological health," and wrote in an UNCED report in August 1991 that:

> *"It is clear that current lifestyles and consumption patterns of the affluent middle-class . . . involving high meat intake, consumption of large amounts of frozen and 'convenience' foods, ownership of motor vehicles, small electric appliances, home and work place air-conditioning, and suburban housing are not sustainable. . . . A shift is necessary toward lifestyles less geared to environmental damaging consumption patterns."*

From his platform as UNCED secretary general, Strong has forcefully advocated a new economic order based on the re-distribution of the developed world's industries and wealth to the Third World. Strong is indeed an arch socialist.

The Trilateral Commission recently published a book, *Beyond Interdependence: The Meshing Of the World's Economy and the Earth's Ecology.* David

Rockefeller wrote the foreword and Maurice Strong wrote the introduction, saying in part:

> *"This book couldn't appear at a better time, with the preparation for the Earth Summit moving into gear . . . it will help guide decisions that will literally determine the fate of the earth. . . . Rio will have the political capacity to produce the basic changes needed in our international economic agendas and in our institutions of governance."*

Strong has established what could be the global headquarters for the New Age movement in the San Luis Valley of Colorado at the foot of the Sangre de Cristo Mountains near Crestone, Colorado. He and his occultic wife, Hanne, call the Baca an international spiritual community which they hope will serve as a model for the way the world should be if humankind is to survive—a sort of United Nations of religious beliefs. The Baca (as the center is called) is replete with monasteries; the Haidakhandi Universal Ashram, a Vedic temple where devotees worship the Vedic mother goddess; amulet-carrying Native American shamans; a $175,000 solar-powered Hindu temple; a mustard-yellow tower called a ziggurat; a subterranean Zen Buddhist center complete with a computer and organic gardens; a house full of thousands of crystals; and even Shirley MacLaine and her New Age followers.

In 1978, a mystic informed Hanne and Maurice Strong that "the Baca would become the center for a new planetary order which would evolve from the economic collapse and environmental catastrophes that would sweep the globe in the years to come." The Strongs say they see the Baca, which they call "The Valley Of the Refuge Of World truths"—"as the paradigm for the entire planet and say that the fate of the earth is at stake." Shirley MacLaine agrees—her astrologer told her to move to the Baca, and she did. She is building a New Age study center at the Baca where people can take short week-long courses on the occult! *Apparently, the Kissingers, the Rockefellers, the McNamaras, the Rothschilds, and other Establishment New World Order elitists all agree as well—for they do their pilgrimage to the Baca—where politics and the occult-the New World Order and the New Age—all merge. Watch Maurice Strong and watch the Baca!*

Much of the above information about the Strongs and the Baca comes from an interview entitled "The Wizard Of the Baca Grande," which Maurice Strong conducted with West magazine of Alberta, Canada in May 1990. Strong concluded the interview with a thought provoking, apocalyptic story from a novel he says he would like to write:

> *"Each year the World Economic Forum convenes in Davos, Switzerland. Over a thousand CEOs, prime ministers, finance ministers, and leading academics gather in February to attend meetings and set the economic agendas for the year ahead.*
>
> *"What if a small group of these world leaders were to conclude that the principle risk to the earth comes from the actions of the rich countries? And if the world is to survive, those rich countries would have to sign an agreement reducing their impact on the environment. Will they do it? Will the rich countries agree to reduce*

their impact on the environment? **Will they** **agree to save the earth?**
"The group's conclusion is 'no.' The rich countries won't do it. They won't change. **So, in** **order to save the planet, the group decides: isn't** **the only hope for the planet that the indus-** **trialized civilizations collapse? Isn't it our** **responsibility to bring that about?**
"This group of world leaders form a secret society to bring about a world collapse. It's February. They're all at Davos. These aren't terrorists—they're world leaders. They have positioned themselves in the world's commodity and stock markets. They've engineered, using their access to stock exchanges, and computers, and gold supplies, a panic. Then they prevent the world's stock markets from closing. They jam the gears. They have mercenaries who hold the rest of the world leaders at Davos as hostage. The markets can't close. The rich countries . . . ? ? ?"

This writer seldom finds time for novels, but a year or so ago, he read two novels by Frank Peretti entitled *This Present Darkness* and *Piercing the Darkness*. Both deal with the New Age, globalists, world government, and the forces of spiritual darkness and light. Both remind this writer of Maurice Strong and the Baca. They make for excellent entertainment and an interesting perspective in light of current developments worldwide.

George Bush: The Environmental President

George Bush is in trouble in the polls, so George Bush has decided to run as a conservative, and to play

330—Toward a New World Order

down his environmentalist record. Bush, therefore, feigned reluctance to go to the Earth Summit, and refused to sign several treaties which would have ultimately committed America to hundreds of billions in new environmental costs and aid to poor countries. Bush can be expected to have a change of heart toward these "Green treaties" *after* the election, if he is re-elected

As *Time* magazine (June 22, 1992) pointed out:

"The environmentalist' president seemed to be caught between two constituencies he holds dear—on one side conservative business leaders who oppose spending on the environment, and on the other side conservationists whose support he courted in 1988."

He counted their votes and opted to be a pro-economic growth advocate *until after the election.* Remember, Bush said "he would do anything to get re-elected." As Lenin said: "We advance through retreat." The reality is that Bush, the self-proclaimed "environmental president," has greatly strengthened the Environmental Protection Agency "gestapo" over the past four years (he even tried to elevate the EPA to cabinet-level status); he appointed William Reilly, a radical establishment socialist and Maurice Strong-type environmentalist to head the EPA; he helped push through the Clean Air Act which will ultimately cost U.S. businesses hundreds of billions of dollars, will cut millions of U.S. jobs, and shut down hundreds of thousands of U.S. businesses; he helped push through protection for the northern spotted owl, which has cost 30,000 jobs (and ultimately over 100,000) in the Pacific Northwest; and *via the EPA and other government agencies has pushed through thousands of environmental regulations which restrict land use of private property and place socialist controls on businesses. Under Bush, Americans have, for the first time, begun to be imprisoned for "environmental crimes."*

Bush has good reason to "low profile" his radical environmentalist agenda in an election year where *hundreds of thousands of Americans have lost their jobs because of his environmental policies. But it should be remembered that Bush is also "the New World Order president" (although he has been told to "low profile" his NWO agenda as well, until after the election). The Establishment sees the radical environmental agenda as their quickest route to the New World Order, and Bush can be expected to redouble his efforts for both agendas after the election (if he is re-elected). In short, Bush's well-publicized reluctance to aid and abet the goals of the recent Earth Summit is as phony as a lead nickel.*

Media Brainwashing Of the Public Regarding Environmentalism

"Tell a lie, tell it often enough, and people will believe it." —Adolf Hitler

The American public has been massively brainwashed by the liberal Establishment-controlled U.S. media regarding the "environmental crisis." From Ted Turner's "Captain Planet" environmental program for children to a daily newspaper column in most major newspapers entitled "Earth Week: A Diary Of the Planet"; from thousands of pro-environmentalist television programs to radical environmental curriculum in almost all public schools; the American people are being brainwashed with "save Mother Earth," "the planet is dying," "report and punish environmental crime," propaganda.

Hundreds of feature articles in news magazines such as *Time, Newsweek,* and *U.S. News and World Report* keep telling us that the environmental crisis threatens the future of the world—even more than the "late great cold war and now 'non-existent nuclear threat' " A recent *L.A. Times* article (May 26, 1992) entitled "Youth's Ecology Concerns Affect Parent's Purchases" described how "children point out environmentally sound products and mothers and fathers buy them." The *Times* article went on:

> *"To cultivate favor with young conservationists, businesses are using recycled products, forming alliances with environmental groups, and trying to understand young people like never before. . . . Clearly, children are having an impact, and a growing impact, on their parents' purchasing, because of environmental information.*
>
> *"Environmental Research's sister company, Infocus Environmental, is interviewing 1,000 children and their parents and 300 teachers to figure out what it takes to appeal to their green side. In a recent survey by Environmental Research, parents said they didn't buy Dove Bars because their children said the ice cream used too much packaging. But parents bought Arm & Hammer detergent because their children told them it was non-toxic.*
>
> *"Some toy makers tried a green hook after the 20th anniversary of Earth Day in 1990 created an explosion of environmental conscious-ness, particularly among children. A few suc-ceeded, such as Hasbro's GI Joe Eco-warriors.*

Mattel is taking an indirect approach. Last year, it created a new position of vice-president of environmental affairs. Mattel has also created an environmental mission statement.

*"Hartman Group in Newport Beach tells its clients to support school programs, youth environmental groups, and environmental projects, and to **buy ads on environmental shows on TV because that's where children learn about the environment.** . . . 'At the end of the day, you are going to have to have an environmentally sound product just to play in the game.' Carl Frankel, editor and publisher of Green Market Alert, says: 'The place to sell the environment is to the kids.' "*

Time magazine (June 22, 1992), adding to the propaganda barrage, wrote on children's involvement in the Earth Summit to save the planet:

*"The more than 300,000 pledges by children to do something for the planet, that were posted on bulletin boards next to the Tree of Life in Flamengo Park, raises hopes that **the next generation may mature with a deep awareness of the perils of waste and pollution. The question is whether they will learn that lesson in schools, or whether it will be imposed upon them by a world run to ruin by their parents.**"*

How long will it be before children are being taught by their teachers, text books, or televisions to turn in their parents or neighbors for "environmental crimes." It's already happening in certain neighborhoods around

America, where children are paid by the local government for reporting "litterbugs" and other "environmental criminals."

The July 9, 1991 *Houston Chronicle* carried an article entitled "Pollution: The Dirtiest Of Deeds," and subtitled "Corporate Crimes Ranked In Survey," which said:

> *"Pollution is a more serious crime than insider trading, price fixing, or anti-trust violations, and top executives could be held liable, says the results of a recent survey.* **'These results erase any doubt that the American public has been highly sensitized to environmental concerns,'** *said a director of Arthur D. Little, who commissioned the survey. . . .*
>
> *"Of those surveyed, 84 percent gave environmental damage a ranking of 8 to 10* **making it the crime considered most serious.** *. . . Environmental offenses were considered most serious by people under 45 years of age, by college graduates, and by people with annual household incomes of $35,000 or more. . . . Three out of four said corporate executives should be held personally liable if their corporation causes damage to the environment."*

The Earth Summit

> *"The Earth Summit must establish a whole new basis for relations between rich and poor, North and South, including a concerted attack on poverty as a central priority for the 21st century. This is now as imperative in terms of our environ-*

*mental security as it is on moral and humani-
tarian grounds. We owe at least this much to
future generations, from whom we have borrowed a fragile planet called Earth."*
                                    —Maurice Strong

Billed as the "mother of all summits," with up to
30,000 government officials and environmentalists from
167 countries in attendance, the June 3-14 Earth Summit
was the biggest gathering of world leaders ever held.
Described by *Time* magazine as a "New Age carnival," the
summit (and related activities) was attended by the Dalai
Lama of Tibet, thousands of New Agers and occultists
(including John Denver and Shirley MacLaine), numerous
leftist groups, and virtually every environmental group in
the world—7,892 non-governmental organizations from
167 countries.

As the *Wall Street Journal* said: "The summit on
Mother Nature was asking: 'What is needed to save the
world and how much is the world willing to do to save
itself?' " The Audubon Society called the Earth Summit
"the most important meeting in the history of mankind,"
and Maurice Strong said at the opening session of the
summit:

*"Nothing less than the fate of the planet is at
stake. . . . No place on the planet can remain an
island of affluence in a sea of misery. . . . We're
either going to save the world or no one will be
saved. I think we're at a real point of civilization
change. We must, from here on in, all go down
the same path. . . . There may not be another
chance."*

The *Rocky Mountain News*, in a May 31, 1992 article entitled "Agenda For Rio: Save the Planet Earth," posed a question:

> *"Who is killing planet earth? Styrofoam-crushing, beef-eating, gasoline-guzzling, air conditioner-blasting Americans and their partners in the developed nations? Rain forest-razing, sewer-fouling, baby-booming peasants of the Third World? Air-poisoning, river-killing, radioactive waste-leaking, dirty coal-burning denizens of formerly communist Eastern European countries? **All of us** are killing planet earth!"*

Many environmentalist leaders touted the summit as an ecological Bretton Woods, just as world leaders crafted the post-World War II international financial system in New Hampshire, the leaders of the post-Cold War era would lay the foundations for the "era of sustainable development." Lester Brown, president of Worldwatch Institute, said: "I think when we look back, we will see the Rio conference as the event that marked the end of an era and the start of a new one."

The Goals Of the Rio Earth Summit

The June Earth Summit in Rio was not just about the pseudo-environmental crisis; it was not just about clean air, clean water, acid rain, global warming, or endangered species: *it was about massive wealth redistribution from the industrial countries (i.e., the North) to the Third World countries (i.e., the South)—from the rich to the poor countries. It was about massive global socialism, people control, and world government. It was also an*

unprecedented global media platform for militant anti-American eco-propaganda with emotional diatribes about America's alleged crimes against the global environment.
The summit was concerned with writing a World Constitution which will deal with ways and means of eliminating pollution; cutting down the alleged "global warming"; cutting down on the emission of carbon dioxide; stalling the rate of ozone depletion; adopting plans to prevent overpopulation, acid rain, nuclear fallout, and to promote clean water and clean air; and *depriving landowners of the right to use their land in any manner other than that permitted by UNCED or its local or regional representative.* Their broad goals include:

1. *A Massive Global Wealth Redistribution Scheme*—
   Maurice Strong and other summit leaders are demanding a $625 billion a year (for a decade) wealth transfer from the so-called wealthy countries (epitomized by the U.S.) to the so-called poor countries—with $125 billion per year coming from America. The U.S. is being pushed to contribute $70 billion per year to this Third World Green fund (this is in addition to the $55 billion we already pour out annually to developing nations).
2. *Imposition Of a System Of Global Environmental Regulation*—including onerous taxes on energy fuels, and on the populations of the United States and other industrialized nations. The developed countries should limit production and consumption, and cut back dramatically on the use of the automobile, electrical appliances, air conditioning, etc. The same formula for "sacrifice by the rich nations to save the planet" was summarized well some 12 years earlier by Kansas Senator James P.

338—Toward a New World Order

Pearson, who said: "Profits must be cut, comforts reduced, taxes raised, sacrifices endured."

3. *Elimination Of Property, Hunger, and Disease In the Third World*—Only if these are eliminated, the environmentalists say, will the poor Third Worlders stop polluting planet earth.

4. *Establishment Of a Global Environmental Protection Agency*—to duplicate the efforts of the American EPA on a worldwide basis and prosecute environmental crimes on a global basis.

5. *Population Control*—is high on the Green agenda, although the issue was low-profiled at the Earth Summit. Strict population control is high on the agenda of UNCED and the Green movement. As the Greens see it, there are too many people on Mother Earth (and the 5.4 billion will double in the next 10 to 15 years); the more people there are, the more pollution there is; the more highly developed the people are, the more resources they consume. *So, one of UNCED and the Greens' chief goals is to restrict population growth by whatever means possible.* Biology professor Garrett Harden (an influential Green spokesman) recently wrote:

*"It is a mistake to think that we can control the greed of mankind in the long run by an appeal to conscience. . . . **The only way we can cherish and nurture other and more precious freedoms is by relinquishing the freedom to breed, and that very soon.**"*

The U.N. Population fund defends the Chinese population control regime, which uses mandatory abortion and sterilization, female infanticide, and incarceration of uncooperative parents. Paul Ehrlich, another Green population controller, in his books *The Population Bomb* and *The Population Explosion,* praises the Chinese approach but calls it inadequate. *He recommends a Chinese-style population control program supervised by the U.N., and the adding of sterilants to water and food supplies.*

It is very significant that *the Greens are very preoccupied with population growth in America.* The Club of Rome would like to see the U.S. population reduced to 75 million—they don't say what will happen to the other 175 million Americans (perhaps Russian nukes or AIDS can solve that problem). In *Earth Day—The Beginning,* David Brower declared:

> *"That's the first thing to do—start controlling the population in affluent white America, where a child born to a white American will use about 50 times the resources of a child born in the black ghetto."*

For the first time, during the writing of this book, this writer has begun to understand the relationship between the Rockefeller-backed Planned Parenthood, the abortion and euthanasia movement on the one hand, and the Green movement on the other. *Both groups want to shrink the world's population to save Mother Earth and our scarce resources.* Both are preoccupied with death, and opposed to life. As Deuteronomy 30:19 says, *"I call heaven and earth to record this day against you, that I have set before you life and death, blessing and cursing: therefore, choose life, that both thou and thy seed may live."*

Conclusion

Very few major changes in the world (including wars or even cold wars) happen by accident or are spontaneous—there is a strategy, a plan, and a planner behind most. The global environmental (or Green) movement is no exception! Today, the internationalists' dream of a New World Order is being moved ahead rapidly by the efforts of our "environmental president," the liberal Eastern Establishment, the Green movement, the United Nations, and a plethora of New Age, leftist, and communist groups all over the world, including the worshippers of Mother Gaia, the Goddess of Planet Earth.

The insane anti-business, anti-private property, people-controlling Gestapo-like behavior of the EPA and our environmental bureaucracy begins to make sense if one can see the larger picture of the environmental movement being used for the abolition of U.S. sovereignty, the U.S. Constitution, and private property, and the subjugation of America into a one-world socialist government.

Chapter Sixteen

Merger Or Surrender:
The Red Dawn Scenario

The December 11, 1989 *Newsweek* cover story "Super Partners—An Ambitious Game Plan for a New Era" says a lot about where we are and where we are headed. For over 50 years, Eastern Establishment insiders have talked about a merger with Russia, about merging common interests of America and Russia, about world government, and, more recently, about the New World Order. In reading through several hundred publications and over 500 articles for the preparation of this book, this writer came across the terms "new world" or "new world order" at least 150 times. This is no coincidence.

The agenda of the liberal Eastern Establishment in America and Europe ever since they helped finance the Bolshevik Revolution in 1917, and helped to finance the Soviets in the 1920s, 1930s, and 1940s, right up through the present, has been global government. This is obvious in studying the publications of the CFR, the Trilateral Commission, and other Establishment groups. They see Russia as an important vehicle (or tool) to be used to help bring about this world government or so-called "New World Order." Russian-backed revolutions and the establishment of their own foreign policy machinations against countries like China in the 1940s; Cuba in the 1950s; Iran, Nicaragua, Rhodesia, and the Panama Canal giveaway in the 1980s; and South Africa, South Korea, and Central America in the early to mid-1990s is all designed to set the stage for world government in the 1990s.

South Africa will be one of the last major dominoes to fall to communism (i.e., in one to three years), via an ANC government; the United States of Western Europe is to emerge in 1992 and beyond; Eastern and Western Europe are to merge into one large economic and political bloc, and the world government (New World Order) dreamed of by Bush, Kissinger, Shultz, Brzezinski, Rockefeller, and their Establishment associates is supposed to emerge in the mid to late-1990s via a global merger of the East and West.

A few minor wars (such as those in Central America and the Middle East) are envisioned along the way, *to preoccupy and divert the attention of the masses*, but a government of, by, and for the elite is scheduled to emerge before the year 2000. *This is the Establishment agenda; this is the New Age movement agenda. But this writer does not think that this is the agenda of Russia.* (It should be remembered that the best laid plans of mice and men and elitists sometimes go astray.)

The Red Dawn Scenario

The Russians may have another agenda. *It is called Red Dawn.* If one studies the writings of Lenin, Stalin, Manuiliski, Andropov, and Russian leaders right down through Gorbachev, one will conclude that the Russian leadership from 1917 to the present has never deviated from the Marxist/Leninist goal of world domination. Capitalism in general and America in particular are their number one enemy and obstacle to achieving this dream.

Western liberals are appeasers; from Bush to Kennedy, from Kissinger to James Baker, from Rockefeller to Armand Hammer (Lenin's old crony and far more than just a "liberal") they keep telling us that "communism is dead," that the "Cold War is over," and that "Russia is now our partner." But the Marxist/Leninists who run the Kremlin, who run the KGB, and who run the Russian military, have never been stronger, nor more dedicated to the destruction of America. *The present retrenchment, retreat, and "humbling" of the communist bloc is simply the communist dialectic (e.g., two steps forward, one back, then two forward, etc.) in action, the sixth* glasnost *since 1921, and the greatest strategic deception in modern (perhaps of all) history.*

Proud, arrogant people are easy to manipulate, and America's liberal Eastern Establishment leaders are proud, arrogant men—today, more so than ever, because they believe they have their dream of world government almost achieved, almost in hand. As such, they can be manipulated by the communist leadership for their own ends. From Lenin to Gorbachev, the communist leadership has talked of the necessity for using wealthy finance capitalists (e.g., like the Armand Hammers, the David Rockefellers, the Dwayne Andreas', and thousands more) to help finance their world revolution. The communist leadership understands these men's greed and lust for more and more wealth. It also understands their lust for power, and world domination via their "New World Order," or global government, scheduled to emerge in the mid-1990s.

So, the communist leadership, headed at this writing by Boris Yeltsin, is willing to go along with their "New World Order" schemes, with the reunification of Germany and then Europe (albeit under neutral banners). That communist leadership is willing to grovel before their Western benefactors, smile, bow, and humbly admit their mistakes—and beg for forgiveness and ask for financial and industrial help to change their ways.

But at a point in time (this writer believes in the mid-to late-1990s) the Russians, the greatest masters of deception in history, will launch their final drive for world domination, will double-cross their liberal Western capitalist benefactors, and will attack the United States of America. You see, they don't see the elitist "New World Order" crowd dominating the globe—they see themselves dominating through their overwhelming military might, through their stealth, their deception, and their audacity. (Both historical and contemporary Russian writers and strategists have long said that they would attack us when we were at peace with them.) That will be the beginning of the Red Dawn scenario.

Note: History is replete with examples of such strategic deceptions and double-crosses. *For example*, the ancient Greeks who sailed their fleet away from Troy, in defeat and humiliation, leaving behind a gift, a war reparation, a giant wooden horse. A proud and gullible Troy fell that very night.

For example, an Oriental ambassador, humbled by America's trade prowess in the Pacific, bowed in humility before our proud and powerful president, seeking conciliation and improved relations with America. Ten minutes later, his emperor's navy and air force were attacking our unprepared American fleet in Pearl Harbor on December 7, 1941.

For example, after signing a non-aggression pact with Stalin in 1939, whereby Russia and Germany would carve up Poland, Hitler double-crossed Stalin and abruptly turned and invaded Russia in 1941.

The Red Dawn scenario (made into a movie based upon an official U.S. government strategic scenario) hypothesizes that: Western Europe goes neutral, NATO collapses, and a communist-(Russian)-backed revolution sweeps through the Caribbean Basin, Central America, and Mexico. America, weakened by three decades of disarmament and appeasement, has its major Strategic Air Command bases, missile sites, and naval ports (but not cities, for the most part)—about 400 hundred targets in all (as estimated by Codevilla)—nuked.

These nuclear missiles are launched from Soviet submarines *currently* a few miles off the U.S. east and west coasts, from MiG fighter bombers launched across the southeastern United States from Cuba, and across the polar ice cap. America, of course, because of 25 years of disarmament treaties, has no nuclear defenses whatsoever. A feeble retaliation from a handful of U.S. submarines does minimal damage to a well-defended Russia.

Within hours of the attack, the Russians launch an airborne and armored division into an undefended and disarmed United States through Alaska and Mexico. This airborne/armored invasion by Russians, Cubans, Nicaraguans, and other East bloc troops quickly cuts North America in half and the political survival of America becomes problematic.

Is the Red Dawn Scenario Plausible?

In this writer's opinion, and that of a number of defense and intelligence analysts he knows, it is! The Russian strategy for the conquest of America has long been "internal demoralization, plus disarmament, plus external encirclement, will lead to nuclear blackmail and eventual surrender or conquest." Perhaps a George Bush, or his successor, with a nuclear gun to his head, will simply surrender—the present "partnership" will reach a "new level of accommodation." Or perhaps the Russians will opt for Red Dawn. The point is the elements for the launching of a Red Dawn scenario are now moving into place. These elements include:

1. Vastly superior Russian military strength versus the U.S.;
2. A neutral Europe and the termination of the NATO military alliance (which secures Russia's western flank);
3. Revolutionary communist governments in Cuba, Nicaragua, and eventually, throughout Central America and Mexico;
4. Larger standing armies in Cuba and Nicaragua (combined) than America now possesses;
5. A very porous, undefendable border with Mexico stretching 2,100 miles from Brownsville to Tijuana;
6. Millions of Latin refugees in the southwestern U.S., with millions more coming in each year— thousands of these are KGB, DGI, or other East bloc agents, Spetsnaz, etc.;
7. A total absence of U.S. air defenses against submarine-launched missiles (e.g., from Russian subs on the U.S. east and west coasts, or the Gulf of Mexico), from Cuban or Central American-based aircraft, or from Russia across the polar ice cap;
8. Huge stores of prepositioned conventional weapons in Cuba, Nicaragua, and eventually, throughout Central America and Mexico; and
9. A sparsely populated and largely undefended Alaska, virtually adjacent to Russia, and already

(*at this writing*) being infiltrated by Russian agents and Spetsnaz.

Conclusion

Very few Americans will be able to comprehend, accept, or be willing to believe the analysis in this book. The "peace propaganda," to the contrary, is enormous and overwhelming. We are the "Pollyanna people," we want good news, not bad. We love people who tell us what we want to hear (like George Bush or Ronald Reagan), and we hate people who tell us what we don't want to hear. Today, we hear our leaders telling us that "there will be peace in our day," but the Bible warns us to beware when men cry "... *Peace, peace; when there is no peace.*" 1 Thessalonians 5:3 says, "*For when they shall say, Peace and safety; then sudden destruction cometh upon them, as travail upon a woman with child; and they shall not escape.*"

We live in the age of deception. Our leaders are deceiving us as they push us into a world government, into the "New World Order." The Russians are deceiving us as they feign peace, brotherhood, the end of the Cold War, and the death of communism—even as they prepare for war. The Russians are currently purging the inefficiencies and dead wood from their system; building their economic strength via massive Western financial/industrial infusions; trying to take out the few remaining anti-communist countries (e.g., South Africa, South Korea, the Philippines, Chile, Taiwan, El Salvador, Israel); neutralizing Western Europe and NATO; "lulling the Americans to sleep with the greatest overtures of peace and disarmament known throughout history"; expanding their military lead over America; and getting prepared for the final onslaught against America in the mid- to late-1990s.

Chapter Seventeen

The 1990s:
The Decade of Deception,
Decision, and Destiny

---

*"At what point is the approach of danger to be expected? I answer, if it ever reaches us, **it must spring up among us,** it cannot come from abroad. If destruction be our lot, we must ourselves be its author and finisher. As a nation of free men, we must live through all times or die of suicide."*
—Abraham Lincoln, 1837

"The strength or weakness of a society depends more on the level of its spiritual life than on its level of industrialization. Neither a market economy nor even general abundance constitutes the crowning achievement of human life. If a nation's spiritual energies have been exhausted, it will not be saved from collapse by the most perfect government structure or by any industrial development. A tree with rotten core cannot stand."
—Alexander Solzhenitsyn

"In Germany, the Nazis came for the communists, and I didn't speak up, because I was not

*a communist. Then they came for the Jews, and
I did not speak up, because I was not a Jew.
Then they came for the trade unionists, and I
didn't speak up because I wasn't a trade unionist.
Then they came for the Catholics, and I was a
Protestant, so I didn't speak up. Then they came
for me. . . . By that time, there was no one left
to speak up for anyone."*

—Martin Niemoller,
Protestant clergyman

The 1990s are shaping up to be the most critical
decade in modern history—perhaps in all of history. As
the leaders of the Eastern and Western worlds talk of
peace, prosperity, and unity, something very different
appears to be approaching like a freight train out of
control. Three giant movements all seem to be converging
in the 1990s, as they struggle for world power:

1. The Russian quest for world domination;
2. The New World Order quest for a one-world
   government; and
3. The New Age movement's quest for world government by the year 2000.

These three movements overlap, cooperate, and
sometimes compete; but all three love the common goal of
a world united under their domination by the year 2000.
The *Russians* are implementing an elaborate and
Machiavellian script, drafted by Yuri Andropov and the
KGB in the early 1980s, a script designed to lower (or
eliminate) the threat perception in the West, designed to
get the West to disarm, and at the same time build up the
U.S.S.R. with massive financial, industrial, and tech-

nological aid. The Russians will be in a position to take their great leap forward and to impose their will on much of the West by the mid- to late-1990s.

The *New World Order movement*, made up of America's liberal Eastern Establishment, the Bilderburgers, Socialist International, the Club of Rome, and other European and global socialist groups, believe that they can establish their global government during the 1990s. These groups are dramatically accelerating their efforts to this end, and believe that their more than 200-year-old goal of world government is almost within their grasp. Since the founding of the Illuminati in 1776, this group has planned and schemed, has precipitated and manipulated wars, revolutions, and depressions in order to advance their one-world socialist order. They believe they now have an open field, with virtually no opposition, for their dash to the finish line.

The *New Age movement*, with its roots in the same Far Eastern religion, occultism, and mysticism which gave rise to the Nazi's Third Reich and World War II, is now rising virtually all over the world—as it looks forward to the public debut of its messiah—the Maitreya. This movement, like a creeping ubiquitous fog, pushed by some powerful, unseen hand, is spreading irresistibly across the planet. Its adherents, from all strata of global society, believe their New Age government and society will be in place by the year 2000—that we will witness the dawning of the Age of Aquarius.

All three of these movements have several common denominators:

1. Their quest for a global government by the year 2000;
2. Their disdain for Christianity, Christians, the

Bible, and traditional Judeo-Christian values;
3. Their disdain for the nation and people of Israel; and
4. A supernatural, satanic dynamic which energizes them.

These movements, and the satanic power behind them, will give rise to the greatest explosion of evil, and the greatest restriction of human freedom and liberty in modern history during the decade of the 1990s. Indeed there is today an explosion of evil all over the planet which has few parallels in history—much of that evil is subtle, deceptive, and not discerned by the great majority. It is incredible how few people in our day (including Christians) can even recognize evil, let alone take an active stand against it.

America, and indeed most of the West, are in rapid decline today: economic, monetary, social, political, moral, and spiritual. It's axiomatic that most people in a declining nation, empire, or civilization cannot see the decline—so gradual is the descent. But in the latter stages of the decline, the decay or rot begins to become more and more apparent. America is in the latter stages of decline in the late 1990s.

A country which leads the world in homosexuality, promiscuity, pornography, divorce, abortion, violent crime, drug usage, alcoholism, and child abuse; a country which embraces its enemies while betraying its friends; and a country which turns it back on its spiritual, Christ-centered heritage while believing itself to still be the greatest—is ready for a major fall. It happened to Rome, Babylon, Persia, Assyria, and Greece—it could happen to America in the 1990s.

America has been blessed with abundance and

prosperity beyond any nation in history; and yet, like pre-revolutionary Russia, as a nation we have forgotten God. God raises up nations and leaders and he also puts them down. This writer believes that the Lord's umbrella of protection over America is now being removed, and that America is about to enter a period of divine judgment. That judgment will be four-fold:

1. Economic/financial disaster;
2. The explosion of the AIDS plague;
3. A powerful oppressive government which will take our freedom; and
4. Military/political attack by communism and Russia.

The financial debacle, analyzed in Chapters Five and Six, is upon us. For over two decades, we have abused our financial system and the consequences of that abuse is now becoming obvious. America's coming financial explosion cannot be avoided. But individuals can protect themselves and their families by taking some of the actions recommended in Chapter Seven.

AIDS and a whole host of deadly viruses are now spreading rapidly through the U.S., Western Europe, Africa, and much of the Western world—a result of rampant homosexuality, heterosexual promiscuity, and nearly total violation of God's rules of sexual behavior, monogamous marriage, etc. The extent and severity of the AIDS crisis in America has been systematically covered up by a liberal government interested primarily in teaching an immoral generation how to have "safe sex"— and is five to ten times more widespread and easily transmitted than officially acknowledged. By the time America wakes up to the magnitude of the plague, tens of millions of Americans will be dying and an overextended medical and financial system will be at the breaking point.

In ancient Israel, when the Jewish people and/or their leaders wandered far enough away from God, or became sufficiently sinful or wicked, God would judge Israel (or Judah) with military conquest by the large, well-armed, and evil nations of that day. The Lord used Babylon, Assyria, Rome, and others as a hammer of judgment against the immoral and wicked generations of those days. These divine judgments are described in Isaiah, Jeremiah, Daniel, and throughout the Old Testament. Before this decade is history, this writer believes that God will use Russia and international communism (which is certainly *not* dead) as a hammer of judgment against a sinful and wicked American people and their leaders.

Note: God's coming judgment against America will first be directed against the church—against apathetic, complacent Christians and their leaders—who, as Revelation 3:16 says, *". . . Because thou art lukewarm, and neither cold nor hot, I will spue thee out of my mouth."*

Meanwhile, we live in a day of deception, confusion, danger, and a blinding acceleration of global events. The decade of the 1990s is witnessing the most incredible deception in modern (if not all of) history. If evil, atheistic, Marxist/Leninist communist revolutionaries like Boris Yeltsin, Mikhail Gorbachev, and Nelson Mandela can be sold to the people of America and the West as men of peace and brotherhood and perhaps even Christians; if Gorbachev can be voted in polls across America, Western Europe, and the rest of the free world as the most popular man in the world; how difficult will it be to sell the Antichrist to the masses as a great man of peace, as the "messiah" who will save the world from self-destruction?

In Matthew 24, in the Olivet Discourse on what Christians could expect to be happening before His return, Jesus warned four times to beware of deception: that evil men, false christs, and false prophets would arise and deceive the great majority, including Christians (the elect). Certainly the decade of the 1990s is a decade of incredible deception, as we are told that communism is dead, the Cold War is over, peace has arrived, and as we plunge toward global government.

Are there any other signs of the return of Christ, of the approaching of the Armageddon scenario described in Daniel, Ezekiel, Revelation, Matthew 24, etc.? The "signs of the times" which Jesus (and the prophets) said would appear before His second coming seem to be proliferating:

1. The union of Western Europe;
2. The plunge toward global government;
3. The gigantic military buildup of Russia—referred to as Gog and Magog and the king of the north in Ezekiel and Revelation;
4. The massive Russian arms buildup in the Middle East, where the Russians have prepositioned almost $100 billion in military equipment;
5. The move toward a cashless society and the computerized numbering and monitoring of people in America, Europe, Australia, and around the globe;
6. The plunge toward a global currency and a central bank;
7. The gigantic increase of wickedness (or evil) described in Matthew 24:12;
8. The "wars and rumours of wars" described in Matthew 24:6;

9. The famine and earthquakes described in Matthew 24:7; and
10. The plagues (e.g., AIDS) described in Revelation 9:13-18.

When Jesus was asked in Matthew 24:3, ". . . *What shall be the sign of thy coming and of the end of the world?*" He described a period of deception, wars, rumors of wars, famines, earthquakes, and wickedness which would precede that coming. And in Matthew 24:32 He said, *"Now learn a parable of the fig tree; When his branch is yet tender, and putteth forth leaves, ye know that summer is nigh: So likewise ye, when ye shall see all these things, know that it is near, even at the door."*

It would certainly appear that the 1990s could see the world enter the countdown to Armageddon. Or it could be that we are just entering another period of economic and political convulsions such as we saw in the 1930s during the Great Depression and before the outbreak of World War II. Regardless of what may be coming in the 1990s, Christians are admonished to take a stand *for* Jesus Christ and *against* evil. Many Christians who are looking forward to the second coming of Christ use that as an excuse to do nothing in the way of financial preparation, political action, or preparing for difficult times for themselves and their families. This writer believes that a "do nothing" position on the part of Christians is apathetic, is complacent, is wrong, and is in violation of the Word of God. Jesus said to "occupy until He returns." And Proverbs 27:12 says, *"A prudent man foreseeth the evil, and hideth himself; but the simple pass on, and are punished."* If the return of Christ is 20, 50, 100, or 1,000 years away, in the meantime, America and much of the West are about to lose their freedom.

Christians and/or conservatives who understand the issues described in this book should be making the following preparations for the turbulent rollercoaster 1990s:

1. Reduce or elimimate your debt and get liquid;
2. Establish a food reserve program for your family;
3. Learn how to become more self-sufficient and less dependent on the "system" for survival;
4. Develop hunting, fishing, shooting, and gardening skills and acquire the tools needed for those endeavors;
5. Acquire firearms (and ammunition) for the protection of your family, or your country if necessary;
6. Acquire precious metals—up to 30 percent of your net worth; and
7. Establish a second source of income which you and your family can fall back on in tough times (see Chapter Seven for more details).

Edmund Burke said, "All that is necessary for evil to triumph is that good men do nothing." Well, good men and women (including Christians) have been doing nothing for a long time and evil is waxing more powerful every day. We are in a spiritual and a political battle, and it must be fought on both planes. Readers need to get involved politically on a local, state, and national level. You need to support and participate in patriotic, pro-American, anti-communist, pro-family, pro-traditional values organizations such as the Conservative Caucus, the John Birch Society, Focus on the Family, Summit Ministries, Concerned Women for America, Southwest Radio Church, Gun Owners of America, and more (see the Appendix for resources).

If you do decide to make physical preparations, or get involved in the political battle for freedom in America, be warned: you will face opposition, and you will come face to face with evil, and that evil will seem to be winning. You cannot fight the battle without God's strength, wisdom, and guidance. This writer tried it in the past and failed. You need to have a personal relationship with God, and with His Son, Jesus Christ. This is your only guarantee to be on the winning side.

John 3:16-18, 36 says, *"For God so loved the world, that he gave his only begotten Son, that whosoever believeth in him should not perish, but have everlasting life. For God sent not his Son into the world to condemn the world; but that the world through him might be saved. He that believeth on him is not condemned: but he that believeth not is condemned already, because he hath not believed in the name of the only begotten Son of God . . . He that believeth on the Son hath everlasting life: and he that believeth not on the Son shall not see life; but the wrath of God abideth on him."*

When you get discouraged, read Psalm 37:1-2, 7, 9, 14-15, which says, *"Fret not thyself because of evildoers, neither be thou envious against the workers of iniquity. For they shall soon be cut down like the grass, and wither as the green herbs . . . fret not thyself because of him who prospereth in his way, because of the man who bringeth wicked devices to pass . . . For evildoers shall be cut off: but those that wait upon the Lord, they shall inherit the earth . . . The wicked have drawn out the sword, and have bent their bow, to cast down the poor and needy . . . Their sword shall enter into their own heart, and their bows shall be broken."*

Pray for your country, for its leaders, for conservative and Christian leaders, and for God to thwart the evil plans of the New World Order and the New Age groups, as well as the Russian leadership. 2 Chronicles 7:14 says, *"If my people, which are called by my name, shall humble themselves, and pray, and seek my face, and turn from their wicked ways; then will I hear from heaven, and will forgive their sin, and will heal their land."*

And finally, remember, God is still in control of history, of nations, and of individual's lives, *and He is the winning side!*

Chapter Eighteen

Encouragement for the Remnant

"Even so then at this present time also there is a remnant according to the election of grace."
—Romans 11:5

In every declining civilization there is a small "remnant" of people who adhere to the right against the wrong; who recognize the difference between good and evil and who will take an active stand for the former and against the latter; who can still think and discern and who will courageously take a stand against the political, social, moral, and spiritual rot or decay of their day.

Members of the *remnant* in every declining civilization are always a small minority—they are defined by quality, not quantity. They are often unpopular or ridiculed for the stands they take and the principles they adhere to. They often feel alone in the context of where they live, work, go to school, etc.—like "a voice crying in the wilderness." This writer has spoken and written for 30 years on many of the topics which are regularly analyzed in his monthly newsletter, the *McAlvany Intelligence Advisor*—and has addressed over 2,000 audiences around the world on the political, financial, and spiritual decline of America.

For a long time, it bothered this writer that only a small percentage of the people he addressed understood the message, felt a sense of urgency, and acted upon it.

However, as the idea that "the majority is always wrong" began to sink in—that there is only a small minority of thinking people who will take a stand for good and against evil (e.g., the *remnant*) in any country or civilization—then this writer began to forget the numbers (the masses) and to concentrate on teaching the *remnant*.

Many (perhaps most) of the readers of this book are unofficial members of the *remnant*: conservative, God-fearing, pro-family, pro-sound money, pro-Constitution, pro-traditional values individualists who see the socialist/secular humanist/globalist juggernaut which is descending on America and who hate it and will oppose it with every fiber of their being. Many readers have written to describe how they feel that *they* are like "a voice crying in the wilderness"—at home, at school, at work—how friends or family either ignore or laugh at their concerns about the country and its direction. Many have described the flak they have received from people to whom they have given copies of this writer's newsletter.

If you ever feel alone or get discouraged about the direction of the country, or your friends' or family's indifference to it, the following article by the late Albert Jay Nock, originally published by the Foundation for Economic Education, should pick you up a bit as it does this writer when he reads it. *The message is, you are not alone!*

Isaiah's Job

The prophet's career began at the end of King Uzziah's reign, say about 740 B.C. This reign was uncommonly long, almost half a century, and apparently prosperous. It was one of those prosperous reigns, however—like the reign of Marcus Aurelius at Rome, or the administration of Eubulus at Athens, or of Mr. Coolidge at Washington—where at the end, the prosperity suddenly peters out and things go by the board with a resounding crash.

In the year of Uzziah's death, the Lord commissioned the prophet Isaiah to go out and warn the people of the wrath to come. "Tell them what a worthless lot they are," He said. "Tell them what is wrong, and why, and what is going to happen unless they have a change of heart and straighten up. Don't mince matters. Make it clear that they are positively down to their last chance. Give it to them good and strong and keep on giving it to them. I suppose perhaps I ought to tell you," He added, "it won't do any good. The official class and their intelligentsia will turn up their noses at you, and the masses will not even listen. They will all keep on in their own ways until they carry everything down to destruction, and you will probably be lucky if you get out with your life."

Isaiah had been very willing to take on the job—in fact, he had asked for it—but the prospect put a new face on the situation. It raised the obvious question: Why, if all that were so—if the enterprise were to be a failure from the start—was there any sense in starting it?

"Ah," the Lord said, "you do not get the point. There is a Remnant there that you know nothing about. They are obscure, unorganized, inarticulate, each one rubbing along as best he can. They need to be encouraged and braced up because when everything has gone completely to the dogs, they are the ones who will come back and build up a new society; and meanwhile, your preaching will reassure them and keep them hanging on. Your job is to take care of the Remnant, so be off now and set about it. . . ."

What do we mean by the *masses* and the *remnant*?

As the word *masses* is commonly used, it suggests agglomerations of poor and underprivileged people, laboring people, proletarians. But it means nothing like that; it means simply the majority. The mass-man is one who has neither the force of intellect to apprehend the principles issuing in what we know as the humane life, nor the force of character to adhere to those principles steadily and strictly as laws of conduct; and because such people make up the great, the overwhelming majority of mankind, they are called collectively the masses. The line of differentiation between the masses and the Remnant is set invariably by quality, not by circumstance. The Remnant are those who, by force of intellect, are able to apprehend these principles and, by force of character, are able, at least measurably, to cleave to them. The masses are those who are unable to do either.

The picture which Isaiah presents of the Judean masses is most unfavorable. In his view, the *mass-man*, be he high or be he lowly, rich or poor, prince or pauper, gets off very badly. He appears as not only weak-minded and weak-willed, but as by consequence knavish, arrogant, grasping, dissipated, unprincipled, unscrupulous. . . .

As things now stand, Isaiah's job seems rather to go begging. Everyone with a message nowadays is, like my venerable European friend, eager to take it to the *masses*. His first, last, and only thought is of mass-acceptance and mass-approval. His great care is to put his doctrine in such shape as will capture the *masses'* attention and interest. . . .

The main trouble with this *mass-man* approach is its reaction upon the mission itself. It necessitates an opportunist sophistication of one's doctrine, which profoundly alters its character and reduces it to a mere placebo. If, say, you are a preacher, you wish to attract as large a congregation as you can, which means an appeal to the *masses*; and this, in turn, means adapting the terms of your message to the order of intellect and character that the *masses* exhibit. If you are an educator, say, with a college on your hands, you wish to get as many students as possible, and you whittle down your requirements accordingly. If a writer, you aim at getting many readers; if a publisher, many purchasers; if a philosopher, many disciples; if a reformer, many converts; if a musician, many authors, and so on. But as we see on all sides, in the realization of these several desires the prophetic message is so heavily adulterated with trivialities, in every instance, that its effect on the *masses* is merely to harden them in their sins. Meanwhile, the *Remnant*, aware of this adulteration and of the desires that prompt it, turn their backs on the prophet and will have nothing to do with him or his message.

Note: The more mediocre the message, the larger the audience; the more hard-core the message, the smaller the audience.

Isaiah, on the other hand, worked under no such disabilities. He preached to the *masses* only in the sense that he preached publicly. Anyone who liked might listen; anyone who liked might pass by. He knew that the *Remnant* would listen. . . .

The *Remnant* want only the best you have, whatever that may be. Give them that, and they are satisfied, you have nothing more to worry about. . . .

In a sense, nevertheless, as I have said, it is not a rewarding job. . . . A prophet of the *Remnant* will not grow purse-proud on the financial returns from his work, nor is it likely that he will get any great renown out of it. Isaiah's case was exceptional to this second rule, and there are others—but not many.

It may be thought, then, that while taking care of the *Remnant* is no doubt a good job, it is not an especially interesting job, because it is, as a rule, so poorly paid. I have my doubts about this. There are other compensations to be gotten out of a job besides money and notoriety, and some of them seem substantial enough to be attractive. Many jobs which do not pay well are yet profoundly interesting as, for instance, the job of the research student in the sciences is said to be; and the job of looking after the *Remnant* seems to me, as I have surveyed it for many years from my seat in the grandstand, to be as interesting as any that can be found in the world.

What chiefly makes it so, I think, is that in any given society the Remnant are always so largely an unknown quantity. You do not know, and will never know, more than two things about them. You can be sure of those, but you will never be able to make even a respectable guess at anything else. You do not know, and will never know, who the Remnant are, nor where they are, nor how many of them there are, nor what they are doing or will do. Two things you will know, and no more; first, that they exist; second, that they will find you. Except for these two certainties, working for the *Remnant* means working in impenetrable darkness; and this, I should say, is just the condition calculated most effectively to pique the interest of any prophet who is properly gifted with the imagination, insight, and intellectual curiosity necessary to a successful pursuit of his trade.

The fascination—as well as the despair—of the historian, as he looks upon Isaiah's Jewry, upon Plato's Athens, or upon Rome of the Antonines, is the hope of discovering and laying bare the "substratum of right-thinking and well-doing" which he knows must have existed somewhere in those societies, because no kind of collective life can possibly go on without it. He finds tantalizing intimations of it here and there in many places. But these are vague and fragmentary; they lead him nowhere in his search for some kind of measure of this substratum, but merely testify to what he already knew a priori—that the substratum did somewhere exist. Where it was, how substantial it was, what its power of self-assertion and resistance was—all of this tells him nothing.

Similarly, when the historian of 2,000 years hence, or 200 years, looks over the available testimony to the quality of our civilization and tries to get any kind of clear, competent evidence concerning the substratum of right-thinking and well-doing which he knows must have been here, he will have a devil of a time finding it. When he has assembled all he can get and has made even a minimum allowance for speciousness, vagueness, and confusion of motive, he will sadly acknowledge that his net result is simply nothing. A *Remnant* was here, building a substratum like coral insects; so much he knows, but he will find nothing to put him on the track of who and where and how many they were and what their work was like.

Concerning all this, too, the prophet of the present knows precisely as much and as little as the historian of the future; and that, I repeat, is what makes his job seem to me so profoundly interesting. One of the most suggestive episodes recounted in the Bible is that of the prophet Elijah's attempt—the only attempt of the kind on record, I believe—to count up the *Remnant*. Elijah had fled from persecution into the desert, where the Lord presently overhauled him and asked what he was doing so far away from his job. He said that he was running away, not because he was a coward, but because all the *Remnant* had been killed off except himself. He had gotten away only by the skin of his teeth, and, he being now all the *Remnant* there was, if he were killed, the True Faith would go flat. The Lord replied that he need not worry about that, for even without him the True Faith could probably manage to squeeze along somehow if it had to; "and as for your figures on the *Remnant*," He said, "I don't mind telling you that there are 7,000 of them back there in Israel whom it seems you have not heard of, but you may take My word for it that they are there."

At that time, probably the population of Israel could not have run too much more than a million or so; and a *Remnant* of 7,000 out of a million is a highly encouraging percentage for any prophet. With 7,000 of the boys on his side, there was no great reason for Elijah to feel lonesome; and incidentally, that would be something for the modern prophet of the *Remnant* to think of when he has a touch of the blues. But the main point is that if Elijah the prophet could not make a closer guess on the number of the *Remnant* than he made when he missed it by 7,000, anyone else who tackled the problem would only waste his time.

The other certainty which the prophet of the Remnant may always have is that the Remnant will find him. He may rely on that with absolute assurance. They will find him without his doing anything about it; in fact, if he tries to do anything about it, he is pretty sure to put them off. He does not need to advertise for them nor resort to any schemes of publicity to get their attention. The prophet of the *Remnant* does not need these techniques. He may be quite sure that the *Remnant* will make their own way to Him without any adventurous aids; and not only so, but if they find him employing such aids, as I said, it is ten-to-one that they will smell a rat in them and will sheer off. The certainty that the *Remnant* will find him, however, leaves the prophet as much in the dark as ever, as helpless as ever in the matter of putting any estimate of any kind upon the *Remnant*; for, as appears in the case of Elijah, he remains ignorant of who they are that have found him or where they are or how many. They do not write in and tell him about it, nor yet do they seek him out and attach themselves to his person. They are not that kind. They take his message, much as drivers take the directions on a roadside signboard—that is, with very little thought about the signboard, beyond being gratefully glad that it happened to be there, but with very serious thought about the directions.

This impersonal attitude of the *Remnant* wonderfully enhances the interest of the imaginative prophet's job. Once in a while, just about often enough to keep his intellectual curiosity in good working order, he will quite accidentally come upon some distinct reflection of his own message in an unsuspected quarter. This enables him to entertain himself in his leisure moments with agreeable speculations about the course his message may have taken in reaching that particular quarter, and about what came of it after it got there. Most interesting of all are those instances, if one could only run them down (but one may always speculate about them), where the recipient himself no longer knows where or when nor for whom he got the message—or even where, as sometimes happens, he has forgotten that he got it anywhere and imagines that it is all a self-spring idea of his own.

Such instances as these are probably not infrequent, for we can all no doubt remember having found ourselves suddenly under the influence of an idea, the source of which we cannot possibly identify. "It came to us afterward," as we say; that is, we are aware of it only after it has shot up full-grown in our minds, leaving us quite ignorant of how and when and by what agency it was planted there and left to germinate. It seems highly probable that the prophet's message often takes some such course with the *Remnant.*

If, for example, you are a writer or a speaker or a preacher, you put forth an idea which lodges in the gray matter of a casual member of the *Remnant* and sticks fast there. For some time it is inert; then it begins to fret and fester until presently it invades the man's conscious mind and, as one might say, corrupts it. Meanwhile, he has quite forgotten how he came by the idea in the first instance, and even perhaps thinks he has invented it; and in those circumstances, *the most interesting thing of all is that you never know what the pressure of that idea will make him do.*

Note: When you get discouraged about the moral, social, economic, spiritual, and political decline all around us, and the inability of those around you to comprehend it, dust off this article and re-read it. It will help put things in perspective.

Appendix

Resources For the
Troubled 1990s

I. Organizations

Focus on the Family
Colorado Spgs, CO 80995
(719) 531-3400

The John Birch Society
P.O. Box 8040
Appleton, WI 54913
(414) 749-3780

Southwest Radio Church
P.O. Box 1144
Oklahoma City, OK 73101
(405) 235-5396

The Conservative Caucus
450 Maple Ave. E.
Suite 309
Vienna, VA 22180
(703) 893-1550

Summit Ministries
P.O. Box 207
Manitou Spgs, CO 80819
(719) 685-9103

Gun Owners of America
1025 Front Street
Suite 300
Sacramento, CA 95814
(916) 443-5909

Concerned Women for America
370 L'Enfant Promenande SW, Suite 800
Washington, D.C. 20024
(202) 488-7000

Christian Financial Concepts
(Larry's Burkett's ministry of helping people get out of
    debt, budget, etc.)
P.O. Box 100
Gainesville, GA 30503
1-800-722-1976

Fighting Chance Foundation
Art Robinson
P.O. Box 1279
Cave Junction, OR 97523
(503) 592-4142

II. Books

New Lies For Old
 Anatoly Golitsyn

Deception
 Edward Jay Epstein

Mesmerized By the Bear
 Raymond S. Sleeper

Red Cocaine
 Joseph Douglass

Red Horizons
 Ion Pacepa

Jubilee On Wall Street
 David Knox Barker

None Dare Call It Conspiracy—Part II
 John Stormer

The Coming Economic Earthquake
 Larry Burkett

When the World Will Be As One: The Coming New World Order In the New Age
 Tal Brooke

Free Speech Or Propaganda: How the Media Distorts the Truth
 Marlin Maddoux

Financial Guidance
 Dr. James McKeever

Where Is the Food?
 Lindsay Williams

Tappan On Survival
 Mel Tappan

Through the Fire
 Dimitru Duduman
 (Hand of Help, P.O. Box 3494, Fullerton, CA 92634)

III. Newsletters

McAlvany Intelligence Advisor
P.O. Box 5150
Durango, CO 81301

Howard Phillips' Inside Washington Report
450 Maple Ave., East, Suite 309
Vienna, VA 22180 — (703) 287-6782

The New American
395 Concord Avenue
Belmont, MA 02178 — (617) 489-0605

The Reaper
P.O. Box 84901
Phoenix, AZ 85071 — (602) 252-4477

Money Strategy Letter
P.O. Box 1788
Medford, OR 97501 — (503) 826-9877

Ron Paul Investment Letter
1120 NASA Boulevard, Suite 104
Houston, TX 77058

World News Digest
P.O. Box 467939
Atlanta, GA   30346 — (404) 399-1877

Straight Talk
P.O. Box 60
Pigeon Forge, TN 37868

Don Bell Reports
P.O. Box 2223
Palm Beach, FL 33484

The Holt Advisory
P.O. Box 2923
West Palm Beach, FL 33402

*Low Profile: Your Monthly Guide to Privacy
    and Asset Protection*
(Mark Nestmann)
P.O. Box 84910
Phoenix, AZ 85071
1-800-528-0559

IV. Videos

South Africa: Revolution and Betrayal (1 hour)
Soviet Strategy For Conquest Of the World (2 hours)
Mesmerized By the Bear: The Great Soviet Deception
(2 hours)
Red World (1½ hours)
Toward A Soviet South Africa (2 hours)

For information, write to:

McAlvany Intelligence Advisor
P.O. Box 5150
Durango, CO 81301

If the information in this book is of interest to you
and you would like to receive it on a regular, updated
basis, you are encouraged to subscribe to the *McAlvany*

Intelligence Advisor—Don McAlvany's monthly monetary, economic, political, geopolitical newsletter. *MIA* is written from a conservative, biblical perspective and is an attempt to help wake up and prepare Americans in general, and Christians in particular, regarding the political, geo-strategic, and financial crises which are approaching. Subscribers are encouraged to copy and distribute copies of *MIA* to friends, relatives, pastors, leaders, etc. For information, write to:

McAlvany Intelligence Advisor
P.O. Box 5150
Durango, CO 81301

Price: $95 per year; $165 per two years

For information or assistance with precious metals, government or municipal bonds, or other securities, survival food reserves, or financial consultation, call:

ICA
166 Turner Dr.
Durango, CO 81301
(800) 525-9556

ICA is a 20-year-old investment brokerage and consultation firm owned and managed by Don McAlvany.